THE NATION'S CITIES

Wide World

The modern, prize-winning Boston City Hall epitomizes American city government's look toward the future.

THE
NATION'S
CITIES......

Change and Challenge

Patrick Healy III 1910-

HARPER & ROW, PUBLISHERS
New York, Evanston, San Francisco, London

FIRST EDITION

Designed by C. Linda Dingler

Library of Congress Cataloging in Publication Data

Healy, Patrick.
  The Nation's cities, change and challenge.

  Includes bibliographical references and index.
  1. Cities and towns—United States. 2. Federal-city relations—United States. 3. Municipal government—United States. I. Title.
HT123.H4 1975   301.36′3′0973   74–1817
ISBN 0–06–011803–2

MaJ 4/75   4/71

To Markey

CONTENTS

ILLUSTRATIONS

Preface

The United States of America became the most powerful nation in world history for a multitude of reasons. Basic, perhaps, is its governmental system. And the success of that federal system depends upon effective and responsive city governments, which must deliver the services affecting the lives of the citizens. To do so more efficiently, the cities in some states began at the turn of the century to cooperate on a statewide basis in exchange of information, experiences, and research for better methods. They formed state leagues of municipalities to facilitate that process and to unite in collective action to seek from rurally dominated state legislatures the removal of restrictions on their powers and financial resources. In 1924 the state leagues came together and formed the American Municipal Association, now known as the National League of Cities.

The next fifty years were perhaps the most dynamic period in American history. This book is basically a review of city government in the United States during those fifty years—its development, its changing problems, programs, and structure; its ability to cope with public needs in the context of the rapid urbanization that has taken place over that span; and a defining of trends that might indicate something of the future. Some might call it a history of "urbanization." Yet modern historians, such as Roy Lubove, prefer the term "city-building," because urbanization, as such, is an abstraction. Cities are the entities with which one must deal, in the final analysis. They are created by concrete decisions over time, not by factors of demography and ecology, which a number of sociologists in recent years have labored to establish as the focal points of urban research to explain "urbanization."

The idea for the book came from Raymond L. Bancroft, managing editor of *Nation's Cities*, the monthly magazine of the National League of Cities. He suggested it as one of the actions to commemorate the fiftieth anniversary of the organization, which now represents through its state leagues some fifteen thousand municipal governments, including as direct members some five hundred of the nation's biggest cities. The development of this intermunicipal cooperation is a significant part of this review.

Despite the fact that the American Municipal Association changed its name to the National League of Cities in 1964, the names are used interchangeably in the text, regardless of time periods.

It has been my privilege to be a participant or close witness in most of this half century of dramatic change and development, beginning more than forty years ago when Morton L. Wallerstein first employed me, fresh out of the Maxwell Graduate School of Public Administration at Syracuse University, in the city government field as field consultant for the Virginia Municipal League. I shall be forever grateful to him for that opportunity, which led a few months later to my appointment as the first full-time executive director of the North Carolina League of Municipalities. Eventually, after World War II service in the Navy and an interim in private business, I served for eighteen years as executive vice-president of the National League of Cities.

Ray Bancroft assisted me in preparing the first outline for this book, in selection of photographs, and in his contributions to the chapter "Modernizing City Hall." My daughter, Nancy Lee Healy, was a great aid as my research assistant, particularly on the early chapters, and as critic of the entire manuscript. I also wish to acknowledge the research help of Michael Lucas and of the library staff of the League of Cities and Conference of Mayors. Ronald Torrence contributed to the chapter "City Hall's Worsening Fiscal Dilemma." For his tactful suggestions, his understanding, his skillful editing, and for his contributions to the chapter "The Long, Hot Sixties—Innovation and Turmoil," I am deeply grateful to Simpson F. Lawson. With all this good help, however, I assume full responsibility for the entire contents of the book.

My secretary of twenty years, Beverly Collins, exhibited her usual patience and skill in typing, retyping, and retyping the manuscript, and I appreciate her many suggestions as to content.

Finally, I wish to express appreciation to my "partner," John J. Gunther, executive director of the United States Conference of Mayors, and to my successor as executive vice-president of the National League of Cities, Allen E. Pritchard, Jr., and to their respective officers and governing boards, for making it all possible.

THE NATION'S CITIES

In many important respects the story of America's cities is the story of the nation. The cities exemplify the features which characterize America, in the minds of her own people and in foreign lands as well. America is a melting pot in which nationals of a hundred countries become citizens of the United States: the cities are the caldron in which assimilation occurs. America is a machine, a technological marvel which is symbolized most dramatically by the city—its factories, its transportation and distribution systems, its skyscrapers and its subways. America is opportunity: the chance to find a job and make a living, the right to strive toward (if not always immediately to achieve) equality of treatment, the challenge to forge one's individual destiny. Here, too, the cities stand most clearly and unequivocally for "the American way.". . . If America is not yet one vast metropolis, its cities nevertheless set the tone and determine the character of national life.

—Roscoe C. Martin, 1962

... 1

City Governments in Transition

The literature of the cities in America is rich and varied, and the story of their emergence has often been told. It is an exciting account. It *is* the story of the nation.

From their evolution in colonial times through their westward expansion, from their post–Civil War corruption and misrule through their reform and more efficient management, the cities have a history marked by change. They have been profoundly influenced by changes in technology. Perhaps the most dramatic changes—not only technological, but economic, social, and governmental—have taken place in the past fifty years.

During this last half century, technology revolutionized transportation, communication, agriculture, and industry. It produced the automobile age, increasing the number of motor vehicles on the roads from less than 10 million to more than 120 million traveling more than 1 trillion miles annually, 20 million of them trucks, many of those hauling 700 million tons of intercity freight. It introduced radio broadcasting, which became a national obsession as the number of commercial broadcasting stations increased from one to 7,200; then television, which, according to a 1972 Roper poll, is the prime source of news for 64 percent of the American people, the only source for 33 percent. It reduced the number of persons needed on the farms from 32 million to less than 10 million working more than 1 billion acres. And its innovations in industrial and mineral production made

America the most powerful nation in history.

The gross national product climbed from $88 billion to nearly $800 billion in constant (1958) dollars, while average personal income rose from $639 per capita to $3,261.

The 1930s ushered in a broad program of social insurance—unemployment compensation, old-age and survivors' benefits, and, later, medical care for the aged—plus a variety of federally aided assistance programs for the needy. And the past twenty years have witnessed significant improvement in racial relations and in the opportunity for advancement by racial minorities.

How to cope governmentally with all this rush of change has been an intergovernmental problem—federal, state, local. Yet, in the final analysis, it is the cities with which one must deal. Here is where the action is, where services affecting the lives of the citizens must be delivered. Here is where the nation's complex and interrelated problems—social, economic, political—come to rest in their most aggravated form. Here governmental services are most in demand, most expensive, and most complex in administration.

And the cities, also, have come on with a rush. America changed from a rural nation to a nation more than 70 percent urban in little more than the last fifty years. It has been an era of startling contrasts in generally accepted concepts of city government responsibilities—from the rapid increase of new housekeeping functions with emphasis on "businesslike" efficiency to today's emphasis on people-oriented policy planning by city governments to improve the quality of urban life. It was a dynamic period marked by the banding together of the responsible representatives of hundreds, then thousands, of city, town, village, and borough governments in state and national associations to cooperate in meeting the challenges of the times and to bring together their combined influence to shape national domestic policies.

It is significant that the National League of Cities was born at the beginning of this era, just fifty years ago, after a quarter century of experience had demonstrated the value of intermunicipal cooperation at the state level in making possible more responsive and efficient municipal government. Its role in the changing concepts of city government responsibilities and the change in concept of its own role have never before been told. This book is an effort to do so, and at the same time to focus on city governments in transition.

Who would have forecast as recently as 1965, for example, that before another ten years would pass, mayors of more than 150 large cities would become responsible for administering social and educational programs, such as coordination of the myriad manpower training and development activities funded by federal and state governments? Is it any more far-fetched to predict that within still another ten years many mayors will be running the public school system? Or a housing program?

Or who in 1965 would have believed that within ten years three of the nation's ten largest cities—Cleveland, Los Angeles, and Detroit, each with a majority white population—would elect black mayors?[1] Or that a leading city in the Deep South, Atlanta, would do the same? Or a hundred other cities? It took about fifty years of change in population patterns—rural migration to the cities and the spilling over of city population into suburbs—plus another twenty years of change in attitudes to make that possible. These were changes stimulated in part by the school-desegregation mandate of the United States Supreme Court in 1954 and its enforcement by the federal courts; by the passage of three broad civil rights acts in four years, including the Voting Rights Act of 1965; in short, by the whole civil rights movement of the 1960s.

On November 7, 1967, the voters of Cleveland elected Carl B. Stokes as the first black mayor of a large American city after a summer in which more than a hundred cities were rocked with racial violence. On the same day, Richard G. Hatcher became the first black mayor of a "medium-size" city—Gary, Indiana, with a population of 175,000, 53 percent black. Because of the tenseness of the summer these elections had enormous significance and attracted national attention. Perhaps blacks could, after all, be persuaded to use the power of the ballot box rather than the power of fire bombs. Perhaps, too, since both Stokes and Hatcher got significant shares of the white vote, whites were learning to share power.

In 1969, just twenty years after Atlanta blacks voted for the first time in a city primary, Maynard Jackson was elected as the first black vice-mayor. After the election, in which he got 54 percent of the vote, he said: "Clearly the emergence of the black elected official is one of the most significant developments of the last fifty years."[2]

In 1973 Jackson became the first black mayor of Atlanta, winning 59 percent of the vote in a city of half a million people, 51 percent of them black. In the same year the nation's third-largest city, Los Angeles, only 18 percent black, elected its first black mayor, Tom Bradley, who shortly thereafter was elected the first black president of the National League of Cities, a voluntary association representing some 15,000 cities, towns, and villages across the land. Likewise Detroit, the fifth-largest with 1.5 million people, 44 percent black, elected its first black mayor, Coleman A. Young. Altogether 107 American cities had black mayors in 1974, including nineteen new ones in the South and including the nation's capital and ninth-largest city, Washington, D.C., which is 71 percent black.

The emergence of the black elected official has indeed been a significant development. And yet other ethnic groups have risen to political power in various cities at different times—Irish, Germans, Italians, Poles, Jews—some of them at the time no more highly regarded by some of the remaining populace than Negroes. It is the process of assimilation, "the American way." And, as Roscoe Martin has said, the cities are the caldron.

However, a more fundamental development has been the change in concept of city government responsibilities. An examination of the problems and priorities of four cities over the past fifty years will illustrate the rapid transition that has taken place in city government. Rock Hill, South Carolina, Lowell, Massachusetts, Atlanta, and Milwaukee were chosen as representative of small, medium-size, and large cities. These brief histories provide insight into how the mayors and other citizens perceived their cities' problems at various stages of development from 1924 to 1974.

Rock Hill is located in the heart of the Piedmont region, sixty-five miles north of the state capital at Columbia and twenty-five miles south of Charlotte, North Carolina. Still a rural town of 8,800 in 1924, it was among the many small cities benefiting from the industrial migration to their region as Northern textile producers were lured away from places such as Lowell, Massachusetts, by the lower wage demands of the South. Five cotton mills had been built in Rock Hill before the turn of the century, and in 1920 another large one opened. The town's municipal affairs were efficiently handled under a council-manager charter adopted late in 1913, Rock Hill being one of the first twelve communities in the nation to adopt that system, which has since been put into effect in some two thousand others.

When the home-county delegation to the state legislature sounded out Rock Hill leaders in 1924 about their priorities in a forthcoming session, the local group expressed the need for a rural police system that could deal with traffic violations, assistance in the settlement of the Catawba Indians, aid in curtailing the dispensing of Jamaica ginger, and continued appropriations for home and farm demonstration work.[3] Legislators of 1974 should have such "demands" to deal with from their constituents! The people approved of their town government, as evidenced by Mayor J. B. Johnson's reelection that year without opposition to serve his second of five successive terms; and the same city manager, W. P. Goodman, was retained for twelve years, from 1921 to 1933. The big event in municipal government in 1924 was the establishment of the town's first public park as a memorial to the Confederate dead.

With its population quadrupled to nearly 40,000, Rock Hill in 1974 had fourteen public parks and playgrounds with more on the way, five neighborhood centers, a dozen special services from family planning to a workshop for school dropouts, all under a full-fledged parks and recreation department. It had a mayor's community relations committee, a youth service agency, and a commission for a Model City program, the latter headed by the mayor, David Lyle.

That the citizens still approved of their city government was indicated by the continuity in office of its responsible officials: the mayor first elected in 1964, other councilmen in 1964 and 1967, and the mayor pro tem, Charles A. Reece, Jr., serving continuously since his first election in 1957. City Manager Max Holland was appointed in 1965 after serving as manager of three smaller cities.

The manager's administrative structure, approved by the city council in 1972, shows how far management techniques can evolve, even in small cities. He has three principal assistants: a director of finance, an assistant city manager for community development, and an assistant city manager for community services. Except for the departments of health and civil defense and the offices of city attorney, city recorder, and city solicitor, all other departments are grouped under the broad authority of one of the two assistant city managers.

Thus, under "community development" are gathered the departments of administrative services, engineering, housing and renewal, housing services, planning and management, public information, and social and economic development. Incidentally, the planning and management department not only works on planning studies and zoning matters, but also works with the Model City program and prepares for other departments most of the applications for state and federal funds. The "community services" departments oversee fire, police, public works, recreation, utilities, and a central garage.

The city is fortunate in owning its own electric utility distribution system, which, while closely following rates charged by private utilities in the area, provides a net return to the general fund that helps keep property taxes at a low 15 percent of total city revenues. Another big factor in keeping the property tax down in recent years has been the growth in the amount of state and federal taxes returned to the city through the efforts of the Municipal Association of South Carolina, the National League of Cities, and the United States Conference of Mayors. These inter-governmental transfers had risen from zero fifty years ago to more than 30 percent of Rock Hill's total revenues by 1974.

Rock Hill's modern municipal government, like that of hundreds of other progressive American cities in the seventies, reflects the city's new concern with "people problems." While still occupied with the physical problems of growth, including redevelopment of blighted areas, and the efficient rendering of good housekeeping services, city officials are now devoting much time and energy to improving the "quality of life" in the city—a new municipal function never dreamed of as a municipal responsibility, as such, fifty years earlier. Imagine a small city in 1924 in South Carolina, or anywhere else for that matter, having a mayor's community relations committee, a youth service agency, departments of housing services and social and economic development. No way!

In 1924 Atlanta's 62,800 black citizens, constituting 31 percent of its population, were disfranchised, and none of them, of course, held elective office. And yet racial relations in that city were considered comparatively good as a result of the work of the Atlanta Inter-racial Committee, organized after World War I. A black minister in 1920 gave credit to the "Atlanta Plan" for securing for its blacks their first park for recreation and their first public high school.

"But I think the chief result of the work of this organization," he continued, "has been the spirit it has generated. . . . It would be impossible, under present conditions, for an outbreak between the races to occur here. This is remarkable, being in the heart of the state that has so often led the Union in her red record of lawlessness."[4] The "spirit" of Atlanta continued high during most of the next half century.

Atlanta had risen from the ashes of the Civil War and a population in 1870 of 21,789 to more than quadruple that size at the turn of the century. Its growth had been assured by its location as a crossroads of railroads in the early 1850s, central to most of the Southeast. By 1970 the thriving trade center had grown to half a million inside its limited boundaries, which did not keep pace with its urbanization. Its metropolitan population was 1,597,816 in 1973, the eighteenth largest in the United States.

On January 7, 1924, fifty years before Maynard Jackson entered city hall, Atlantans turned their radio dials to WSB at 7 P.M., an hour before the station normally went on the air, to hear Mayor Walter A. Sims deliver the first annual message to the city council ever broadcast in the city. Sims recited public works accomplishments and needs in the rapidly growing city—new sewer lines, street improvements, new schools and clinics, police substations, and firehouses. Mayor Sims called upon the council committee in charge of the police department "to purge it of all who are not in thorough sympathy with enforcing the law" and admonished them to "require the men to patrol their beats."

Automobile traffic had reached a sufficient volume to permit Sims to recommend establishment of a traffic bureau, and parked cars dotted the streets in such numbers during business hours that street cleaners and garbage collectors were ordered to do their work at night, a practice, Sims boasted, that "has proven to be the correct method."

In an appeal for economy, the mayor complained that the expense of government had risen rapidly, partly as a result of a recent bond issue. He warned the council against emulating officials in other areas who, he said, "have gone wild on issuing bonds." He called for charter changes that would extend the city limits, halve the thirty-six-member council to eighteen, and abolish the board of education, which the mayor proposed to replace with a committee of five councilmen.[5]

Note that city departments were still being administered by committees of the council or by boards, a holdover from the system in vogue in the 1890s. Atlanta was then, and still was through 1973, operating under the "weak-mayor" plan, in which the mayor's limited power includes appointing the council committees and holding the threat of veto over their ordinances. In some weak-mayor cities he doesn't even have a veto.

The more modern "strong-mayor" plan centralizes responsibility for administration in the elected mayor, who appoints his own department heads to assist him. In this sense the mayor is truly the chief executive, while the council's role is to determine policy, including the forms and amounts of taxation. The voters can thereby more easily understand the system and who is responsible for what.

Occasionally, however, by sheer force of personality and leadership, a mayor of a weak-mayor city can achieve sufficient influence to coordinate the administration and accomplish good results. Atlanta's long-time mayor William B. Hartsfield was such a man. Serving in that position for a total of twenty-three and a half years until 1961, he used to like to hear people describe him as "a strong mayor working under a weak-mayor charter." And he was. His two great frustrations were the rural-dominated state legislature and the mentality of voters in rural Georgia—"stick whittlers," he called them—who favored only candidates for public office who were the most vociferous in their anti-Negro stands. His slogan for Atlanta was "a city too busy to hate."

Referring to that slogan in his inaugural address January 7, 1974, Mayor Jackson asked, "Are we a city too busy for love?" Citizen concern, he said, must be translated into action for such objectives as economic growth and prosperity for *all,* a voice for the young in city government, a balanced diet for all children, decent, safe, and sanitary housing for all Atlantans, safe streets and homes secure from the threat of violence, and the abolition of racism and sexism.

Improving the "quality of life" was the concern of Atlanta's mayor in 1974. Like his predecessor of fifty years earlier, Maynard Jackson was also concerned with crime. But while Mayor Sims could dismiss the subject by admonishing the police to "patrol their beats," Mayor Jackson termed crime to be "foremost among our problems, other than the need for increased interracial communication." He vowed "death on the drug trade" and called for the "creation of a new, vigorous moral spirit in the

Wide World

Traditional "housekeeping" functions such as street cleaning have been among the key services performed by city governments. Here a New York City street sweeper carries away debris from a 1937 May Day parade.

community to help young people find new, purposeful roles in society," a new climate based on awareness that, in the words of Aristotle twenty-five centuries ago, "poverty is the parent of crime."

It was significant that Atlanta's first black mayor entered office with more power than any of his white predecessors. A new city charter took effect on the day of Mayor Jackson's inauguration. Under it the mayor became, in fact, a strong mayor—a chief executive with department heads appointed by him. No longer did committees of the city council run the departments. They now served as policy committees appointed by the president of the council, with the mayor having the responsibility to execute the policies.

Milwaukee has an even longer tradition than Atlanta of strong leadership exerted by "weak mayors." The tradition was started by Daniel W. Hoan, who had been city attorney for six years before his election as mayor in 1916 for a tenure that did not end until twenty-four years later, in 1940. He was swept into office on a Socialist ticket that also included twenty-one of the twenty-five aldermen in a protest by the voters against the graft, vice, and corruption that had flourished in the city since before the turn of the century. In his book, published a quarter of a century later, Hoan described that era:

The task of rehabilitating Milwaukee's government began in 1910. That year marked the close of a dark period in the city's history. The stewardship of this community had been in the grasp of the sinister and slimy hand of special interests, divekeepers, crooked contractors, petty racketeers, and political bosses. This city was then as graft-ridden as any other.[6]

Only two years out of law school, the young city attorney had already achieved a certain measure of fame by drafting in 1909 for the Wisconsin Federation of Labor what became the first workmen's compensation act in the United States and preparing the necessary brief supporting its constitutionality. His biographer, Edward S. Kerstein, describes its enactment by the Wisconsin legislature in 1911 as "a historic milestone in the cause of the working man. . . . It also catapulted [Hoan] into political office."[7]

A study made in 1931 for the President's Research Committee on Social Trends showed that the city of Milwaukee in that year was performing about three hundred municipal activities, one-fifth of them initiated in the fifteen years since Hoan became mayor. For example, the period 1916–20 saw the development of many health activities, including venereal disease clinics, public health field nurses, and compulsory pasteurization of milk. Routine procedures were improved through centralization of purchasing and standardization of positions and salaries. Twenty-four new activities were undertaken in the next five years, nearly a third associated with the growing influence of the automobile, and twenty-nine in the next six years, eleven of which broadened the scope of health and welfare services.

Hoan's pride in his accomplishments was indicated in the introductory note to his book: "I have not attempted to record all of the virtues and accomplishments of our Milwaukee government, but only enough of them to justify our assertion that no other city in the world has accomplished so much in genuine governmental improvement in so short a period of time. I make this claim in all due modesty and without fear of successful contradiction."

Hoan attributed his defeat in 1940 to a "decision to get a new common council or get the hell out of the job. I was sick and tired of the streetcar company financing and electing my common council. I had to live with them [the aldermen], and they were meaner than hell."[8]

After a wartime interval, Frank P. Zeidler became mayor for twelve years, 1948–60. Fellow mayors on the executive committee of the National League of Cities admired his intellectual leadership in that body during the 1950s. Generally low-keyed and not so flamboyant as Hoan, Zeidler projected the image of the scholar and intellectual in city hall rather than that of the politician.[9] Although he was able to lay a foundation for organizational change in several executive functions, the city council's strong attachment to aldermanic prerogatives and his own philosophical aversion to executive domination precluded any basic structural changes.

Zeidler's successor, Henry W. Maier, has had no such philosophical aversion to executive leadership. In fact, he has made a careful study of the subject and has developed a theory of urban leadership, which he set forth in a book, *Challenge to the Cities: An Approach to a Theory of Urban Leadership,* published in 1966 during his second term as mayor.

Milwaukee's tradition of keeping a good mayor in office for long tenure is being continued with Henry Maier, who was reelected for a fourth four-year term in 1972. From the outset he clearly understood the structural shortcomings of his office, and developed a plan to cope with the situation. Because of the council's strong position, he determined to avoid giving any appearance of undermining aldermanic prerogatives. He also was careful not to appear to threaten the relative autonomy of many of the line departments which had been developed as structural impediments to strong administrative leadership.

By carefully following these tactics, he has been able to increase the chief executive's power and thus enable the city to deal more effectively with such major activities as community renewal, economic development, and city finances, while at the same time increasing governmental efficiency. For example, under a charter that doesn't authorize the mayor to formulate a budget, Mayor Maier, for all practical purposes, regularly prepares one. A recent scholarly analysis of Mayor Maier's executive leadership concludes that "he has altered the basic influence relationships to the point where his position now encompasses probably as much political power as that of most big-city mayors, except Chicago's Richard J. Daley."[10]

Maier's peers throughout the country expressed their recognition of his leadership qualities by electing him president of the National League of Cities in 1963 and of the United States Conference of Mayors in 1971.

Milwaukee has needed such leadership during the turbulent

times that have marked urban life in all large cities during the sixties and seventies. In contrast to its image fifty years earlier as a community of friendly and peaceful burghers, the events of recent years, largely the result of forces beyond local control, have challenged its earlier complacency. Milwaukee Professor Henry Schmandt has written:

For Milwaukee, as for its prototypes elsewhere, there has been no escape from the pressures of modern urban society and the concomitant tactics of confrontation politics, crisis precipitation, creative disorder, civil disobedience and militant activism. Milwaukeans, to the horror and disbelief of many, have witnessed angry confrontations between blacks and whites, the seizure and burning of draft records, mass protests against the Vietnam War, hunger marches, student disorders in the high schools and local universities, the spread of marijuana smoking among their children and the increased use of drugs, the growth of an extensive "hippy" colony, the publication of underground papers, and a police strike. They have heard their public officials vilified and their police called "pigs" . . .[11]

These are the kinds of problems confronting mayors and councilmen in all big, and some not so big, American cities today. Fifty years earlier, Mayor Hoan's big problem was initiating new municipal services. Today Mayor Maier is saying in his book: "The day of the simple municipal service government is gone. A new era has arrived, in which the big test of a mayor is whether he can cope with the demands and needs for economic, social, and physical development."

Lowell, Massachusetts, mentioned earlier as an exporter of textile mills to such Southern cities as Rock Hill, South Carolina, has undergone a remarkable transition from economic disaster in the twenties to a spectacular rebirth of hope and opportunity in the seventies.

Known as America's first industrial city, it was created by enterprising Bostonians seeking to recapture the commercial prosperity they had lost before and during the War of 1812. In the new era that began in 1815, Boston capital was put into cotton manufacture and the development of new mill towns inland where water power was available. By the time Lowell was incorporated as a city of 2,500 in 1826, two textile mills were being powered by water from the Pawtucket Falls on the Merrimack River, thirty miles northwest of Boston. Production grew rapidly as other companies were established, and Lowell soon became the leading American textile center. But aging industrial plants and higher production costs (wages and taxes) caused a gradual decline in Lowell's output, and by the turn of the century it had lost its competitive advantage. Although its economy was revived by a severe need for textiles and munitions during World War I, employment fell sharply when the war ended. Lowell recovered again during a textile boom in 1923, then collapsed in 1924. The textile mills there went out of business or moved elsewhere, mainly to the South.[12] Its population peaked at 124,000 in 1924 and fell to 95,000 fifty years later. During this period, and especially since 1950, chronic unemployment, blighted areas, abandoned housing, and high taxes have been symptoms of its urban distress.

Lowell's commission form of government, adopted in 1911, was replaced in 1944 by a council-manager charter. When James Sullivan, former city manager of Cambridge, Massachusetts, became city manager of Lowell in 1970, he discussed Lowell's problems with Professor John F. Collins at the Massachusetts Institute of Technology's Alfred P. Sloan School of Management. Collins, former mayor of Boston and former president of the National League of Cities, had been working since 1968 with Professor Jay W. Forrester in applying systems dynamics to urban problems. Forrester described the results in *Urban Dynamics,* published in 1969.

Sullivan recognized similarities between Lowell's history and the life cycle of a hypothetical city traced in the book. He offered Lowell as a site for testing the model, and the Department of Housing and Urban Development awarded a contract to MIT in mid-1972 for urban dynamics research, part of which included creating an urban dynamics model for application to Lowell. Throughout 1973 the city manager, his assistants, the Model City director, two city councilmen, the director of planning, the local director of manpower training, and several Lowell residents met biweekly to review the HUD-sponsored research and to relate Lowell issues to urban dynamics.[13]

The program has enabled the city to identify the dynamic causes of its problems and to test and evaluate many alternative policies that might be used to bring social and economic improvement. It is a departure from the traditional urban management, which usually focuses on short-range and direct consequences of proposed policies. For example, the immediate benefits of, say, a low-cost housing program might impel decisionmakers to take action without considering that the consequences might very well be unfavorable and go unnoticed until long after project completion. The program has enabled the city of Lowell to establish a set of goals and a program of action with the dynamic consequences properly identified. It represents an outstanding innovation in policy planning.

If these brief sketches of the life and times of four American cities show nothing else, they show that cities, whatever their size, have always been attuned to national events and moods in any historical period. When Henry Ford cranked up automobile production lines in Detroit, Rock Hill, Atlanta, Milwaukee, and Lowell soon felt the results in their streets and in their budgets for traffic control. Unprecedented demand for khaki during World War I brought new life, if only temporarily, to Lowell's dormant textile mills. Wall Street crashed, and the thud caused tremors that brought widespread defaults on municipal bonds around the country, as a later chapter will show.

None of this is meant to minimize the very significant individual differences in the cultures, growth patterns, political traditions, and demographic profiles of cities. The "spirit of Atlanta" may be no more than a Southern blend of fraternity and boosterism, but Atlantans have shown a capacity to avoid the grim kind of racial polarization that has at times paralyzed other cities. Furthermore, they have kept the spirit alive while surrounded by a rural noose of Jim Crowism. Lowell's urban dynamics model is just one of many diverse experiments in systems analysis in use in municipal government, and countless other cities still rely on sound intuitive reasoning in policy planning.

Not even mentioned here are the rich and varied patterns of neighborhoods within cities. No city of any appreciable size is without several sections enriched by ethnic flavor and traditions or a heritage of grandeur or quaintness that can be traced to life styles of earlier generations.

But most importantly, these case studies and myriad events that will be described in later chapters of this book illustrate an enormous municipal capacity for change. They reveal a strong responsiveness to waves of reform. But they also show a steady, encouraging incremental adjustment to adversity as well as prosperity. Changes in technology and in energy converters and fuel have dramatically changed the shape and location of cities in America and the urban environment everywhere. The energy crisis that finally burst fully upon public awareness in late 1973 may well change further the shapes of cities and of all civilization in the years ahead. The nation's commerce and industry will continue to expand. New groups will emerge to exert claims on the cities' resources and officials' time. The city-building process will continue. Coping with this inevitable change will require drawing on the best of the municipal traditions of the past and combining them with imaginative but realistic experimentation. The remainder of this book will review many tested examples of the former and preview some of the more promising manifestations of the latter.

The Evolution of Cities in the United States

By the middle of the seventeenth century, Boston "freemen" were electing three selectmen to carry out decisions of the settlement's annual town meeting and designating lesser functionaries, such as night watchmen, to enforce curfews, to patrol the streets after dark, and to warn of fires. A 1666 ordinance forbade householders to empty filth in the streets. Another regulation required that garbage be thrown from the drawbridge into the Mill Creek. The town specified the depth of privy vaults. By town vote, every family had to equip itself with leather buckets for fire fighting, and adult males were expected to join the bucket brigade when the alarm sounded. Overseers of the town's poor provided care at public expense. Beginning in 1643, Boston, and later most Massachusetts towns, adopted a system of free public schools, financed by income from the lease or sale of town lands.

Thus, more than a century before the American Revolution brought independence and a constitution to the Commonwealth of Massachusetts, Boston had an incipient governing body, a basic police force, a sanitation code, fire regulations, a welfare caseload, and a public school system.

Not all the municipal governments of the five embryo cities that were flourishing in colonial America by 1700 were as sophisticated or as independent as Boston's. But the history of urban expansion is replete with demonstrations that it is the cities of this nation that from the beginning have had to cope with "cutting-edge" responsibilities caused by ever-broadening social and economic forces over which they had little or no control.

Towns, and the cities that many of them became, were the first of the three traditional layers of government—local, state, and national. From the standpoint of satisfying the human wants that are most important in the daily lives of people, cities and towns must be judged most essential. Yet the draftsmen of the early state constitutions were allowed to usurp power which the local governments—the first to develop and the first to come to the minds of aggrieved citizens—granted to them.

Unfortunately, the present revenue relations between state governments and municipalities are almost the same as those conceived when the colonial governments discarded their royal charters for constitutions that recognized the state as the supreme political institution, limited only by restrictions imposed upon it and by powers delegated to a national authority. Thus, the framework and intergovernmental relations of the American political system are the product of colonial and Revolutionary times.

Municipalities perform functions that have been granted to them by states, usually through *permissive* state authorizations, although some services have been made mandatory. Attempts of cities to undertake any activities not specifically authorized by the state bring them into conflict with state authority as expressed by existing statutes and charters. Even the so-called charter cities with "home rule" privileges seldom have complete freedom to determine their activities. When they want to undertake experimental functions, they, too, must first go, hat in hand, to the state for authority.

For the simple needs of the early settlers this was no great problem. The colonists tended to come from an urban background—shopkeepers, tradesmen, artisans, mechanics, and day laborers. Ever since the arrival of those European colonists during the mid-seventeenth century, the development of this country has been largely urban. New England from the very beginning was an area of towns, settled by English Puritan or Pilgrim religious dissenters. The Dutch founded New Amsterdam primarily to promote commerce. The Catholics who established Maryland as a religious haven and the Quakers who settled Pennsylvania were not basically agriculturists. It was chiefly trade advantages, such as good harbors and access to productive hinterland, that gave Boston, Charles Town, South Carolina, Newport, Rhode Island, New York, and Philadelphia the ascendancy they enjoyed by 1700. At that time they dominated American economic life, although they had only 9 percent of the total colonial population.

The forces in their creation derived from expansion of world trade under English and Dutch leadership. Joint-stock companies were replacing kings and merchant princes as sponsors of large-scale overseas ventures. The corporate form of business organization, which supplied continuity and financial backing of numerous shareholders, was replacing medieval methods of financing. Their commercial enterprises centered in the young colonial towns. The Dutch West India Company's settlement on Manhattan was five years old, with three hundred inhabitants, when the Massachusetts Bay Company started building their town in 1630. The bigotry of the Bay colonists' theocracy led dissidents to found Newport on Narragansett Bay in 1639, dedicated to religious toleration and freedom of thought and practice. Royal patentees laid out Charles Town in 1672, a thousand miles down the Atlantic coast in South Carolina, and settled it in 1680. William Penn two years later laid out the village of Philadelphia on the wooded stretches of the broad upper Delaware River, a hundred miles from the sea. This "City of Brotherly Love" was destined to become in seventy-five years not only the foremost city in British North America but also the second largest in the English-speaking world.

As the glimpse of early Boston public life indicates, municipal government in the colonial centers was simple. Yet citizens of those towns developed a strong sense of loyalty to local government that could coexist with an inclination to flout strictures of the British crown. In *The Rise of Urban America,* Dr. Constance

McLaughlin Green notes that "the self-respecting Bostonian recognized his duty [to town administration even in the face of official ineptness] and behaved accordingly. He might smuggle valuable goods into port under the nose of royal customs collectors, but he would not dream of evading local taxes and would serve conscientiously if elected to local office."[1]

As in the 1970s, there was great diversity in the forms of town governance. Like all New England settlements, Newport decided its municipal affairs in town meeting, where selectmen were chosen to carry out decisions. Unlike Boston, though, Newport allowed any newcomer who acquired property and settled permanently to participate in town government. The smaller town required fewer or simpler regulations than Boston's and saw no need for extensive official supervision. It acted before Boston, however, in setting aside land for support of public schools. And it was generous in providing relief for legitimate residents in need of help—widows, orphans, and impoverished aged.

Manhattan's story was different. Directors of the Dutch West India Company, planning originally only for a trading post, did not encourage the rise of a self-governing community. They preferred to keep tight administrative control over the settlement and to limit expenditures for streets, sanitation, and similar services. Even after the surrender to the English in 1664, mayors and councilmen were appointed by the royal governor of the province. A new charter in 1731 ostensibly gave property owners a voice in municipal affairs, and yet the royal governor continued to control appointments to the principal municipal offices. Sanitation was lax. Care of the needy was of little public concern, and publicly financed education hardly existed.

The royal charter for the province of South Carolina made no provision for town government. Consequently Charles Town's affairs were run completely by the colonial Assembly. The town itself included more than 25 percent of the population of the province but had only four of the thirty members of the Assembly. The planters and merchants, who composed a majority of the legislature, gave small consideration to the town's needs.

They dismissed education as a family or church matter, although a school was opened in 1712, with the encouragement of a £10 annual appropriation by the Assembly sixteen years earlier. But this school charged tuition. A charitable organization paid the fees of most of the poor boys who attended. After a series of disastrous fires, the legislature levied a tax on the town about the turn of the century for purchase of buckets, ladders, and a fire-fighting water pump. But it was not until a conflagration wiped out three-quarters of the town in 1740 that a law was passed requiring stone or brick for all new construction. The Assembly looked to private charity to care for the needy until an annual tax was levied on the town by an act of 1712, to be administered by the vestry of a church. Thus, a system that allowed townspeople no control of local affairs resulted in deficiencies in education, sanitary regulation, fire protection, and poor relief, although the plantation owners and exporters were thriving.

In spite of the most spectacular cultural and economic growth of all the colonial towns, governmental institutions in Philadelphia were very little, if any, better than those in Charles Town or New York. Its charter was modeled on New York's, so that Philadelphia was as handicapped in the exercise of municipal authority as Manhattan—a corporation of mayor and council not responsible to the public and with very limited taxing powers. So far as ordinances governing sanitation, drainage, street extension, and police and fire protection are concerned, the record of both town corporations was a story of neglect. Fortunately, it was the concerted efforts of private citizens in the Quaker tradition of community responsibility that created an orderly Philadelphia.

While these five principal seaport trading centers were developing, rapid settlement was taking place in their respective agricultural hinterlands. Newer towns were beginning to compete with the early leaders. Homesteaders steadily pushed farther westward, and secondary towns multiplied to serve as their local centers of trade. New towns joined forces with the old in seeking aid from provincial legislatures to build roads into the back country. Although the total population of the five major cities had grown to 53,380 by 1743, their proportion of total colonial population had dropped to only 5 percent. But those five cities were still the unifying centers of colonial life, and their leadership in combination with the statesmen of rural Virginia was largely responsible for organizing the successful revolution against the British, beginning with the Declaration of Independence in 1776.

The first official United States census in 1790 showed a population of nearly 4 million—3,172,000 whites and 750,000 Negro slaves. Only one out of twenty of the new American republic's population was classified as urban—that is, living in towns of 2,500 or more—down from the 10 percent urban proportion of one hundred years earlier. Not until 1830 did the urban percentage reach again its level of 1690.

Noticeable by the middle of the eighteenth century was a growing resentment of people in the rural areas toward the cities. In their dependence on the seaports for European manufactured goods and markets for their own produce and furs, they believed they were victimized by wealthy city merchants. Constance McLaughlin Green wrote: "The antagonism of the country bumpkin toward the city slicker mounted from the late 1750s onward, a hostility that would endure for two hundred years until automobiles, telephones, radio, and television largely obliterated basic differences between rural and urban life in America."

At the same time, city dwellers complained that the rural population was disproportionately represented in the provincial legislatures and that the tax burden consequently fell more heavily on townspeople. Even in New England, where the town meeting and a high degree of local autonomy enabled the cities to handle their municipal problems without constant interference from the provincial legislatures, tax inequities created resentment of city toward country.

By the end of the war in 1783, each of the thirteen states had drafted its own state constitution providing for a legislature based on its colonial model, which continued to underrepresent the cities. All those constitutions required officeholders to be property owners, and most of them required property ownership as a qualification for voting for presidential electors, representatives in Congress, and members of the upper house of the state legislature. The legislatures, in turn, elected the two United States senators.

Westward migration was spectacular, beginning shortly after the Revolution, and the trans-Appalachian country bred its own urban communities. Serving at first as distribution centers for commodities between the seaboard and the interior, they soon became markets in their own right where local manufacturers traded with the country dwellers. By 1807, Pittsburgh was already smoky from factories. Two years later, two cotton mills were operating in Cincinnati. And throughout the Ohio Valley many settlements sought to follow their example.

The westward movement duplicated the colonial pattern of settlement. "The towns were the spearheads of the frontier," University of Chicago historian Richard C. Wade wrote. When the British acted in 1763 to halt the flow of settlers across the Appalachians, "a French merchant company prepared to survey the streets of St. Louis, a thousand miles through the wilderness," Wade declared.[2]

Though to a much lesser degree than the colonial towns, most of the towns of the West predated formation of the states that asserted legal parenthood over them. Saint Louis was settled half a century before Missouri became a state. Louisville and Lexington were established ten years before Kentucky gained independence from Virginia, and Cincinnati was a decade old before Ohio was separated from the Northwest Territory.

Meanwhile, scores of new cities came into existence in the East, generally where water power was available for industrial purposes. Both in New England and in the Middle Atlantic states the movement of population from country to town was beginning, as well as migration from city to city. Long before the great European immigration of the 1840s, the leading cities began to increase rapidly in size.[3]

In 1806 Oliver Evans developed a lightweight, high-pressure steam engine, paving the way for operation of Robert Fulton's steam ferry on the Hudson River the following year. The manufacture of steamboats in Cincinnati beginning in 1818 made possible a thriving river commerce. Every town along the Ohio and Mississippi benefited, as did the new towns that sprang up during the digging of the Erie Canal from the Hudson River at Albany to Buffalo on Lake Erie. Its completion in 1825 gave impetus to settlement of northern Ohio and the territory beyond, and the canal traffic put New York City permanently ahead of its rivals on the east coast for commercial and financial leadership.

But Baltimore, which had risen fast after the Revolution to become the third-ranking city in the country, was not to be outdone in the competition for Western trade. After studying the English experience with a railway, Baltimoreans started construction of the Baltimore and Ohio Railroad in 1827, to connect over the mountains with the Ohio Valley. Within the first five years traffic was rolling in volume into Baltimore, and by 1857, when the rail line entered Cincinnati, the venture had made the Chesapeake Bay port an important outlet for Western products, challenged only by New York and New Orleans.

New York began building railroads at the end of the 1820s. Philadelphia, Pittsburgh, Boston, and other cities soon followed suit, city enterprise creating the railroad age. New towns sprang up along their routes, and existing towns grew to become cities. The nation was on a course of industrialization, prompted first by the steamboat and then by the railroad. While the attraction of new, free land continued to draw men westward, still the 1840s and 1850s saw cities grow and multiply at a faster rate than in any other period of national history. Only the South, clinging to its plantation economy, failed to share in the commercial and industrial expansion and growth of cities.

Newly arrived immigrants in increasing numbers provided plenty of cheap labor for this expansion, mostly from northern and western Europe—Scandinavians, Germans, English, Scotch, and Irish—and from French Canada. The poorest of them, usually illiterate, settled in the cities. The Irish in particular, unskilled and semiskilled laborers and their families seeking to escape the poverty imposed on them for generations by their English masters, crowded into the Eastern seaboard cities after the potato famine struck Ireland in 1847. Immigrants were not readily accepted by the established native-born until they more than proved their loyalty to the Union side in the Civil War by providing soldiers well beyond their quota—in the case of the Germans, more than double.

Meanwhile, the pressures of Jacksonian democracy were changing the composition and character of the electorate. As state after state extended voting privileges to all males over twenty-one years of age, city after city amended their charters to eliminate the ownership of property as qualification for holding public office. The affluent were no longer in charge, and the quality of city administrations began to change, usually for the worse. The phenomenon of the "political boss" appeared by the 1850s in New York, Boston, Philadelphia, and half a dozen other cities. He headed a "machine" based on "ward heelers" who rounded up the votes of the native-born poor and the newly naturalized citizens to control the government of the city. Constance McLaughlin Green has explained this incipient new order as "the deliberate withdrawal of the 'first families' from civic responsibilities."

"Furthermore," she added, "men caught up in the excitements of accumulating riches in land speculation, railroad building, banking, and industrial promotion were loath to give time to municipal problems. In the post–Civil War era that washing of the hands would become more general and the consequences far more obvious."[4]

She refers, of course, to the notorious misrule of cities for three or four decades after the Civil War, an era which led one observer to declare in 1890: "With very few exceptions, the city governments of the United States are the worst in Christendom —the most expensive, the most inefficient, and the most corrupt."[5]

And yet Dr. Green's assertion that the decline in good and

honest city government was due to the abdication of the affluent from civic responsibilities seems too easy an explanation. For example, as late as the 1890s Providence still allowed only property owners to vote. They elected businessmen to the city council. This council, according to Ernest S. Griffith, "then awarded Aldrich, the state boss, a perpetual franchise [for a utility], which he sold out at an enormous profit. He went to the Senate through wholesale bribery of rural voters,* with money contributed by the sugar magnates for whom as congressman he had arranged a protective tariff."[6]

More likely, the era of governmental corruption could be blamed on the abdication of the affluent from moral standards of ordinary human behavior. The avarice and greed of many businessmen, land speculators, financiers, and their lawyers to profit from opportunities in the frenzied post–Civil War expansion of industry, railroads, and trade led the most ruthless of them to take the shortest way to quick riches. They simply bribed those equally immoral and unscrupulous politicians in a position to grant favors. And that, likewise, is too simplistic an explanation for the breakdown in ethical city government. Many factors contributed to the general malaise. There is no single answer.

In a diagnosis of what he calls "The Cancer of Corruption," Ernest S. Griffith traces many governmental abuses to the use of a third party in the receipt of graft. He wrote:

Respectable business interests could hire a political lawyer at high fees or contribute lavishly to campaign expenses—both completely legal transactions—and then ask no questions about the uses to which the money was put. Undoubtedly the lawyer was one of the chief channels for buying votes on city councils for franchises, just as campaign expenses were one of the principal sources for funds with which votes were purchased and repeaters hired at election—not to mention the withholding of astronomical sums by the party ring or boss who received the gifts. . . . These devices are far from having fallen into disuse in the 1970s

*Meaning those in the state legislature, which at that time still elected the U.S. Senators.

although the *quid pro quo* is probably not often mentioned explicitly. Covering of tracks by "loans" was then, as it is now, another device for transmission of funds. To this day mayors and councilmen who are lawyers may still be legally placed on a retainer, whether or not they do any legal work in return.[7]

He could have added that state legislators and members of Congress who are lawyers can do the same.

But Griffith is convinced that in the late nineteenth century "large scale profits fell more to the corrupters than to the corrupted." Without condoning the behavior of either, he finds evidence of some positive consequences in some petty kinds of graft. "Small-scale, lower-echelon corruption in the denizens of the cities . . . almost certainly fell on the plus side of the 'democracy of access' and humanization, social mobility, and integration of the ethnic groups into the nation."

One of the "great depressions" was the panic of 1873, following the inflationary boom after the Civil War. The last link in the first transcontinental railroad had been completed with the ceremonial driving of a golden spike into the ties near Ogden, Utah, to mark the joining of the Union Pacific and Central Pacific Railroads in 1869. As already noted, the railroad-building era had started some forty years earlier and had resulted in a spreading network, much of it financed by cities eager to be on the "main line" and to reap hoped-for benefits from this new, fast, and more flexible mode of transportation. In New York State alone some two hundred cities and towns had already extended loans to the railroads before 1870, and for the nation as a whole local bonds for railroad-related projects had grown to $185 million. Widespread abuses by the promoters of many of the earlier railroads led to the bankruptcy of a majority of them when the depressions of 1873 and 1893 hit, and the credit of cities was often brought down with them. To curb the local financial abuses of the period, more than half of the states by 1880 had constitutional limitations of city debt, many of them aimed at restricting municipal subsidies to the railroads and other corporations.[8] The abuses resulted from extravagance, overoptimism, and some-

Wide World

Horse-drawn fire apparatus in Dorchester, Massachusetts, responds to its last alarm in 1925.

times corrupt decisions in the post–Civil War period, especially in the two or three years preceding the panic. In addition, tax and debt limitations were placed in state statutes and city charters.

Some of the financial excesses were the result of rapid expansion of city functions. The census of 1860 showed that nine cities each had a population of more than 100,000, including the then-independent city of Brooklyn. Twenty-five others had more than 25,000, and another four hundred, each above 2,500, would today be qualified as urban. Altogether the urban population was 6,216,500, or one out of five Americans compared to the one out of twenty in 1790.

But municipal services had not kept pace with this growth. Unpaved streets were the rule, so that a heavy rain turned them into a sea of mud. Garbage collection in the smaller cities was done mostly by pigs which freely roamed the streets as scavengers. Sewers were rare, and flush toilets were nearly nonexistent. Philadelphia early in the 1800s was the first city to build a public waterworks, an outgrowth of the yellow fever epidemics of the 1790s. Over a hundred other municipal water systems were installed before the Civil War, inspired more by real estate promotion and recognition of the need for high-pressure water to fight fires than by any knowledge yet of the germ theory of disease. In the absence of public health administration, epidemics of typhoid, dysentery, and other diseases were common, aggravated by housing congestion in the slums that were appearing in the larger cities. Horse-drawn street railways that appeared in New York, Philadelphia, and Boston in the midcentury were only beginning to encourage the spread of new housing beyond a radius of walking distance to work. Constables and the small numbers of uniformed police that came into existence in the 1850s were no match for the crime that flourished in the darkness of unlit streets. The meager system of poorhouses and orphan asylums maintained by private charity and local tax money was inadequate to assist increasing numbers of people in desperate need. Yet one public service that had become accepted everywhere except in some areas of the South was free, tax-supported public schooling.

The Civil War temporarily checked the expansion of industry, the growth of railroads, and the rate of immigration that had been responsible for urban growth of the 1840s and 1850s. However, it all resumed with a rush soon after the war ended in 1865. New inventions and manufacturing processes, aided by cheap immigrant labor, expanded industry, making towns into cities, small cities into big cities, and big cities into metropolises. New towns and cities continued to rise with the westward spread of the railroads and the opening of new land to homesteaders. In 1870 the number of cities over 100,000 had increased to fourteen, those over 25,000 to fifty-two, and there were 663 incorporated communities of more than 2,500. The total urban population was 9,902,361.

In spite of the coincident growth of municipal graft, corruption, and misrule that accompanied this development, services expanded rapidly if not efficiently. Street paving proceeded briskly to the city limits, then was often torn up to lay new gas, water, and sewer lines. Although private companies usually supplied the gas, most municipalities built or enlarged their own waterworks. Public health boards were created and city health officers appointed. By 1875 most cities had uniformed, salaried police forces; they had existed only in the seven largest cities and the national capital in 1865.[9]

The Chicago fire of 1871 prompted cities to improve their fire defenses. Many of them increased water pressure; bought new equipment, including steam engines and telegraph alarms; instituted building inspections for fire hazards; and replaced politically powerful volunteer companies with paid departments. The expansion of all these and other municipal functions not only created golden opportunities for graft in the award of franchises and of contracts, but it enlarged the opportunities to load the public payrolls with jobholders appointed without regard to merit under a patronage system that rewarded the party faithful and strengthened the political boss and his machine. As municipal debts mounted and local tax burdens increased, it is no wonder that the panics of 1873 and 1893 prompted alarmed businessmen in the cities to persuade the rural representatives who dominated the state legislatures to restrict city activities and impose tax and debt limitations.

Reform movements inevitably followed exposure of the worst scandals and abuses. But even with honest mayors and other local officials, the structure of most city governments did not lend itself to efficiency and "businesslike" government. City charters, invariably complex, were usually patterned after the structure of state government. They often provided for a mayor elected at large and a bicameral council elected by wards or districts. Committees of the council administered various city activities. This system of administration by committees of unqualified, part-time amateurs began to be replaced about 1870 by numerous boards or commissions, although councilmen for decades afterward were reluctant to give up entirely the prerogatives and sense of power that went with determining policy and administering specific functions. The replacement of the council committees by boards was considered a reform of sorts. It brought a nonpartisan or bipartisan specialization and continuity to a function and thereby made its administration more "businesslike." Health boards, school boards, park boards, fire boards, police boards, public works boards, and water boards became common. Under either system, responsibility was diffused, and so the multiboard system began to be replaced by the grouping of functions under a single board. This could be considered the forerunner of what later became the commission form of city government, but with the exception of school, park, and library boards, the board system began to die out by 1890. It gave way for an interim to the strong-mayor plan, under which department heads were responsible as administrators directly to the elected chief executive.[10] Later the commission and then the council-manager plans became prevalent.

Although numerous citizen-sponsored reform efforts had been organized in individual cities earlier, it was not until 1894 that a sustained national movement got under way, possibly inspired by desires for economy as a result of the depression that started the year before. The earlier reformers had differing priorities and concepts of needs, although there was general agreement on four principal objectives: (1) the need for civil service reform and the abolition of patronage; (2) nonpartisanship in deciding local municipal issues on their own merits as having no relationship to national or state partisan contentions; (3) a reform of nomination and election processes to assure competition, wide participation, a secret ballot, and honest counts; (4) freedom of cities from interference in local affairs by the state legislature (municipal home rule), including greater freedom in adopting new functions. Of course, everybody was for "honesty" and "efficiency."

On January 25, 1894, citizens from twenty-seven cities met in Philadelphia at the joint call of the Municipal League of Philadelphia and the City Club of New York. Among the 105 signers for that first "National Conference for Good City Government" was Theodore Roosevelt. The result was the formation in May that year of the National Municipal League,[11] not to be confused with the state leagues of municipalities, sometimes called municipal leagues, that were formed later. At succeeding annual conferences it became clear to the members and participants that there was not one, or even four, solutions to the problem of achieving "good city government," that it was, in fact, extremely complex, and that it must be approached comprehensively. A committee was appointed in 1897 to develop a program for the organization. Its reports were discussed at the succeeding two conferences, and a final version was adopted at the 1900 session. Ernest S. Griffith describes it as "by all odds, the most thoroughly studied, far-reaching, and prestigious report ever drafted by anybody in the municipal field."[12]

The report, according to a summary by Griffith, included proposals that cities be given broad authority to enact ordinances and provide a wide range of services; that they be granted extensive taxing and regulatory powers; that civil service commissions, appointed by the mayor, be established to make job classifications, conduct examinations, and insulate appointments from political influence; that, with the exception of self-liquidating projects, the debt level be limited to a percentage of assessed valuation, and that property be taxed at a specified percentage of assessment; that utility franchises be limited to twenty-one years and that they be granted only after adequate publicity; that such utilities be subject to a gross-receipts tax; that municipal ownership of utilities be permitted; and that elections, conducted by secret ballot, be nonpartisan as far as possible.

The report advocated the mayor-council form of government under which the mayor would serve a two-year term and would have full powers of appointment and removal, would have limited veto of ordinances and an item veto of appropriations, and would have authority to prepare a budget which council could reduce but not increase. Ideally, said the report, council should be a unicameral body, with members elected at large for six-year, overlapping terms. Its sessions should be public and it should have the power to determine the organization of the executive branch.

The report reflected the mood of the most concerned and thoughtful citizen observers of the municipal scene. In general, they were disposed to broaden legislative and administrative powers but determined to place firm restraints on fiscal affairs. They sought to establish a system of political accountability by mayoral appointees, but they were bent on curbing patronage by isolating civil servants from politics and on pressing for safeguards against graft. And they wanted city hall as far removed from party politics as possible.

A proliferation of books and articles on local government appeared during this time. This great surge of publications emphasized structural reform. Studies on local government published about twenty years earlier usually dealt with engineering, sewage systems, paving, fire fighting, public health, and educational administration. The discussion of organization and management of city administration added a new dimension to the textbooks.

During the first fifteen years of the twentieth century, the evolution of city administration from confusion and "conspicuous failure" to the beginnings of a generally well organized system has been described as "startlingly rapid" and as a period of greater progress in the improvement of municipal services than the entire nineteenth century.[13] It has become known as the Progressive Era.

For the city governments themselves, however, improvement in structure and methods to promote efficiency, expansion of services, and addition of new services usually required legal authority that could come only by changes in state laws. The so-called Dillon rule had become the accepted legal dictum that cities could have only those powers specifically granted to them by the state. They had no implied powers and no inherent right of local self-government. In addition, as has been noted, the abuses and excesses of the preceding decades had resulted in limitations and restrictions imposed on them by the states. Technological advances, such as electrification of street railways beginning in 1887 and telephone communication, facilitated the spread of housing and the beginning of suburban development, adding to the demands on cities for expansion of services. Legislatures dominated by a combination of venal city politicians and rural representatives who were suspicious of cities, if not actually hostile toward them, frustrated early efforts for improvements sought by a growing number of well-intentioned mayors. Governors and the executive branch of the states were equally unsympathetic, in some instances for partisan or political reasons, in others for lack of knowledge or understanding.

To discuss these problems and others, city officials in a few states began to meet together in statewide conferences and to organize state leagues of municipalities for cooperating in presenting a united front to the state government. Four such leagues were formed in 1898 and several more in the next dozen years. These leagues began to serve also as a medium through which city officials could exchange experiences and ideas concerning improved methods and efficiency, a process of evolution that will be described in succeeding chapters. Such leagues became an important factor in the growth of professionalization of top-ranking municipal administrative personnel, and ultimately were pioneers in the development of in-service training programs. But their most important function was seeking state legislation and administrative decisions beneficial to cities. In this and in other services, as well as in the improvement of city-state relations, they were eminently successful in many states, although in more than half the states they were not to come into their own until about the 1930s.

As the twentieth century ushered in a municipal renaissance, industrial expansion continued to absorb the swelling volume of immigration—which by this time had changed in character, with most of the new arrivals coming from eastern and southern Europe. At the same time an even greater number of native-born

Americans were leaving their rural birthplaces and crowding into the cities. Thomas Edison's experiments had given birth to the electrical industry. The internal combustion engine, which had been invented several years earlier, was perfected in about 1901. These events, followed by the introduction of assembly lines into automobile factories, created new complicating factors in urban growth. By 1910 the United States had been transformed from a rural to a predominantly industrial nation and a world power. The population of its 2,405 municipalities was rapidly overtaking that of the rural areas.

However, the social problems that accompanied this rapid urbanization were accumulating and going largely unresolved, although the controlling grip of the "robber barons" on the great corporate trusts had been broken and the adoption of a graduated federal income tax in 1913 began to check the accumulation of huge fortunes. Still, industrial strife continued, compounded by racial and ethnic antagonisms, as unions sought to organize the workers. The further industrial expansion and general prosperity that followed World War I ended in the Great Depression of the 1930s, a decade which marked the beginning of direct city-federal relations as the states demonstrated their inability to cope.

During World War II rural workers flocked into cities in search of job opportunities. This great migration continued after the war as technological innovations and mechanization of agriculture displaced the need for manual laborers on the farms. A later chapter deals with the profound impact of this phenomenal relocation.

"From humble beginnings in the early days of settlement the city has thus traced a varied course," wrote historian Arthur M. Schlesinger in 1940. "In Europe the urban community emerged by imperceptible stages out of the town economy and culture of the Middle Ages; by comparison the American city leaped into being with breath-taking suddenness."[14]

Once in being, the infant American cities had little time to establish traditions. They were forced immediately to assert the authority needed to guarantee the freedoms and to curb the excesses of wilderness settlements. They then had to acquiesce as the states expropriated a broad range of powers and stood athwart the "middle tier" that was for decades a virtually impassable barrier between federal and local government.

As we have seen, most of the major cities of the West were established as thriving outposts, far in advance of the frontier at most any given time in history. During a period of industrial expansion, cities served as ports of entry and schools of citizenship for waves of immigrants. Cities not only became hubs of the transportation system; they furnished much of the capital to build the "spokes." For years electorates countenanced the most revolting scandals but, fortunately, they contained the civic leaven to bring about desperately needed reform. A growing cadre of municipal officials, swept into office on the crest of enthusiasm for this new era of "good government," began to search for ways to translate reform rhetoric into actual practice. The next chapter deals with their quest.

John G. Stutz, founder of the National
League of Cities in 1924, as he appeared
then and fifty years later.

Wichers—Topeka

...3

Cities Unite to Improve Efficiency

"There is no denying that the government of cities is the one conspicuous failure of the United States," wrote Lord James A. Bryce, the British scholar, in 1888.[1]

The failures, including those detailed in the last chapter, were equally conspicuous to native-born observers. The harsh judgments of Lincoln Steffens *(The Shame of the Cities)* and other so-called muckrakers at the turn of the century reached a far wider audience than Lord Bryce's scholarly pronouncement. The momentum generated by the writings of these critics and other revelations of corruption, waste, and inefficiency provided a wide range of issues for the agenda of the foremost citizens' reform group, the National Municipal League, for many years after its founding in 1894. This nonpartisan group of good-government advocates wrestled with such basic problems as how to guarantee honest elections, how to keep profligate patronage dispensers from flooding city departments with incompetents, and how to organize city government so that municipal employees were accountable to the voters for the duties they were charged with carrying out.

As an aroused citizenry began to "throw the rascals out" and elect more honest, responsible persons to city offices, the new breed of mayors, councilmen, and administrators sought to become better informed on methods to increase efficiency. Their desire to create a mechanism for systematic exchange of experiences, ideas, and information and their need for changes in state laws to authorize new methods prompted them to form statewide leagues of municipalities. The cities in five states had organized such associations by the turn of the century, and by 1924 the cities in thirty-two additional states had followed those examples. Some existed for only a short time, in some cases because their only objective was to mobilize sufficient strength to secure from a reluctant, rural legislature some legal authority for a specific city need. That accomplished, such an organization lapsed for lack of a continuing, year-round program of service.

And yet the institutional response of city officials to the demands for reform and efficiency continued to center on the development of more effective state leagues of municipalities. This was because only the state could grant to local governments the powers that cities needed to perform an expanding range of functions for their constituents. Many cities sought to change their structure of government, which also required sanction by the state, either by general or special laws or by the granting of home rule powers under which local communities could determine their own structural systems.

These were some of the reasons why, in 1924, cities in more than half the states organized primarily at the state level, and why there was so little impetus for a national organization.

A short-lived national organization, the League of American Municipalities, had been defunct by 1916. At its first convention in Columbus, Ohio, in 1897, the 418 delegates from 101 cities in twenty-three states had agreed to open the membership to any municipality in the United States or Canada.[2] Two factors apparently contributed to its demise. First, its main purposes were the holding of annual conventions and maintaining a central information bureau on municipal government. It did not attempt to establish policy on national issues and press for legislation— hardly possible, anyway, in a binational organization. Second, its alleged mismanagement, climaxed in 1912 by the loss of all the league's records, discouraged potential city members. It collapsed after four more poorly attended conventions. The league started two magazines, *City Hall,* its official organ, published until about 1911, and *Modern City,* a periodical established in 1915 that failed to survive the death of the organization.[3]

In the 1920s there was very little of common interest to hold cities together in a national organization other than a desire of many of their officials to improve efficiency—some say as a result of public concern after the muckraking exposures at the turn of the century. A central clearing house of information and experience could help them improve efficiency, but that was not enough to hold the support of elected policy leaders. Furthermore, there was then, and there still is, a rapid turnover of elected officials. This can range from 30 percent to 60 percent annually. Most of them are interested in achieving a better record of efficiency than their predecessors and are interested in learning about better methods of municipal government. Yet it seems that by the time they have mastered their jobs they leave office, not always voluntarily. Therefore, it is more reasonable to expect appointed officers to provide continuity of effort to advance efficient administration, particularly where appointees are chosen on the basis of merit and have achieved career status.

Some groups of appointed officers had begun to develop standards of professionalism and had formed specialized societies and associations. Fire chiefs organized nationally in 1873, waterworks operators in 1881, police chiefs in 1893, public works officials in 1894, civil service and personnel officials in 1906, finance officers in 1906, city managers in 1914, building code officials in 1915, and city planners in 1917. Those fledgling professional societies began to fill the need for exchange of technical information and experience on a national basis in their particular functions, albeit with limited resources.

But a national association of city *governments*—municipal corporations, represented by their elected officers—needed the cohesive force of mutual national policy objectives implicit in direct city-federal relations. Until the 1930s there was no significant direct relation between cities of the United States and the national government. In fact, as late as the middle 1920s such a modest proposal as that made by Secretary of Commerce Herbert Hoover to establish within the Department of Commerce an organization to give technical aid and assistance to municipalities, in the same way that he was so successfully aiding business enterprise, received a negative response from President Coolidge. The President, a former governor, held the opinion that because local governments were merely creatures of the state governments, there should be no direct communication between the federal government and the local governments except through channels established by the states.[4] The cities' problems were with their state governments. Hence, it is understandable that the League of American Municipalities had withered away.

As already noted, thirty-seven state associations of city governments had been formed by 1924, all organized since 1891, when Indiana became the first state to record the formation of a league of municipalities. The Indiana league soon died out but it was revived in 1899, the same year a league was formed in Michigan. Leagues were organized in Iowa, California, and Wisconsin in 1898.

Frank G. Pierce, with Des Moines Mayor John MacVicar co-founder of the Iowa league, and its first executive secretary, pioneered many of the practices adopted by successful leagues in other states. The Iowa league, for example, set a precedent when it decided to follow the European example whereby municipal corporations, not individual officials, were enrolled as members and paid for its operations. Pierce was one of the ten founders of the national association of state municipal leagues, the American Municipal Association, formed in 1924.

Apparently the first need for collective action in the states organizing these early leagues was the strength of union to secure desired municipal legislation. But their proceedings expressed the need for information clearing houses, conferences to permit city officials to exchange ideas, and research. They also pooled their strength and talents to present the public position on issues involving public utility service and rate-making.[5]

Some of the first thirty-seven state leagues gained strength and recognition as the power in municipal affairs in their states. Others functioned inadequately and still others soon became inactive. By 1924 leagues were functioning in only twenty-one states. John G. Stutz, who provided the inspired leadership that brought the state leagues together in a permanent national organization, reflected in 1926 on the frustrations the leagues faced in their formative years.

Sometimes, Stutz said, an organization's enthusiasm departed upon the resignation of its organizer, and it dissolved. Stutz's catalogue of obstacles also included short-sighted and indifferent city officials, the failure of cities to see tangible benefits in membership—often the case with leagues that failed to develop publicity or provide sufficient services—and executive secretaries who were not qualified, poorly paid, or unable to devote sufficient time to organization work. Finally, he said, the war delivered the knockout blow to a few tottering leagues.

Stutz listed factors that had contributed to the growth of most successful leagues in the United States and Canada: annual conferences, information services, regular publications, employment of a field agent, permanent headquarters, policies of encouraging inquiries and visits from city officials, and strong efforts to secure desired legislation and to deal with problems of statewide scope. "A competent, well-paid secretary," Stutz emphasized, "is one of the best guarantees for a successful organization." Opinion was divided, he said, about the value of league affiliation with universities, an alliance some leagues had formed.[6]

The most basic and important ingredient for success listed by Stutz was and still is without question "a competent, well-paid secretary," full-time, of course. The secretary—more commonly called the executive director today—is the key to the whole operation of the league and its success or decline. If he is as dedicated as he should be, he will never convey that impression of himself. He will maintain low visibility. Pushing his officers and other elected officials to the forefront, he will remain in the background, directing the staff work and seeing that the required job gets done. Quietly and without credit for himself he prepares speeches, statements to the press, and testimony to legislative committees as necessary to assist his association leaders to convey the association's objectives in the best possible public image, based on careful staff research and reporting of verifiable facts. By developing a dependable clearing house of information, he will constantly strive to make it easier for responsible officials to do a better job for their constituents. He will provide the intellectual leadership. He will provide the continuity that is essential through changes of administration and all the vicissitudes of partisan (or nonpartisan) politics as city officers, through the periodic vagaries of the fickle public, are retired from office.

Kenneth E. Kerle reached the same conclusion in his scholarly and detailed study of the League of Kansas Municipalities in 1967:

Most leagues possess the democratic trappings of elected governing bodies and public official committees designed to formulate suggestions, discuss alternatives, and present recommendations at the conferences and conventions for delegate approval. In fact, however, most of the suggestions and alternatives emanate from the executive directors and staff members of the leagues. These are the people who initiate the planning, organization, and operation of programs and proposals. A weak or lethargic director is likely to be a sign of a stagnant league.[7]

John Stutz was one of the early examples of the "competent secretary," but few today would consider him "well paid." His starting salary as director of the League of Kansas Municipalities was $2,200, rising to $6,255.27 five years later. He used more than $2,000 of that personal income in 1925 for trips to international municipal meetings in Quebec and Paris. When he retired after thirty-five years of service to the League of Kansas Municipalities his salary was $10,800. He may have been well paid within the context of state and local government salary scales in 1955, the year of his retirement, but his income was woefully insufficient compensation for the contribution he made toward better local government. Unfortunately for Stutz, the national average income for this type of position started rising about the time he retired. By 1972 at least twenty-five state leagues were paying their directors more than $20,000, plus fringe benefits.

Stutz had not come on the organizational scene in 1917 when the secretaries of six state leagues met in Detroit under the auspices of the National Municipal League and organized the short-lived Conference of State Leagues of Municipalities. A second annual meeting, scheduled in New York the following year, was never held, and the conference became inactive.

The man whose presence probably ensured that the second national organizational effort did not meet the same fate was born in a sod house—a dugout—on a Kansas farm, January 1, 1893. John Stutz attended Kansas State College, the University of Kansas, and, after World War I service as a lieutenant in the United States Army, the University of Chicago, where one of his professors was Dr. Charles E. Merriam. He sought employment as a city manager, but was persuaded in 1920 to become executive secretary of the League of Kansas Municipalities. The Kansas league, organized in 1910, was affiliated with the University of Kansas Extension Division. At Kansas, Stutz also taught municipal government and directed the Municipal Reference Bureau, an adjunct of the league which drafted model ordinances and dispensed information. Destined to become the cities' "man for all seasons," he was already wearing three hats in his first job.

Stutz made it his business to study the methods used by other organizations in order to apply their successes to his own operation in Kansas. He personally visited the secretaries of nine state municipal associations. With the encouragement of Morris B. Lambie, executive secretary of the League of Minnesota Municipalities, and of Frank G. Pierce, secretary of the League of Iowa Municipalities, he invited the secretaries of all the twenty-one state municipal organizations then functioning to attend a meeting on December 12 and 13, 1924, at the University of Kansas in Lawrence. After citing the advantages of personal contact, rather than the limitations of correspondence, in the interchange of ideas, methods, and experiences, he proposed the following agenda for the meeting: legislative methods, research and the compilation of special bulletins, information service for city officials, general legal service, ordinance revision service, accounting and auditing service, publication of official organs and convention proceedings, and maintaining library service for city officials.

The ten who attended can rightfully be called the founders of what is now known as the National League of Cities. Besides Stutz, they were: Don C. Sowers, Colorado Municipal League; A. D. McLarty, Illinois Municipal League; Frank G. Bates, Indiana Municipal League; Frank G. Pierce, League of Iowa Municipalities; Bates K. Lucas, League of Michigan Municipalities; Morris B. Lambie, League of Minnesota Municipalities; Harry A. Barth, Oklahoma Municipal League; Robert D. Jackson, League of Texas Municipalities; and Morton L. Wallerstein, League of Virginia Municipalities.*

Before these founding fathers adjourned, they concurred in a denunciation of the spoils system by their guest speaker, Dr. Frederick K. Guild, chairman of the University of Kansas department of political science. The Jacksonian doctrine underlying the spoils system, Dr. Guild argued, constituted a formidable barrier to standardization of public service positions and kept alive a skepticism toward experts in government. For a group of experts on government dedicated to standardization of public service roles, this speech identified one of the major challenges they faced. Another was spelled out in two papers presented at that charter meeting. The papers dealt with the problems of getting rural-dominated legislatures to pass needed municipal legislation.

Some of the needs of the cities in the ten states represented

*The other eleven states in which leagues were actively functioning with varying degrees of effectiveness in 1924 were: California, Florida, Nebraska, New Jersey, New York, North Carolina, Pennsylvania, Tennessee, Utah, West Virginia, and Wisconsin.

included: use of the state gasoline tax on city streets in addition to arterial highways and rural roads, authority to enact zoning ordinances, authority to levy special tax assessments against property abutting public improvements, home rule authority to enable cities to enact their own local legislation, equalization of property tax valuations, and authority to make and adopt city plans.

It is quite obvious from the records of that 1924 meeting and of meetings for many years thereafter that the professionals who ran the affairs of the state organizations of cities were concerned primarily with efficiency in city government and with ways to persuade reluctant state legislatures to make that possible in many fields. Some league leaders, however, expressed broader concerns. Morris Lambie of the Minnesota league, for example, believed that "the research of any league should not be confined to city problems only, but should begin with a consideration of state government, its organization and functions; special assessments, accounting and indebtedness of states and cities should come in for a considerable amount of study." And he envisioned a set of model ordinances in pamphlet form, giving the history of the need and uses of each ordinance and a thoroughgoing account of the experience of other cities with a similar ordinance, including court decisions affecting its validity. He advocated studies of home rule charters in states that authorized them. The Colorado league secretary said his office was studying state government and was instrumental in securing the preparation and consideration of that state's first comprehensive, accurate state budget. Also under way in Colorado were studies of the financing of higher education, and agricultural interests in the state had asked the league to make a study of taxes. A downward revision of utility rates was a common objective of some leagues.

The delegates adjourned after endorsing a tentative plan of organization to be submitted to the members and prospective members for vote by letter ballot. John G. Stutz was elected the first executive secretary of what was temporarily called the Association of American Municipal Organizations. Morris B. Lambie became its first president and Morton L. Wallerstein its first vice-president. At the second annual conference, held in Chicago, December 17–19, 1925, the same officers were reelected, a constitution was adopted, and the name became officially the American Municipal Association.* The executive secretary reported that total expenditures of the association that year were $149.44, paid for out of dues of $65 and a gift of $100, leaving a balance of $15.56. Forty-six years later, Stutz revealed that it was he who had made the $100 gift.[8]

The reason for the use of "American," rather than "United States" or "National," was that "American" was intended to include the state municipal organizations of both the United States and Canada. The Union of Canadian Municipalities, organized in 1901, was represented at the 1925 meeting in Chicago but, although they remained eligible until 1947, participation in the new association by municipal associations of Canadian provinces never materialized.

A significant decision was made by the founders when they decided that the basic purpose of their new organization, as expressed in its first constitution, was "to collect and exchange information upon municipal affairs, which may serve to assist the respective state municipal organizations in the promotion of approved methods of municipal government." Note that the service was to assist "the respective state municipal organizations," and they were to be its only members. Individual cities were not to be eligible for membership until more than twenty years later. Note also the emphasis on promoting "approved methods" of municipal government, which had been the basic purpose of the defunct League of American Municipalities. If a national association of cities could not be successful, perhaps a federation of state associations could be more effective, at least in the collection and exchange of information on municipal affairs.

The choice was made only after considerable discussion and

*In 1964, forty years after the first meeting, the name of the organization was changed to the National League of Cities.

advice from an outsider, Dr. Charles E. Merriam, a nationally recognized professor of political science at the University of Chicago.

"So far as the structure of the organization is concerned," Dr. Merriam said in his 1925 address, "this ought to be the real center of municipal power. . . . That power, of course, will not be a commanding or controlling power. It will be the power of information or the power of service, the power of intellectual leadership without any power of force back of it." He urged the new American Municipal Association to encourage and develop organized municipal research. "We had better develop more science in city government, more information, more research, more service, and more technical advice," he concluded.[9]

Charles E. Merriam was addressing an audience of less than two dozen persons, which prompted him to remark: "I have seldom talked to a smaller group with larger possibilities." Thirty-five years later his son, Robert E. Merriam, Assistant to the President of the United States, addressed the annual conference of the American Municipal Association at New York City in 1960, when its attendance had grown to 1,500.*

In the discussion that followed Charles Merriam's 1925 address, the delegates grappled with the question of what type of association they wanted. It was pointed out that at that time it was merely an association of secretaries of state leagues of municipalities. Dr. Richard R. Price, who had organized both the Kansas and the Minnesota leagues, put the issue clearly:

"The whole issue is bound up in what you want to make it. Are you thinking of making it a conference of the permanent secretaries of your state leagues? Is that to be the object? Is it to be a conference for discussing methods and plans and principles to obtain wisdom from a multitude of counselors, or is it meant to be an official congress of delegates of states? You can't think clearly until you know which of these things you are driving at."

*The fiftieth annual meeting was attended by more than 5,000 at San Juan, Puerto Rico, in 1973.

Dr. Merriam pointed out that a "conference" of secretaries would be primarily a study of the technique of running the state leagues, while a "congress" would deal with urban problems. He again emphasized the strength of union. "The thing that has the striking, driving power is the combination of cities," he declared.

Asked by the presiding officer whether there is "a driving power among cities" and whether there is a community of interest among the cities of the state, John Stutz provided the answer that seems to have become the basic philosophy of the organization: "I think that is the only way you could have it, that is, through the state organizations. I think that is the reason the League of American Municipalities died. It was so scattered it could not keep up the interests of the states, and it failed. I think if you want to have a successful national association you must have it through the state leagues."

A year later, in his president's address at the third annual conference, in Saint Louis, November 9–11, 1926, Morris B. Lambie was saying: "We know that at present [the American Municipal Association] is nothing more than a conference group, that it has no intention of representing any individual league, that it is not militant, and that it has no set association policy or program. I doubt if any of us have thought very much about the activities of the association for the immediate future or about the desirability of its asserting itself beyond the present field."

Lambie himself, however, had thought about it enough to have formed an adamant, inflexible position. As the association's president during its first two years and as an influential spokesman during the first ten annual meetings, he used his influence to keep the association from becoming a policy spokesman for cities or their state leagues. Thus, right into the economic and social crisis of the Great Depression in the 1930s, attempts were made to keep the potentially powerful association a mere political eunuch.

The Golden Twenties—Boom!

While the executives of the state leagues of municipalities continued their struggle for identity, American cities were striving to keep pace with the expanding economy of the boom years that followed the postwar depression of 1920–21. Swift and far-reaching technological advances dramatically altered the physical form of cities while less visible social changes planted seeds for urban problems of the 1950s and 1960s. City officials were able to cope adequately with the demands for services growing out of the new affluence. Pressures for social change, however, when identified on rare occasions, were not strong enough in this period to command major attention.

New modes of transportation had begun to change the shape of cities long before the advent of the automobile. Among city dwellers, horses and carriages were mostly for the rich, and so the natural boundaries of cities extended only as far as a man could walk in an hour.* The *voiture omnibus* (vehicle for all), later shortened in English to "bus," was introduced in Paris in the early nineteenth century. It provided public transportation along a fixed route in a large horse-drawn vehicle which any-

*Likewise, the natural boundaries of counties generally extended only as far as a horse could convey a man to the county seat in a day but, with exceptions of rare consolidations, or their outright abolition as in Connecticut and Rhode Island, county boundaries have not changed since the days of the horse.

body could board for a small fee. Soon rails, like those already used in coal mines, were laid to carry such vehicles. Possibly the first such horse-drawn street railway built anywhere was the New York & Harlem Railway. It was built in 1832 by an Irish immigrant, John Stephenson, who became the leading manufacturer of "streetcars," as they came to be called when they flourished after the middle of the century.

The "flight to the suburbs" began long before urban affairs "experts" started using that phrase as shorthand to describe, with varying degrees of scorn, the rapid post–World War II development of outlying land that resulted from the proliferation of automobiles, growth of a modern highway network, and easy financing of home ownership. The flight actually started when the streetcar made it possible for an employee to live beyond walking distance of his job. Cities began to stretch. Boston, for example, which was still a pedestrian city with a three-mile radius as late as 1850, became a suburbanized metropolis by 1900, with a radius of ten miles, due largely to extensions of streetcar lines.

Development of the carbon commutator brush by Belgian immigrant Charles J. Van Depoele made possible an efficient electric motor to replace the horse as a source of power for streetcars. Van Depoele also developed the overhead trolley system to transmit electricity from a central power station to the moving cars. Richmond, Virginia, in 1888, became the first city to have an extensive trolley system, built by Frank Julian Sprague in ninety days. Sprague built eighty motors and equipped forty cars, laid twelve miles of track, erected the overhead trolley wire, and built and equipped a central power plant—all for $110,000. He soon had contracts for a hundred other streetcar systems.[1]

Streetcars became necessary for the promotion of new suburbs by real estate men and suburban investors. Even the notorious sprawl of Los Angeles was begun not by the automobile, but by the streetcar empire of Henry Huntington. Between 1900 and 1913, Huntington extended electric streetcar lines thirty-five miles, connecting some forty incorporated centers. By 1920 he had helped create a dozen new incorporated suburban satellites of Los Angeles.

Another technological breakthrough was also changing the shape of cities—this one vertically rather than horizontally. "The revolution which brought about the most radical transformation in the structural art since the development of gothic architecture in the twelfth century was the invention of complete iron framing on skeletal construction," wrote Carl W. Condit in *The Rise of the Skyscraper.*[2] According to Condit, the first true skyscraper was Chicago's ten-story Home Insurance Building, the achievement of full framing by architect William LeBaron Tenney in 1883–85, and "the first complete answer to the problem of large scale urban construction."

Of course, the elevator was a necessary component. Elevators had been tried earlier in the century for freight, and had been used by passengers in experiments in hotels as early as 1833. Elisha Graves Otis invented a safety device which he demonstrated publicly in New York City in 1854. Otis installed his safety elevators in the new five-story Haughwout Department Store on lower Broadway in 1857, and in 1861 patented a steam-powered elevator. Hydraulic elevators were installed in the Eiffel Tower for the Paris Exposition in 1889, the same year that the new electric elevators first appeared. By the end of the century, high-rise office buildings were appearing in all the larger American cities and mini-skyscrapers in many of the smaller ones. While they contributed greatly to the downtown economic base, they also helped to produce a growing congestion, particularly after the automobile came into widespread use following World War I.

Thus, the cities were stretching out and up. By 1920 the whole urban environment was entering an unprecedented phase of technological change that even by 1975, fifty-five years later, had yet to complete its course. The basic factor bringing about the change was the development of the internal combustion engine, using still another source of energy—petroleum. This engine had been invented before the turn of the century and initially applied to highway vehicles during the 1890s. From an output of some 4,200 cars in 1900, the new automobile industry in the next ten years won a major position in the economy, with a production in 1910 of 187,000 cars valued at $225 million wholesale.

By 1915 nearly 2.5 million cars were in use. Between 1910 and 1920 the industry made the transition to mass production and in the final year of that decade turned out 2.2 million vehicles. The Automobile Age had begun in earnest. The 8 million passenger cars and 1 million trucks on American roads in 1920 had increased to 23 million cars and nearly 4 million trucks ten years later.[3]

The amazing expansion of the auto industry after World War I and its boost of the iron and steel trade were major forces behind the quick economic recovery from the depression of 1920–21. The resulting business boom was accompanied by land and building booms. One economist described the years between 1922 and 1929 as the "Golden Twenties," a period which "raised the economy to unheard of heights of business activity."

The increase in automobile ownership was quickly reflected in city ordinances and administrative procedures. Police departments formed special traffic divisions. Traffic control towers and semaphores were installed in the centers of busy intersections, and by 1921 the first electric signal lights were installed on such towers to make them more effective at night. Cities recording an increase of 8 percent or more in vehicle registration were advised to give "serious consideration to traffic control problems" by an article in the March 1924 *National Municipal Review.*

State leagues of municipalities developed model traffic ordinances. The one drafted by the League of Kansas Municipalities not only prescribed speed limits (fifteen miles per hour at intersections, twelve in school zones, and twenty elsewhere), but it foreshadowed the future plagues of air pollution and smog. It prohibited the visible emission of "an unduly great amount of steam, smoke or products of combustion from exhaust pipes or openings."[4]

The growth in numbers of cars and trucks was accompanied

by a rapidly growing network of paved highways—primary roads to connect the cities and secondary, rural roads to "get the farmers out of the mud." Special taxes on vehicles, accessories, and gasoline soon became the accepted means of raising money for the maintenance and for a large share of the construction of roads. Thirty-six states and the District of Columbia had adopted gasoline taxes by 1924, ranging from one or two cents per gallon in most of them to Arkansas' four cents. These special taxes produced some $100 million in 1920 and over $800 million a year by 1929.

In most states, rural-dominated legislatures forbade the use of state-collected highway taxes for maintenance of the connecting links of the systems inside city limits. This discrimination was one of the motives that impelled cities to form state leagues.

North Carolina pioneered in the use of bond issues to finance road building, and by the early 1920s had connected each of its one hundred county seats with a network of paved highways, giving it an edge over all other Southern states in industrial development. Most states, however, built roads on a "pay as you go" basis. In all states with modern road networks, plant location was no longer dependent on waterways or railways. With such vastly improved facilities for truck transport and the large-scale extension of heavy-duty power-transmission cables, plants could be located almost anywhere along the highways. And in any territory with a reasonably high population density, management could expect to attract daily commuters within a radius of up to thirty miles.

Likewise, the automobile began to change the geography of retail trade and service industries, which were formerly concentrated at the central core where public transit routes came together and where the chief shopping and office buildings were located. Those facilities began to join manufacturing and storage establishments in moving out from the congested central districts of large cities, a trend that is continuing to this day. This trend led one economist in 1951 to envision an almost irreversible pattern of urban blight. "Property owners, municipalities,

Urban traffic in the 1920s was only a preview of more massive congestion problems to come.

and utilities are left with enormous investments in downtown facilities, that, under Automobile Age conditions, can perhaps never be utilized in such a way as to make a fair return on the investment," wrote Edgar M. Hoover.[5] He was unduly pessimistic, for he could not foresee the massive redevelopment of blighted areas that has taken place since then nor the more recent dramatic improvements in public transportation.

It was clear, however, that the automobile had accelerated the exodus of city dwellers, who moved to the suburbs by the thousands, leaving their old city houses to be occupied by lower-income families or to be converted to commercial use. New arrivals from rural areas or from Europe continued to settle in the old centers. While World War I caused a sharp drop in immigration, the manpower shortages that developed in the expanding war industries attracted a mass movement of workers to urban centers from farms and villages until the census of 1920 showed, for the first time, that more than half the population of the United States was living in urban places. Still, the number of persons living on farms that year was 32 million, or 30 percent of the total U.S. population, a percentage that dropped steadily for the next fifty years until the 9.7 million persons living on farms in 1970 constituted only 4.8 percent of U.S. population.

While advancing transportation technology made possible the expansion of cities, electronics engineers achieved a breakthrough that would increasingly intensify the cultural cohesiveness of their dispersing populations. Radio and the growth of commercial broadcasting added to the prosperity of the "Golden Twenties" and possibly altered the daily habits of Americans as profoundly as anything that decade produced. The nation's first broadcasting station, KDKA in East Pittsburgh, went on the air late in 1920, operated by Westinghouse. By 1922 radio had become a national obsession, and the sales of sets, parts, and accessories amounted to $60 million. The sales volume increased steadily until it reached $842,548,000 by 1929. The common stock of Radio Corporation of America went from a 1928 low of 85¼ to a 1929 high of 549.[6]

The forces that created the trends of the twenties and their powerful impacts on cities were national in scope. Most city officials, however, did not consider the social and economic problems caused by those forces to be the responsibility of city government. Some cities, with encouragement from their state leagues, tried to channel growth in an orderly manner through city planning and land-use controls. The practice of zoning was upheld by the United States Supreme Court in 1926, and cities were encouraged to use it by the Department of Commerce under Secretary Herbert Hoover and by the Chamber of Commerce of the United States. Otherwise, the principal concern of cities was for "businesslike" efficiency in the rendering of the increasing number of municipal services.

Only occasionally did a lone voice suggest that the basic problems of the city could not be solved merely through reforms to achieve honesty and efficiency. For example, Professor Charles A. Beard, the economic historian, during the 1917 convention of the National Municipal League, vigorously opposed the reform concept of nonpartisan city elections on the grounds that municipal leaders would have to seek state and federal assistance through political channels to deal effectively with the city's basic problems. He defined these as poverty, overcrowding, unemployment, physical decay, and low standards of life.[7]

Responsible officials made accommodations for the physical changes thrust upon cities by expanding technology but they showed little concern about the social consequences of those changes. They likewise largely ignored the emerging racial and social problems resulting from heavy migration of Negro workers attracted from the rural South by jobs in industries mobilized by the war that continued to expand after 1914.

At the 1924 convention of the City Managers' Association, Professor Howard W. Odum, the sociologist, urged the managers to become involved in the "modern techniques and organization of public welfare," which, he made clear, was not to be confused with "charity." He defined public welfare as "that technique and organization of government which guarantees that democracy shall be made effective in the unequal places." Noting that only about thirty cities had "standard" departments of welfare, he said he knew of nothing about which there was less understanding. "People are not interested," he declared, which apparently was true of most of his audience.[8]

What *did* interest city managers intensely in 1924 was governmental form, departmental organization, budgeting and finances. In an era that placed a high premium on businesslike administration of municipal government, the managers' zeal for efficiency seemed to exceed that of their counterparts in other forms of city government. For this they received recognition outside their profession. City managers "pre-eminently characterize the new management," wrote Professor Leonard D. White in the public administration section of the President's Research Committee on Social Trends.[9]

The first city manager position was established by ordinance in Staunton, Virginia, in 1908, when that city's bicameral city council and mayor concluded that the management of municipal expenditures and personnel by twenty-two council committees was neither efficient nor responsive to the needs of the citizens. The elective public officials voluntarily relinquished their committee work to a new full-time officer called general manager. Sumter, South Carolina, in 1913 was the first to put a manager under a single elective council, something which Staunton was not able to do until 1920. The Staunton council broke all precedent by advertising for applicants for the managership and hiring one from out of town, following the long-standing practice of American school boards in hiring professional school superintendents. It was also in 1913 that the first sizable city, Dayton, Ohio, adopted the plan under a new charter. By the end of that year twelve cities had adopted the system. By the beginning of 1974, over 50 percent of all American cities of more than 25,000 population were operating under the council-manager plan. Its basic principles, as set forth in the *Model City Charter*,[10] are the following:

All the powers of the city are vested in a single small board of elected representatives, usually called the council. The council hires from anywhere in the country a city manager, whom it can replace at any time and for any reason.

The city manager appoints and supervises the heads of all operating departments, prepares and submits the annual budget, attends council meetings without a vote, and brings in much of the business.

The chairman of the council is the mayor, who has a vote but has no veto or other powers. Depending on provisions of the charter, he is either selected by the council from its own membership or chosen in an at-large election, which is usually nonpartisan.

There are no other elective officers. The council appoints an auditor or a firm of professional auditors to conduct postaudits.

In December 1914, eight of the then-existing thirty-two managers met in Springfield, Ohio, to compare notes and organize the City Managers' Association. By 1924 the plan had spread to 308 cities in the United States and to eleven in Canada. The organization's name was changed that year to the International City Managers' Association. As of January 1, 1923, the association established its first permanent secretariat at Lawrence, Kansas, with John G. Stutz as the executive secretary and editor of its monthly *City Manager Magazine,* now *Public Management.*

City managers considered themselves to be a new, highly specialized profession, which, in the words of one of them, had "the same rank and importance as that of doctor, lawyer, minister, or engineer."[11] They adopted a professional code of ethics at their 1924 annual convention in Montreal.

The first code of ethics reflected the young profession's conception of the responsibilities of city managers, specifically regarding the operational nature of management, the public aspects of the professional's job, and the primacy of the city council in the council-manager form of government. The code was amended in 1938, 1952, and 1969. The current version of the code is the result of substantial revision in 1972. "Guidelines for professional conduct" have been published to augment the code by providing suggestions on ways to meet specific ethical issues which may confront an urban administrator. The code, the rules of procedure, and the guidelines have all been published in a special pamphlet.* It is of particular interest to all local government officials in this era of decreasing confidence of the general public in the integrity and credibility of government officials at all levels.

Both the guidelines and the code could well be adopted by any city to govern the conduct of all its officials and employees. Those guidelines dealing with "Conflict of Interest" include a prohibition against acceptance of gifts in any form, "under circumstances in which it could reasonably be inferred that the gift was intended to influence him, or could reasonably be expected to influence him. . . ."

*Available from the International City Management Association, 1140 Connecticut Avenue, N.W., Washington, D.C. 20036.

Another rule provides: "A member should not disclose to others, or use to further his personal interest, confidential information acquired by him in the course of his official duties."

Members are forbidden to represent "any outside interest before any agency, public or private, except with the authorization or at the direction of the legislative body of the governmental unit he serves."

Members may not hold investments in transactions that conflict with official duties, and the guidelines outline procedures for transactions that require special consideration.

Private employment for an interest that creates "a conflict with or impairs the proper discharge of his official duties" is prohibited.

As the managers were developing standards of conduct for themselves in 1924, they were being encouraged to train younger men for the position. Clifford W. Ham, city manager of Pontiac, Michigan, who in late 1935 was to become executive director of the American Municipal Association, urged his fellow managers to create the position of assistant city manager, not only as an aid to more efficient administration, but also to develop a reservoir of younger potential executives for cities searching for qualified managers.

"Practically all cities, with few exceptions, in seeking a city manager now are compelled to go into various other fields to draft men in the hope that their previous training would prove fitting in the new job of public administration," Ham said.[12]

Because of its emphasis on management (the association changed its name to International City Management Association in 1969), its members justifiably attained the image of consummate public administrators. Nevertheless, mayors and other elected officials were no less responsive to the demands for efficiency, which did not diminish with the rising demand for services during the twenties.

Perhaps the best way to reflect the major concerns of municipal government during that decade, whether in cities administered by managers or in those with other forms of government, is to examine the activities of some representative state municipal leagues.[13] It will come as no surprise that paving problems, traffic regulations, zoning, and legislation topped the agenda of the Nebraska league at its 1925 annual convention. The Texas league, for lack of someone to "push it," failed to persuade the legislature to pass a zoning enabling act. The North Carolina league, on the other hand, achieved passage of a similar law. The executive secretary of the Colorado league spent much of his time in late 1924 with the governor and budget commission in preparation of a state budget and in working for legislation that would grant cities a share of state-levied motor vehicle license fees and gasoline taxes.

The Kansas league was providing on contract a range of services to constituent city governments. The Iowa league secured enactment of state enabling legislation for city planning commissions. The New Jersey league organized some of its municipalities to defend zoning cases before the state Supreme Court and drafted a bill "to separate school and municipal districts so that city officials will not have to be criticized for the great increase in taxes caused by school systems."

The Virginia league successfully promoted passage of a constitutional amendment permitting local assessments against abutting property owners for street improvements. The California league prepared model building and plumbing codes and a model zoning ordinance and published a handbook for city officials. The work of the New York league in 1927 ranged from a report dealing with uniform automatic traffic signals to a series of special studies of such diverse fields as school finances, municipal tree work, and crime prevention. This league, formally the New York State Conference of Mayors and Other Municipal Officials, appears to have been the first state association to offer members guidance on welfare problems, announcing in 1928 a conference "of municipal charity officials to discuss unemployment plans and the proposed revision of the Poor Law."

The 1928 convention of the Michigan league dealt with such subjects as garbage collection and disposal, sewage treatment and the financing of sewage plants on a utility basis, and airport design and development.

That composite picture of state leagues of municipalities activity helps reconstruct the scene in which American city government operated in the "Golden Twenties." It was a period marked by the quest of city officials themselves for efficient management methods, their cooperation among themselves to help them achieve that goal through statewide associations, the emergence of a profession of city managers, and the growth of new functions in a booming decade of increasing affluence.

Focusing the Vast Latent Power
of Our Cities

With the attention of the city officials they represented still narrowly focused on management methods and efforts to stay abreast of citizens' expanding demands for services, secretaries of state associations continued to find it hard to look beyond the trees of their individual professional problems to the forest of national policy issues. Their frustration mounted. In 1927, Morton L. Wallerstein, executive secretary of the League of Virginia Municipalities, admonished fellow delegates "to cease floundering and establish the definite scope of this organization." But the "floundering" continued.

In 1928, however, A. D. McLarty issued a challenge to fellow delegates at that year's annual meeting that now seems almost prophetic. He called on the American Municipal Association, "or any other group that is in a position to do it, [to] render an effective service to the larger cities of the country. . . . It seems to me there is a place in this country for a national league of municipalities."

Differences of opinion did not by themselves prevent expansion of the association from an organization of secretaries into an organization of municipalities. Additional funds were needed

Public Administration Center at 1313 East Sixtieth Street, Chicago, headquarters of the National League of Cities until 1954 and of some twenty other national and international public-interest organizations.

to hire a paid staff and keep a headquarters functioning for the broader mission.

An announcement at the 1929 AMA convention that John Stutz had asked to be relieved of his responsibilities as executive secretary raised hopes for such an expansion. Though the league secretaries were reluctant to lose this founding organizer, his proposal added an extra incentive for those who wanted to enlarge the role of the organization. Had Stutz carried out his intention to resign at that time, the association probably would have relocated the secretariat in a place other than Stutz's home base of Lawrence, Kansas, and hired a paid staff. These changes, no doubt, would have added pressures for earlier clarification of the group's objectives. Funds for the changes, however, were not forthcoming, and Stutz was persuaded to maintain the Lawrence headquarters as interim secretary without pay.

Some exasperated pleas for resolution of the identity issue were heard in the 1929 discussions. The representative of the Oklahoma league demanded: "Are we an association of secretaries or are we an association of leagues of municipalities? . . . What are we?"

In replying, AMA President Don C. Sowers of the Colorado Municipal League noted that the association's constitution vests membership in the individual state leagues. "But in practice," he added, "as we all know, we have been a conference group. That is, we have felt any action this organization would take would have no binding effect on any league."

Even as a conference group the fledgling association had become an ever-growing force to strengthen municipal government. By the end of the decade of the twenties, mayors who were presidents of the state leagues were accompanying their executive secretaries to the annual AMA meetings. Successful programs carried out by enterprising state leagues inspired others to conduct similar programs in their own states. How-to-do-it discussions, transcribed verbatim and published in the annual *Proceedings,* included such topics as the administration of an information service to city officials, public personnel training, securing good legislation, regulation of utility rates and services, the programming and management of conventions, accounting and auditing, relationships with universities, and the publication of research reports, news bulletins, and magazines.

The publication of magazines received special attention, especially in the early thirties. With a small grant from the Spelman Fund of New York, the association opened a temporary Chicago office on July 1, 1931, to promote the sale of national advertising in the state magazines. It was anticipated that commissions from ad sales would supplement the foundation grants to be made for a permanent secretariat, but the venture was not a success and was terminated in April 1936.

As evidence of their growing influence, the state leagues and their new national association began to be invited to participate in the work of other organizations. The association's office at Lawrence, Kansas, was designated in 1926 as the American headquarters of the International Union of Local Authorities, and formal affiliation with that group was approved in early 1927. The following year the association became a member of the National Fire Waste Council, a voluntary federation of national organizations which was assisting the Chamber of Commerce of the United States in carrying on a nationwide fire prevention program. It also began affiliation that year with the National Committee on Municipal Reporting, a committee financed by the Spelman Fund to develop standards for improving the quality of reporting by cities to the public. In 1929 the association appointed three representatives on the governing committee of the Municipal Administration Service, an activity begun in 1925 to coordinate municipal research and publications. And in 1930 the association became a member of the National Committee on Municipal Standards, which was concerned mainly with uniform street sanitation records and with uniform crime reporting.

While these linkages expanded the range of concerns of state league officers, outside speakers at annual meetings helped broaden their horizons. Dr. Charles E. Merriam, for example, could foresee a time "when you get all the forty-eight states fully organized" and have "practically all the cities in the United States in combination. . . ." Professor Merriam reminded the league officers that European nations have powerful alliances of cities and pointed to a time when such effective coalitions would function in the United States.

Unions of cities abroad had already intrigued John Stutz. In 1925 he led a small delegation of Americans to Paris to the Third International Congress of Cities, conducted by the International Federation of Local Government Associations, later the International Union of Local Authorities. Stutz was designated the American representative on the general council, the governing board of the International Union. He attended six subsequent congresses and was vice-president from 1936 to 1949.

When in 1926 the secretariat of the American Municipal Association became the American headquarters for the International Union, this made the fifth secretariat managed simultaneously by John Stutz. In addition to his new union responsibilities, he was executive secretary of the League of Kansas Municipalities, director of the Municipal Reference Bureau, executive secretary of the American Municipal Association, and executive secretary of the International City Managers' Association, a position he held until he was succeeded in June 1929 by Clarence E. Ridley.

Headquarters of the City Managers' Association had been established at the University of Kansas in Lawrence in 1922, largely through the efforts of Stutz's good friend Louis Brownlow, then the association's president and city manager of Petersburg, Virginia.

The conglomerate of association headquarters over which Stutz now presided represented a new level of centralization for municipally oriented organizations. But it fell short of his expectations for "a national research organization in the United States," to which he referred in a 1925 report on the merits of international linkages among cities.

Stutz had suggested to Brownlow early in 1923 that they try to enlist the aid of Dr. Merriam in seeking foundation funds for a centralized national bureau of municipal research. The bureau would be located near some university and share headquarters with the City Managers' Association and AMA. In a memorandum to Merriam, drafted in consultation with Brownlow, Stutz outlined what was later to become the Public Administration Clearing House and the agglomeration of organizations of public officials that came to be clustered at 1313 East Sixtieth Street, adjacent to the campus of the University of Chicago. Financed mainly through aid from the Spelman Fund, this concentration was to produce a rapid growth in professionalism in state and local governments.

The role of the Spelman Fund, a relatively small ($10 million) foundation, was critical in the advancement of the state of the art of municipal government and the evolution of institutions that fostered it, including associations of city officials. It was formed in 1928 by a merger of the Laura Spelman Rockefeller Memorial Fund, established by John D. Rockefeller in memory of his wife, and the Rockefeller Foundation. Its purpose was to promote some of Mrs. Rockefeller's principal interests, including improvement of child welfare, interracial relations, and government. After merger the fund's directors decided to concentrate on government, seeking to improve governmental practices, not through citizen reform groups but primarily through national associations of local and state government officials.

Beardsley Ruml was named executive director of the fund; Guy Moffett, his assistant, later succeeded him as director. Charles Merriam was elected to the board and later became chairman. To this triumvirate is due a large share of the credit for bringing the clearing house into being and, currently, for pushing AMA to a clearer definition of itself.

To acknowledge that does not diminish the role of Brownlow and Stutz as conceptual designers and prodders. Louis Brownlow won world-wide distinction as a newspaper reporter before President Woodrow Wilson named him, in January 1915, as one of the three Commissioners of the District of Columbia. He assumed the city managership at Petersburg six years later and soon was elected president of the League of Virginia Municipalities. He established a permanent headquarters for the league and persuaded a young lawyer to become the nonsalaried permanent secretary. That attorney was Morton L. Wallerstein, who was to become one of the ten founders of the American Municipal Association, predecessor of the National League of Cities.

After three years as city manager in Petersburg, Brownlow took a similar position in Knoxville, Tennessee, in 1923. He returned to journalism temporarily and later was a municipal consultant in the development of Radburn, N.J., an innovative suburban garden-city new town whose growth was to some measure halted by the Depression after early stages of development.

Brownlow had retained his contacts in local and state government circles, especially with Ruml and Moffett of the Spelman Fund. Thus the proposal he and Stutz designed got a ready hearing.

After two years of research, the Spelman Fund decided early in 1930 that it ought to encourage formation of a center for national associations of officials in the field of public administration. Spelman grants had financed the Bureau of Public Personnel Administration, now the International Personnel Management Association; influenced the transfer of the headquarters of the City Managers' Association from Lawrence, Kansas, to a building near the University of Chicago campus; and financed establishment in Chicago of the American Legislators Association. The fund also promised support to the newly organized American Association of Public Welfare Officials, now the American Public Welfare Association.

The grants had the effect of stabilizing and providing permanent headquarters for key organizations that were doing excellent work with the part-time staff services of some dedicated volunteers. By shoring up these associations, the Spelman Fund made an immeasurable contribution to better state and local government in the United States.

Among the purposes of the center, which was to be located in Chicago, were the fostering of an exchange of knowledge and experience in public administration, the elimination of duplication in research, closer cooperation among officials, researchers, and technicians, and reduction of the gap between theory and practice.

To achieve these purposes, the center would, among other things:

1. Act as a central clearing house for the exchange of information and results of research.

2. Establish and maintain continuing personal contact with cooperating agencies in the field.

3. Encourage closer relations among organized bodies of administrators, in order to improve the service rendered by each organization to its members and constituents, by placing combined resources of information and experience at the disposal of each organization.

It is significant that the memorandum explaining the proposal included the following limitation: "The Clearing House will advocate no particular form of governmental organization nor support specific political plans proposed for the remedy of administration ills, being concerned solely with making available to those engaged in the operation and study of government such information and results of experience as will assist them most intelligently to decide upon a course of action."

The Public Administration Clearing House closely adhered to the terms of that disclaimer throughout its life. Nevertheless, during the period when the service was located at 1313 East Sixtieth Street, some right-wing groups began to denounce and vilify "terrible 1313" as some kind of Communist conspiracy to destroy local government in the United States. The Clearing House's encouragement of professionalism in local government and its promotion of metropolitan government are apparently what nettled these groups. Their attacks, innuendos, half truths, and falsehoods continue to slip past unwary editors into some weekly newspapers and other publications.

After the decision to go ahead with the project, Dr. Luther Gulick, director of the Institute of Public Administration, presented the proposal to the Public Administration Committee of the Social Science Research Council, which agreed at its meeting in early November 1930 to act as the sponsor for the proposed center. Later that month the proposal was endorsed by the American Municipal Association, the American Legislators Association, and the City Managers' Association. A group of distinguished persons agreed to serve on a board of trustees, including former Governor Frank O. Lowden of Illinois, who became chairman of the board; Newton O. Baker, former Secretary of War and former Mayor and City Attorney of Cleveland; Harry F. Byrd, then governor of Virginia; Richard S. Childs, president of the National Municipal League; and others. Louis Brownlow was named director.

AMA's endorsement of the center came at its seventh annual meeting, in Cleveland on November 14, 1930, a year after the association had failed in efforts to get funds to set up a permanent secretariat that would relieve John Stutz of his part-time duties for the national organization. The Spelman Fund had turned down a formal application for $30,000 annually for five years. The fund apparently advised the association that it must first more clearly define its role as an organization. To assist in resolving this perennial problem of the association, the fund granted $2,500 to AMA's executive committee for studies and reports that would presumably illuminate the issues involved in the impasse.

The committee met for three days in Chicago, August 14–16, 1930. It inventoried all services then being performed by state leagues of municipalities. It tried again to define the purposes and objectives of the national association. It projected work programs—one appropriate to a loose conference group that could be accommodated by the current budget and an alternate one for operation of "a definite organization with sufficient funds to render practical services." And it developed a program for coordinating the efforts of AMA with other municipal organizations. It completed all its tasks but one. That it failed once again in defining the purposes and objectives of the association at the meeting was indicated by the committee's instruction to the secretary to write a letter to each committeeman requesting him to prepare a brief on the subject.

Their recommendations led to some amendments to the association's constitution adopted the following year, one of which finally redefined its purpose. No longer would functions be confined to collecting and exchanging information about municipal affairs to assist the state municipal organizations in the promotion of approved methods of municipal government. The association would now "furnish information *and services* which may assist the respective state leagues of municipalities or substantially similar organizations in performing their functions." At the same time the executive secretary was made an appointed, rather than elected, officer, to be compensated for his services. John Stutz was thereupon appointed executive secretary, but with no funds available for his compensation, to devote "as much time as can possibly be spared from his duties as executive secretary of the League of Kansas Municipalities."

The constitutional changes were made in the hope that they would dispel the misgivings the Spelman Fund had expressed about the association. They apparently accomplished that purpose. Two relatively small grants were immediately forthcoming early in 1931. The third, the one for which Stutz and his cohorts had been working for more than two years, was announced in August. It was for a total of $87,500, to be paid in decreasing amounts over the succeeding four years as financial assistance to an adequate secretariat.

Having accomplished this major financial objective and with his cherished permanent secretariat now in sight, John G. Stutz, on August 5, 1931, tendered his resignation as executive secretary of the organization in order to devote all his time to the work of the League of Kansas Municipalities. The executive committee appointed A. D. McLarty, executive secretary of the Illinois Municipal League, to succeed Stutz temporarily until a full-time executive could be found.

At a meeting three months later in Buffalo, New York, the

executive committee voted to locate the permanent secretariat at the University of Chicago. Thus, the future National League of Cities joined that growing public administration complex that already included the American Legislators Association, American Public Welfare Association, Civil Service Assembly, International City Managers' Association, Municipal Finance Officers' Association, and Public Administration Clearing House.

Louis Brownlow and Guy Moffett were present at that committee meeting. Moffett made a suggestion that Morris Lambie promptly seized to bolster his argument. The meeting's minutes note: "Mr. Moffett felt the AMA should keep clear of controversial matters and could not commit any individual leagues to any specific policy." Lambie, a member of the committee, unsuccessfully attempted to bind the committee to that view.

To this day the National League of Cities cannot commit any individual league or any individual city to any specific policy. Nor can any other association of corporate members, including a state league of municipalities, actually commit its members to anything. That is not the nature of a voluntary association. What it does is to take a position that reflects the consensus of authorized delegates representing a substantial majority of its members. Without "substantial unanimity" these associations don't take a position on controversial matters. When they do, most of their members will support the decisions of their delegates. But they are free to repudiate them. There is nothing binding on the members.

So it is difficult to understand the reasoning of Guy Moffett or Morris Lambie that the organization "should keep clear of controversial matters." It is a sure formula for weakness, if not failure, of an organization of cities seeking to improve municipal government and to serve the best interests of its members. No successful state league of municipalities kept clear of controversial matters, not even the Minnesota league, which Professor Lambie represented. And certainly the earlier experience of the defunct League of American Municipalities should have underscored the point. Its ill-fated attempt to exist only as an information exchange, avoiding any policy stands on controversial matters, steered it into oblivion. Fortunately AMA resolved the issue against the Lambie line by a constitutional change a year later.

The committee also voted to offer the position of executive secretary to Paul V. Betters, then on the staff of the Brookings Institution, Washington, D.C. Betters accepted on November 24, 1931, and became the association's first full-time executive at an annual salary of $6,600 beginning January 1, 1932.

This series of changes could be considered a watershed in the evolution of municipal governance. "Efficiency" in American city government had been fairly well achieved. The new era of concern about national municipal policy was beginning. And the potential power of the American Municipal Association to mobilize the cities to influence national policies was being recognized by most state league secretaries. What Dr. Merriam had told the group six years earlier seemed to be less a distant vision, more a realistic appraisal:

There are unlimited possibilities for this organization in the way of consideration, concentration, and focusing of the vast latent power of our many cities, great and small. It is certainly clear that the 3,000 counties of the United States are dead politically and that the forty-eight states are not very much alive. But in the city government you see signs of vitality, and in this vitality I see the chief promise of American political advancement. It may seem a poor place to look. I suppose Viscount Bryce would turn over in his grave to hear us say the American city is the hope of American dreams, but it seems to me it is.

The Depression Thirties—Bust!

The panic started October 24, 1929, and continued until the price of stocks hit their lows for that year on November 13. Alarmed businessmen tightened their belts, disposed of their inventories, and reduced their work forces. Millions of jobs were abolished. A major depression was under way, and the "Golden Twenties" ended in economic collapse.

The prices of farm products also plunged, and a terrific drought during the summer of 1930 intensified the plight of agriculture and many rural communities. Several brokerage houses went broke, and over a thousand banks failed during 1930. Unemployment grew steadily until by the end of that year the number of jobless totaled approximately 6 million.

By 1932 the number of unemployed had passed 12 million, nearly one-fourth of the nation's work force. None of the sophisticated procedures which today measure even subtle changes in employment at both national and local levels was in use at that time. As a result of the enormous body of manpower legislation that has been enacted in the forty years since the depth of the Depression, localities that are classified by the Bureau of Labor Statistics as "areas of substantial unemployment" now automatically become eligible for such antirecession measures as allocations of job slots under the federal Public Employment Program and preferential treatment to area contractors for defense contracts.

In the early 1930s, the federal government did not even keep official statistics on national employment. Nor had it recognized the need to do so. Tremendous burdens, unparalleled in all history, were thrust upon cities by the most serious economic condition that ever faced the nation. Home owners and other property owners who could not pay their taxes created tax delinquencies as high as 60 percent. In spite of drastic retrenchment in salaries and services, six hundred cities and towns had to default on their bonded debts, and many resorted to the issuance of scrip to pay their employees. A total of 5,741 banks had failed by the end of 1932. And yet in the planning at the national level of measures to alleviate the conditions local authorities had little part.

At the beginning of the Depression, the initiative to meet the challenge came not from the federal or state governments but from some cities. Cincinnati set the example in 1929, when City Manager C. O. Sherrill appointed a citizens committee to stabilize employment. Subcommittees on public works, temporary employment, fact finding, job training and placement, and others had completed their preliminary studies before the Depression really broke. However, the number of unemployed in that city had tripled, rising to 18,000 by November 1930. This prompted Sherrill to urge the annual convention of the International City Managers' Association to appeal to Washington for an emergency loan to tide the cities over the Depression.

President Hoover in November 1929 urged the governors to seek the aid of their cities in "the absorption of any unemployment which might result from the present disturbed conditions." Cities did increase their public works expenditures, thus creating additional jobs, and yet total unemployment continued to increase. Late in 1930 a group of fifty-eight mayors joined in a request to Congress to appropriate $1 billion for public works.[1] However, President Hoover rejected the proposal of his new Emergency Committee for Employment that the federal government undertake a program of public works and extend credit to cities for slum clearance and low-cost housing. As unemployment continued to increase in 1931, Hoover changed his committee to an Organization on Unemployment Relief, charged with the job of stimulating local communities to assume their full responsibility to the unemployed. By the end of that year, C. A. Dykstra, Sherrill's successor as city manager of Cincinnati, was urging his fellow managers at their 1931 convention to seek a federal appropriation, not a loan.

At the same conference, Louis Brownlow, director of the new Public Administration Clearing House, cited a statement by Walter S. Gifford, chairman of the President's Organization on Unemployment Relief, as characteristic of the federal government's position:

First it is the duty of the municipality to take care of this situation [unemployment relief]. If the municipality won't or can't, it is up to the county. If the county won't or can't, then the state. If the state won't or can't, then we will cross that bridge when we come to it.

"So far as I know," Brownlow added, "nobody in authority in the federal government has yet referred to that bridge."

Dykstra complained about the lack of recognition by the federal government of the problems of cities:

What cities need just now from Washington is correlated information on unemployment and a national program of employment agencies and employment distribution. What it gets is the cheerful news that distress is a local and municipal problem. The fact that in such times those who pour into our cities for relief thus add to our local problems is not taken into account.

Several other city managers stated the need for representation of the cities' point of view in Washington, which led to unanimous expression of opinion that a committee representing all municipalities, not just city-manager cities, be appointed to confer with the President's Organization on Unemployment Relief. The ICMA executive committee then authorized its president to appoint such a group.[2]

It was also in 1931 that the mayors began to talk about uniting to demand assistance from the federal government. In July

Mayor Daniel W. Hoan of Milwaukee wrote a letter to the mayors of the nation's largest cities, noting that most cities have definite legal limitations on their taxing and bonding ability. "Isn't it high time," he asked, ". . . that the federal government assume its full responsibility in this crisis without further evasion and shifting of the burden on local communities?" He pointed out that the national government had no similar restrictions on its taxing powers, and he concluded by asking the mayors if they would favor the calling of a meeting in Washington in the fall to discuss this subject.

All who replied except three agreed that unless some action was forthcoming soon, such a meeting should be called, and a flood of letters and telegrams was sent to Washington urging President Hoover to call a special session of Congress to provide the necessary relief. With control of Congress in doubt, however, Hoover demurred. He did set up the Organization on Unemployment Relief and announced a greatly enlarged program of public works.

By standards of today's pressure politics, when a dozen mayors can be mobilized within twenty-four hours to converge on Washington for a day of lobbying on far more narrow issues, Mayor Hoan exercised remarkable restraint. He withdrew his call for a meeting in the capital because, as he explained later in his book,[3] he felt the President's new committee was entitled to a fair chance to show what it could accomplish, and he urged states and cities to cooperate to the fullest extent.

More than a year later, however, when conditions had become much worse, he revived his plea for a united front in Washington to focus attention on the mounting relief load of overburdened cities and to persuade the national government to assume a share of the load. "The mayors of this country are going to be compelled to do something if you don't," he told the directors of the state leagues of cities at the 1932 convention of the American Municipal Association.

At that time there was no national organization through which the responsible heads of cities—mayors or city managers—could express their common needs on matters of national policy. The American Municipal Association could have filled that role. It had just received assurance of financing to enable it to establish a permanent secretariat. Yet two factors militated against its becoming involved. One was that its membership was restricted to state leagues of municipalities, which existed at that time only in some thirty states, and only twenty-two of those were members. Thus, AMA could not truly claim to represent municipalities throughout the country. That could have been remedied if earlier action had been taken to open the membership to individual cities in those states where leagues were not organized, a step finally taken early in 1933. The second factor was the inability of the executive secretaries of the state leagues to agree on the role of their national association.

While the city managers and some mayors were calling for federal help in meeting the unemployment relief problem, the American Municipal Association did not even discuss the subject at its August 1931 annual convention. That lack of concern about the most important problem facing the cities was to change drastically the following year. Meanwhile, the vacuum had to be filled, and the mayors of the nation's largest cities were soon to fill it by organizing the Conference of Mayors as a national association of individual cities with the active support of AMA's secretariat.

The debate about whether the association should continue to be merely a professional society of individual state municipal league executive directors or become an organization to reflect national municipal policy was a hardy perennial at each annual meeting, as preceding chapters have shown. While the dispute had been resolved on a philosophical plane by 1932, resolutions on national policy issues were adopted by a narrow margin and only after resistance by Morris B. Lambie, secretary of the League of Minnesota Municipalities and the unwavering foe of efforts of fellow league directors to "go national" with the association.

It apparently was this resistance that made Mayor Hoan skeptical about the ability of AMA to unite the cities behind any effort to persuade the national government to do anything at all. Shortly after the vote Hoan, with the help of AMA's executive director, Paul Betters, organized the mayors' own association to articulate the cities' needs for national legislation.

Culmination of the debate over the association's mission came at its 1931 meeting. Lambie's immutable position that the group should remain a professional organization came under heavy challenge from Harold D. Smith, director of the Michigan Municipal League, and Morton L. Wallerstein, executive secretary of the League of Virginia Municipalities. Smith was to become state budget director of Michigan and, in 1939, first director of the U.S. Bureau of the Budget in Franklin Roosevelt's newly organized Executive Office of the President.

Smith touched off the final major discussion with a plea to fellow directors to heed the rising demand for an association that would formulate policies with the participation of state league officers and other city officials. "Either this organization will fulfill that need or some new organization will arise to do it," he declared.

Wallerstein echoed that soon-to-be-fulfilled prophecy. He reemphasized the need for a national counterpart of a state league—an organization to which constituent cities and towns could turn for representation in emergencies. "If we are correct in our theory that the electorate elects the officials comprising the [state] league, this ought to be the logical organization to speak in that sort of thing."

Smith's challenge was part of a careful review of the debates of past years on the role of the association. Noting that dues to the association were paid by municipalities, Smith declared: "The organization is obviously, then, not a group of individuals, but a super-organization of cities acting through their respective leagues." Recognizing the frequency of overtures then being made for direct cooperation with, and assistance from, the federal government, Smith asked: "In what ways could the association work with federal departments, provided some other organization does not take over that function?"

In an ensuing colloquy John Stutz of Kansas and Morton Wallerstein of Virginia supported Smith, who added: "Suppose in time it should be shown there ought to be an organization to deal with the federal government. It seems to me the merit of the American Municipal Association might bring some pressure to bear to cause some of the mayors of these larger municipalities to get some action. In other words, it is either a super-organization of cities, acting through their municipal leagues, or it is a professional group of league secretaries."

This was too much for Lambie!

"We have a function as a professional association," he declared, "and I cannot see anything in the future, regardless of what is in the constitution, that will legitimately allow a group of this kind to meet annually and make decisions other than as a professional association of individuals. I know, speaking for Minnesota, we would not allow the American Municipal Association to say any word about the municipal policy or federal government or state government as such, with any understanding that the Minnesota league is thereby committed or involved in that particular situation. You cannot tell what the repercussions would be of the simplest type of statement by such an organization."

He simply couldn't get the point. One can only conclude that, sincere as he was, Lambie could never understand that a national voluntary association of corporate (or municipal league) members could not "commit" its members who did not choose to be bound by decisions of a majority of delegates. And yet, as I have said, his own state league did take policy positions whenever it pressed for enactment of controversial laws by the state legislature. Why he persisted in trying to keep the national association from becoming a strong force for policy objectives that would benefit the cities is incomprehensible.

In contrast, another professor, Dr. Charles E. Merriam, addressing the banquet session of the same 1931 annual meeting, said:

I still think one of the most powerful agencies in city government would be the organization of these city officials into some group which may be called Städtertag or city parliament or American Municipal Association or what not, but it would be *an organization that would reflect the united force and power of the American cities.*[*]

These cities are undoubtedly the centers of financial power. They are the centers of organizing drive. They are going to be the dominant political power in the United States, and their organization on the municipal side will inevitably sooner or later be one of the most conspicuous things in American political life.[4]

It could be that the two contrasting philosophies of the role of the association in the municipal field really pointed up a changing concept of municipal government needs. Lambie was still obsessed with the drive for reform and efficiency, and he saw his role as a state league secretary to be primarily "the promotion of approved methods of municipal government," also evidenced by his zealous participation in the affairs of that foremost citizens' reform group the National Municipal League.

Actually, that era in the history of municipal government in the United States was drawing to a close. Reforms had been accomplished nearly everywhere, with widespread adoption by cities of nonpartisan city elections, the short ballot, civil service, and structures of government that were designed to produce efficiency and pinpoint responsibility, such as the strong-mayor and the council-manager plans. "Boss rule" was declining, partly as a result of such reforms but also because of the ebbing tide of immigration since the Immigration Act of 1924 and of the increasing educational level of the electorate. That last factor was also aided by the new medium of rapid, widespread communication, radio, which had come into its own during the twenties. These more favorable conditions encouraged the growth of professionalism in municipal government service. Exchange of experiences and information on more efficient administrative techniques had increased through such professional societies as

*Emphasis supplied.

the International City Managers' Association, American Public Works Association, American Waterworks Association, Civil Service Assembly, International Association of Chiefs of Police, Municipal Finance Officers' Association, and others.

The big need now was for a national organization that could represent the cities in national domestic policy. Having resolved its long-standing internal struggles, the American Municipal Association had determined to provide that representation, but it was not yet organized to fulfill the role. Fortunately, however, it selected as its first full-time executive director the brilliant and dynamic Paul V. Betters, age twenty-five.

Betters was one of the early graduates of the Maxwell Graduate School of Public Administration, which, since its founding in 1924, had supplied a small but steadily expanding cadre of leaders who were making significant contributions to the improving quality of governance. The school was made possible by a large grant from George Maxwell, a Boston shoe machinery manufacturer and Syracuse University alumnus. Maxwell envisioned it as an undergraduate school whose graduates hopefully would become civic leaders and teachers who would foster loyalty to the nation and a commitment to its traditional values.

To organize the school, Maxwell turned to Frederick M. Davenport, a New York State senator since 1908 who was elected U.S. representative in 1924 and later served as chairman of the Federal Personnel Council. Noting a "lack of enough competent leaders in national, state, and municipal affairs," Davenport urged that Maxwell's purposes for the new school be narrowed. He recommended that it offer a graduate program to emphasize the training of experts for the public service.

Declining Maxwell's offer to make him director of the school, Davenport went to Luther Gulick, director of the National Institute for Public Administration (formerly the New York Bureau of Municipal Research), for counsel on curriculum. Gulick, faced with a shortage of funds for a school at the institute that had been training students for public service, suggested that his school be incorporated into the new school at Syracuse. Davenport, Maxwell, and the university's chancellor agreed, and the head of the institute's Training School, William E. Mosher, was appointed the first director of the Maxwell School, which opened its doors to a class of six graduate students in September 1924.

Davenport and the others believed that the study of government had been "too bookish," dealing almost exclusively with theory and logic, not with human reality. They insisted that undergraduate and graduate training, therefore, should emphasize exposure to the practical workings of government. An explicit requirement of the graduate program was that students spend much of their time conducting their own field research to gain firsthand knowledge.[5]

Paul Betters, who received his master's degree from the Maxwell School in 1929, was a product of such training. Some of his twenty-five contemporaries during the school's first five years included Donald C. Stone, who became assistant director of the U.S. Bureau of the Budget, then dean of the Graduate School of Public Administration at Pittsburgh; C. A. Harrell, city manager of several cities, including Norfolk and Cincinnati; Clarence E. Ridley, the first full-time executive director of the International City Managers' Association; Ridley's successor, Orin F. Nolting; Carleton F. Sharpe, city manager of Saint Petersburg, Hartford, and Kansas City; and several others who became successful in public administration. After receiving his degree, Betters continued his studies at Syracuse for another year, then joined the staff of the Brookings Institution in Washington, D.C., where for a time he was assigned as technical adviser to the governor of North Carolina for the reorganization of the state government. It was from Brookings that he went to the American Municipal Association.

He wasted no time. During the first nine months after opening the association's new headquarters on January 1, 1932, he visited seventeen of the state leagues of municipalities, five of them twice; addressed the annual conventions of six of them; made nearly fifty other speeches around the country; and helped organize an American delegation to the Fifth International Con-

The Depression of the 1930s put extra burdens on city governments. Here is a breadline in New York City in 1935.

gress of Cities held in London in May. Following that, the American group, which included three state municipal league executives, Louis Brownlow, and Guy Moffett, visited the national leagues of cities in the Netherlands, Germany, Austria, Czechoslovakia, Switzerland, France, and Belgium. Betters drafted a lengthy and detailed report on the European unions of cities, which he mimeographed and distributed to the state leagues of municipalities in the United States.[6] He was out of the country for two months on that trip, which explains why he was not present when the mayors of eighteen large cities met in Detroit on June 1, 1932, to survey the plight of their communities and the need for immediate federal assistance in dealing with the unemployment problem.

The meeting had been called by Detroit's Mayor Frank Murphy at the request of a group of Michigan mayors who had met with him two weeks earlier.[7] The group approved a $5 billion federal loan "to be made available immediately for national projects to effectuate the employment of millions of men and in this manner obtain work for our jobless, redistribute purchasing power and thereby stimulate industry." They suggested that a "work army be mobilized as armies were mobilized in 1917 and 1918, for work on national projects throughout the United States." Other resolutions recommended that legislation be enacted for "such financial aid to American municipalities as may be necessary to provide for the conservation of the American people during the depression." Mayor Murphy appointed a committee of seven mayors "to wait on Congress as representatives of this organization and present these resolutions."

Finally, the group authorized Mayor Murphy to appoint a committee to perfect "a permanent organization to establish a closer cooperation [of the executives of the cities of the United States], make a careful study of municipal problems and keep before the government and the people of the nation the vital interests of municipal government."

Thus was the United States Conference of Mayors conceived on June 1, 1932, in Detroit.

A committee of mayors headed by James M. Curley of Boston did travel to Washington and met with the leadership of both houses of Congress and with President Hoover. Although they were not successful in achieving the enactment of a massive public works program, their efforts resulted in the appropriation of $300 million to be loaned through the states for relief. Frederick N. MacMillin, president of the American Municipal Association, called the action "one of the first concrete instances of cooperation in the municipal field on federal matters."

MacMillin, executive secretary of the League of Wisconsin Municipalities, told the association at its 1932 convention that the Conference of Mayors probably would hold another meeting soon to establish a continuing organization with the assistance of Paul Betters. He said he believed that a national mayors' conference would fill a real need on federal legislative matters, especially those affecting larger cities. "As our association is working along similar channels," MacMillin said, "it is essential that there be the closest relationship between the association and the National Conference of Mayors if that body establishes a continuing organization." He suggested that AMA serve as the secretariat of the mayors' conference, thus avoiding duplication in the work of the two organizations.

Upon his return from Europe, Betters moved quickly to help the mayors carry out their objectives in Washington. He utilized the services of Richard E. Saunders as a Washington correspondent to keep the mayors and the state leagues informed about the administration of the new Federal Relief Act.* The relief law, Betters wrote in his first annual report to the American Municipal Association, "puts municipalities in close contact with the national government." He predicted that it would be necessary in the future for cities to maintain an agency in Washington to distribute information and exert influence on national affairs.[8]

*Saunders continued for many years to write the Washington news bulletins for AMA and for other associations located with the Public Administration Clearing House in Chicago.

It can be said with certainty that the year 1932 marked the beginning of a new era of municipal government in the United States—the birth of a direct city-federal relationship, which continues to this day.

The action of a group of mayors in cooperating to formulate an unemployment plan and to present it to Congress and to the President, coupled with the monitoring of the resulting Federal Relief Act by the newly created staff of the American Municipal Association, were the first manifestations of this new relationship.

The changing intergovernmental relationships were recognized by AMA President Frederick MacMillin when, in calling for prompt action at the 1932 convention, he told delegates that "the time has come in this country, I believe, when we can expect to see more and more federal legislation enacted vitally affecting the welfare of cities."

The change was very definitely reflected in the work of that convention. More than half of the program was devoted to papers, speeches, and discussions related to federal relief programs, the Reconstruction Finance Corporation, and advance planning of public works. Resolutions on national policy, though narrowly approved, as already noted, were far-reaching. They included measures calling on the RFC to liberalize its rules on loans to municipalities for self-liquidating projects, appointment of a committee to cooperate with the new Federal Employment Stabilization Board in planning and budgeting for municipal public works, approval of the action of the New York league in calling on the President and Congress to amend the Federal Reserve Bank Act to permit the Federal Reserve Bank to rediscount municipal loans to relieve unemployment and need, and a proposal that state leagues consider joining the call of the Wisconsin league on Congress to permit the Controller of the Currency to issue currency to local governments, which would use their municipal bonds as collateral.

After that controversial and timid start in 1932 of taking policy stands on national issues affecting cities, amendments to the

AMA constitution were adopted by its members late that year, including one that committed the organization to this objective: "The safeguarding of the interests, rights and privileges of municipalities as they may be affected by federal legislation." Thus, the issue was finally resolved after eight years of arguing whether AMA should be merely a professional society or an organization broadly representing the interests of municipalities. The latter was now officially approved, and the association began in 1933 its long history as a spokesman for the nation's cities in shaping national municipal policy.

The 1933 convention saw the adoption of several resolutions relating to federal legislation, and the procedure was formalized by the executive committee in September 1934, when it declared that under the AMA constitution it was proper for the annual convention to adopt resolutions upon which united action by the member leagues seemed desirable and where the sentiment of league representatives was "substantially unanimous." The committee statement said that "this conforms to the policy of individual leagues in taking action upon matters at league conventions although neither the American Municipal Association nor an individual league by such action can commit any member thereof." The committee then directed that a general statement of policy should be prepared to be followed by AMA in representing member leagues in national legislative matters. It further directed that a committee on federal policy be appointed to study and make recommendations regarding federal matters affecting municipal governments and to cooperate with other national organizations of public officials, including the United States Conference of Mayors.

Paul Betters followed this breakthrough by organizing for Mayor Frank Murphy of Detroit a second conference of mayors, held in Washington on February 17, 1933. This one was attended by mayors of twenty-three cities, and again the objective was a $5 billion appropriation by Congress for a construction program to relieve unemployment. Additional resolutions called for broadening the lending powers of the Reconstruction Finance Corporation and for the appropriation by Congress of such additional federal relief funds "as may be necessary," to be made on a direct grant basis to the municipalities of the nation, rather than to the states.

At that meeting Mayor Hoan of Milwaukee introduced a resolution, which he said had been prepared by Betters, recommending that the mayors of cities with more than 50,000 population form a permanent organization "to establish closer cooperation, make a careful study of municipal problems, and keep before the government and the people of the nation the vital interest of municipal governments."[9] Some mayors expressed doubts as to the need for such a permanent organization, citing the existence of state leagues of municipalities and their national organization, but Mayor Hoan explained that the American Municipal Association was in accord with the organization of the mayors. His resolution failed to receive unanimous support, but it did pass, and a constitution was adopted, also obviously drafted by Betters, based on that of the American Municipal Association.

Mayor Murphy was elected as the first president of the organization, Mayor Curley of Boston the vice-president, and as trustees Mayor Hoan of Milwaukee, Mayor William A. Anderson of Minneapolis, and, *in absentia,* Mayor Anton Cermak of Chicago. The latter had shortly before been mortally wounded by an assassin's bullet intended for President-elect Franklin Roosevelt and was to die soon after the meeting.

Paul Betters was appointed secretary, and in a memorandum to the AMA executive committee he reported that "the officers of the Conference have asked the Association to serve as a secretariat for them."[10]

It thus became possible for the United States Conference of Mayors to establish an image of itself among the mayors throughout the country as not only their spokesman on policy matters in Washington, but also as a source of information on all manner of city problems. Each research and information report prepared by the AMA staff in Chicago for the member leagues of

AMA was mailed also to the mayors and city managers of all cities over 50,000 population. Yet the latter received it with a different cover to indicate that it was published by the Conference, rather than its AMA secretariat, and a foreword by Betters would state that it had been prepared by "The Municipal Information Bureau of the United States Conference of Mayors," with no credit to AMA. The mayors were deluged with fifty-one pamphlets and reports in 1933, for example, prepared by AMA or other organizations, ranging in subject matter from "Installment Payment of Taxes in United States Cities" to "Federal Civil Works Administration Rules and Regulations."

In addition, during the last nine months of that year nearly a hundred mimeographed letters, bulletins, and other communications were sent to the mayors, most of them describing the status of the emergency measures being considered by Congress and often enclosing advance copies of new administrative regulations. Many of these were also sent on AMA letterheads to the state leagues, which could then reproduce and mail them to their member municipalities. Of course, those cities over 50,000 had already received them from the Mayors Conference. In 1934 Betters inaugurated an additional publication, a semimonthly four-page newsletter named *United States Municipal News,* showing on its masthead that it was "published jointly by the American Municipal Association and the United States Conference of Mayors."

At the same time the mayors were being solicited to pay dues and become members of the Conference. In the third year of this membership drive, 1935, the Conference collected $19,670 in dues from cities, of which $3,500 was turned over to AMA for "services rendered." The instruction of the AMA executive committee to Betters in early January 1933 to solicit membership in AMA of individual cities in states where no leagues of municipalities existed was largely ignored.

Meanwhile, Betters was making his mark in Washington. In fact, because of his aggressive and able representation of the cities' interests during the fast-moving early months of New

Deal legislation and administrative implementation, he had made such a favorable impression on Federal Emergency Relief Administrator Harry Hopkins that Hopkins asked AMA to lend Betters to him to assist in setting up the new Federal Civil Works Administration, a request granted in November 1933 by AMA's executive committee. Betters announced this in a Mayors Conference bulletin as follows: "As you perhaps know, the United States Conference of Mayors has temporarily loaned the services of its secretary, Paul V. Betters, to aid the Federal Civil Works Administrator, Mr. Harry L. Hopkins, in organizing and getting the Civil Works Program under way. The Conference is in position to promptly handle all inquiries." There was no mention that it was the American Municipal Association, the secretariat for the Conference, that was actually doing the lending!

These and other actions typifying Betters' style of operation began to be considered by some of the state league secretaries, goaded perhaps by Louis Brownlow, as irritants, if not actual acts of duplicity, and led to a confrontation in late 1935 between the AMA executive committee and its executive director. The result was Betters' resignation effective at the end of that year.[11]

Mayor Daniel W. Hoan of Milwaukee was president of the Mayors Conference at the time. He had also been elected vice-president of the American Municipal Association at its 1934 convention, where in a banquet speech he thanked AMA for lending to the Conference of Mayors "the splendid, the efficient services of Paul Betters."

"We have found," Hoan said, "that our organization [USCM] has been a splendid success, due largely to the fact that you loaned us your secretary, and that you, more than anyone else, have sponsored the idea of such an organization's being created. . . . If there is any possibility that we can work closer than we have, I want to say this to you, that the fact that the secretary of the American Municipal Association is also the secretary of our organization has strengthened the Mayors Conference."

During the successive year Hoan as AMA vice-president did not attend any of the three AMA executive committee meetings or the 1935 AMA convention in Knoxville. Neither he nor Mayor Fiorello H. La Guardia of New York, who was to become the next president of the Mayors Conference, had any indication that a breach was developing between AMA and its executive director. Nor were they advised directly by AMA's officers when the break did occur on October 23, 1935, following adjournment of the Knoxville convention.

The new, direct federal-city relationship required some organizational adjustment by the American Municipal Association, originally conceived as a national clearing house for the interchange of ideas and experiences in municipal government, with particular reference to state leagues. Changed conditions, beginning in 1933, thrust it into the position of seeing most of its staff time devoted to national matters. This led then-President Mac-Millin to call on the association for a more militant leadership. But he explained that he had come to that position with a great deal of reluctance. It was a reluctance no doubt shared by many of his fellow directors.

On the other hand, the Conference of Mayors had no hesitancy about exercising "militant leadership." In a display of tireless energy during the first three years of the New Deal, Paul Betters set a furious pace, organizing appearances before congressional committees and conferences with executive departments and agencies, and making speeches in all parts of the United States. He organized a United States delegation to the Lyon Conference of the International Union of Local Authorities in 1934 and annual conferences for both the organizations he served, along with numerous committee meetings. He published *United States Municipal News* and sent a constant flow of other informational bulletins to the state leagues and to mayors. Meanwhile, he kept in constant personal contact with executive directors of leagues of municipalities in twenty-five states, some of them prima donnas, and with the mayors of many big cities, nearly all of them prima donnas.

In addition, Betters supervised the administration of the Chicago headquarters office and the Washington branch office. A substantial grant from the Rockefeller Foundation to AMA made possible the channeling of aid to some twenty-five state leagues of municipalities beginning in late 1933, for employing field consultants to assist municipalities in the emergency PWA, CWA, and relief activities of the federal government, a program also under Betters' direction.

So when AMA and Paul Betters came to a parting of the ways at the end of 1935, the officers of the Conference of Mayors were not about to relinquish such a valuable talent.

The Washington branch office which AMA authorized Betters to establish early in 1934 in a converted residence at 730 Jackson Place, N.W., near the White House, served the Conference of Mayors also. Actually, Betters had leased the building in the name of the Conference. Although the AMA executive committee offered to continue to serve the Conference as its secretariat, its officers decided to stick with Betters. He promptly moved the records and files of the Conference from Chicago to Washington, established headquarters in its building there, and continued the semimonthly *United States Municipal News* as a publication of only the United States Conference of Mayors.

It should be noted that a few of the younger state league executives, notably this author, then in North Carolina, Ed E. Reid of Alabama, and Richard Graves of California, were completely dismayed, even outraged, by the loss of Paul Betters' services to AMA. Although new in the organization, we early sided with those who wanted it to be something more than a professional society of state league secretaries. We believed that it should be a forum for municipal policy in which mayors, councilmen, city managers should take the lead, acting also as its officers and as national spokesmen for municipalities of all sizes. Since that was not then the nature of the association, we highly approved of Betters' aggressive and effective rounding up of the mayors to utilize their collective political clout in Washington at a time when the cities, and therefore the nation, were in deep trouble. And we especially valued having AMA serve as secretariat for the Mayors Conference, even though the mayors were, with a few exceptions like Hoan, kept ignorant of that fact.

Though disconcerting at the time, the split between the two organizations never widened into a serious breach. In fact, Betters occasionally would urge in *United States Municipal News* that the mayors of large cities should actively support their state leagues of municipalities. Both national associations continued to work together and in the same coalitions of other national organizations in behalf of legislation and administrative procedures that would benefit cities. Today the National League of Cities, formerly AMA, and the Conference of Mayors share quarters in the same Washington building, gaining advantages from combined efforts and from the maintenance of a joint staff in many activities.

Paul V. Betters, first full-time executive director of the American Municipal Association (now National League of Cities), 1932–1935, and of the U.S. Conference of Mayors, 1935–1956.

Ernest Martin—Chicago

Clifford W. Ham succeeded Betters as executive director of the American Municipal Association in late 1935 until his death June 8, 1939. He had previously been city manager of Pontiac, Michigan.

City-Federal Linkages Start Working—Recovery!

The beginning of the profound changes in intergovernmental relations caused by responses to the Great Depression probably can be traced to what for its time was revolutionary action by the federal government—creation of the Reconstruction Finance Corporation. Established by Congress early in 1932 on President Hoover's recommendation, the RFC was authorized to make $1.5 billion in self-liquidating loans to states and local governments. The Federal Relief Act, signed by Hoover in July 1932, authorized the RFC to lend $300 million to the states for relief, an action prompted by the unsuccessful appeal by the mayors who met in Detroit a month earlier for a $5 billion public works program.

By November, only $67 million of the $300 million had actually been transmitted to the states. In most of them, despite the desperate need, there was no administrative structure to receive and distribute the money. Traditionally, relief in most urban communities had been the responsibility of private social agencies. Public relief had been largely confined to the maintenance of poorhouses and the support of paupers.

At the request of governors all over the country, Frank Bane, director of the American Public Welfare Association, recently located in Chicago as part of the Public Administration Clearing House complex, tried to repair the grossly inadequate machinery of public welfare. In states with an existing welfare structure, he set up plans for improvement; in others, he established new welfare departments from scratch.

On November 18, 1932, representatives of practically all the nationally organized agencies involved in either public or private welfare and relief were assembled by Frank Bane and Louis Brownlow in Chicago. The result was the adoption of a set of principles that have determined the federal, state, and local administration of public welfare, as far as relief is concerned, since that time. The principal agreement was that "the major responsibility for the relief of destitution rests with government."[1]

After the inauguration of Franklin D. Roosevelt as President in March 1933, many additional emergency measures were enacted which benefited cities. The first was the Federal Emergency Relief Act of 1933, signed by the President on May 13, which appropriated $500 million in direct grants for relief, to be administered through the states. The following month witnessed the enactment of the National Industrial Recovery Act, of which Title I related to industrial matters and was administered by General Hugh Johnson, while Title II related to public works and ultimately came under the administration of Secretary of the Interior Harold Ickes. Title II included a $400 million appropriation for federal aid to highways which for the first time in history authorized the expenditure of federal highway funds within municipal corporate limits. Paul Betters succeeded in having the United States Bureau of Public Roads include in its subsequent regulations the requirement that not less than 25 percent of the $400 million be spent within city limits, a real accomplishment for the cities, which had throughout the country long been discriminated against by rural-dominated legislatures and state highway commissions much more interested in "getting the farmers out of the mud." It also provided for a $3.3 billion public works program under which loans would be made to states and political subdivisions, with the proviso that 30 percent of the cost of labor and materials for such projects could be received in outright grants. Further, it authorized loans for subsidized low-rent housing projects.

When at their Chicago convention in September the Conference of Mayors confronted Secretary Ickes with the slowness and red tape involved in getting any public works under way, it brought to public attention the fact that the program was not putting substantial numbers of unemployed to work. This aided those within the national administration who were seeking a program of outright grants to states and localities for work projects, instead of relief doles, to win their power struggle. On November 7, 1933, the President created the Federal Civil Works Administration (CWA) and appointed Harry L. Hopkins as administrator. Public Works Administrator Harold Ickes made available $400 million to the CWA. The objective of the program was to take 2 million men off the work relief rolls and put them to work as self-sustaining employees on federal, state, and local public projects, beginning nine days later. An additional 2 million would be put to work as soon thereafter as possible. At that time approximately 3 million families were being cared for throughout the country by local relief administrations financed in whole or part by FERA funds. About 2 million adult members of those families were earning relief in the form of wages for part-time employment on make-work projects, and the total amount earned by the members of any one family was less than twenty dollars a month in most of the localities. The new program was designed to make them self-sustaining by placing them on regular pay for a thirty-hour week at the hourly rates prevailing for similar work in the community. It was to help organize this program that Harry Hopkins recruited Paul Betters for three or four weeks.

Fiorello H. La Guardia was elected mayor of New York City that fall. Soon after he took office at the beginning of 1934, he was visited by Mayor Hoan and Betters, who persuaded him to bring New York into the Conference of Mayors and to serve on the executive committee of the Conference. He was elected vice-president at the annual convention the following November. With his ready access to President Roosevelt, La Guardia arranged for the executive committee to meet with FDR at Hyde Park that fall. The mayors, according to La Guardia, "gave the President a real picture of the conditions existing in the cities of the country and made definite recommendations."[2] The execu-

Works Progress Administration (WPA) workers helped cities maintain services during the Depression.

tive committee met again with the President in the spring of 1935 and told him that unemployment relief programs that required cities to borrow money for public works were "simply nonsense" because most cities were unable legally to contract additional debts.

In 1935 Congress made its appropriations for recovery and relief in a huge lump sum of $4.8 billion to be apportioned by the President. An unorthodox method of administering the new funds was set up, under which an office was established to receive applications for projects. After examination and review there, they were transmitted to another new agency, the Advisory Committee on Allotments, which made recommendations to the President on the allotment of funds. Interior Secretary Ickes chaired this twenty-three-member committee, which included the President himself, other federal officials, and five nongovernmental members, including a representative of the United States Conference of Mayors. La Guardia was designated to represent the Conference. In the same executive order the President set up the Works Progress Administration (WPA), which was to be responsible for the coordinated execution of the work relief programs as a whole and was to move as many persons as possible from the relief rolls to work projects or private employment in the shortest possible time. The Federal Emergency Relief Administrator was designated to serve as head of the WPA, and that meant Harry Hopkins.

Although the Public Works Administration continued to carry on, as did many of the other agencies engaged in the battle against unemployment, it was not long until Harry Hopkins' Works Progress Administration emerged as the dominant agency.

La Guardia knew his way around Washington very well after his fifteen years as a member of Congress, and he now had almost weekly contact with the President, PWA Administrator Ickes, WPA Administrator Hopkins, the chief of the Bureau of Public Roads, and the other top government administrators who served on the Allotments Committee. He and Betters made an effective team in representing the cities in Washington. Both the state leagues and the mayors of the larger cities were kept fully informed of developments through a constant stream of bulletins and reports, which, after the formal opening of the Washington office on June 15, 1935, were sent directly from there.

An impressive array of speakers addressed the annual meeting of the Mayors Conference the following November. They included Hopkins, Secretary of Labor Perkins, Attorney General Cummings, Secretary of the Treasury Morgenthau, Senator Robert F. Wagner, and, at a White House reception, President Roosevelt. Elected to succeed Mayor Hoan as president was Mayor La Guardia, who held the position for the next ten years.

Although unemployment remained high and millions of persons were still on relief, conditions by the end of 1935 were improving, both in the nation's economy as a whole and in the financial position of city governments. Senator Wagner reported in his speech to the Mayors Conference that industrial employment and production were at the highest levels in five years, that retail trade and freight car loadings were on a continual upswing, that steel production was stronger and steadier than at any time since 1928, that electric power distribution was setting a new record, and that the profits of 220 representative industrial concerns had increased in the third quarter of that year by 59 percent over the same period the year before. The local governments also were benefiting from passage of the Home Owners Loan Act of 1933, which included a section, inserted in the law at the urgent request of many state leagues of municipalities, requiring payment of delinquent taxes with funds of the HOLC before any home mortgage could be refinanced. More than $190 million in back taxes had been turned over to local treasuries from the passage of that act through August 1935. More than a year earlier, Congress had passed the Sumners-Wilcox Act, the so-called Municipal Debt Readjustment Act. This facilitated negotiations between cities and their municipal creditors for refunding of debts. It led to the restoration of credit for nearly 1,200 municipalities that were in default on principal or interest of their bonded debt. Two years later, the act was declared unconstitutional by a five-to-four decision of the United States Supreme Court, but an amended version was sustained by the Court in 1938. While it remained on the statute books, it probably did more than anything else to restore defaulted municipalities to a better financial condition.

There was more evidence of municipal recovery. In late 1936, *The Daily Bond Buyer* reported that no new defaults had occurred in many months and that of the fifty-four cities of 25,000 or more population which defaulted on bond principal or interest, all but ten were in a position to meet their obligations in cash on time. This was in striking contrast with the picture of earlier fiscal crisis sketched by the financial journal in the same article. It said that "during the worst months of this latest era of defaults out of which American municipalities are now emerging, there were probably more than 3,000 separate local governmental subdivisions behind in payments of some part of principal or interest on their funded, temporary, or floating indebtedness. No complete inventory has been made, nor is it likely that one ever will be compiled." However, such an inventory was made thirty-five years later by the Advisory Commission on Intergovernmental Relations from defaults reported to *The Daily Bond Buyer* from 1929 through 1937, which showed that a total of 4,770 local government units defaulted during that period, as categorized in the following table:

During 1936 and 1937, Betters organized several regional meetings of mayors in most parts of the country, focused primarily on generating pressure on Congress to continue the WPA program with adequate appropriations. At the same time he attempted to organize city administrators into seven "departments" of the Conference of Mayors, thus presenting a competitive challenge to corresponding associations that had headquarters with the Public Administration Clearing House in Chicago, such as the American Public Works Association, the Municipal Finance Officers' Association, and the American Public Welfare Association. It does not appear that this move met with much success,

Incidence of Defaults by Type of Local Government Unit: 1929–37
(in millions)

Type of Government Unit	Total Number[a]	Number in Default[b]	Percentage of Total Number in Default	Net Debt of All Units, 1933[c]	Indebtedness of Defaulting Unit[d]	Percentage of Debt in Default
Counties	3,053	417	13.7	$ 2,391	$ 360	15.1
Incorporated municipalities	16,366	1,434	8.3	8,842	1,760	19.9
Towns and organized townships	20,262	88	.4	344	10	2.9
School districts	127,108	1,241	.9	2,040	160	7.8
Reclamation, levee, irrigation, and drainage districts	3,351	944	28.2			
Other special districts	5,229	646	12.4	1,599[e]	400[e]	25.0[e]
Total	175,369	4,770	2.7	$15,216	$2,690	17.7

[a]Based on number in William Anderson, *The Units of Government in the United States* (Chicago: Public Administration Service, 1934), pp. 1 and 24.
[b]Based on all defaults reported to *The Daily Bond Buyer* from 1929 through 1937.
[c]U.S. Bureau of the Census, *Financial Statistics of State and Local Governments, 1932* (Washington, D.C.: U.S. Government Printing Office, 1933).
[d]Indebtedness at time of default as reported to *The Daily Bond Buyer.*
[e]Combination of reclamation, levee, irrigation, and drainage districts and other special districts.

although it did result ultimately in the formation of three new national associations: the National Institute of Municipal Law Officers, which Charles S. Rhyne, later to become president of the American Bar Association, has served as general counsel continuously since 1937; the National Institute of Governmental Purchasing, of which Albert H. Hall has been executive vice-president since its founding in 1944; and the International Institute of Municipal Clerks. In 1937 Betters moved to broaden the support of the Conference by reducing the population requirement of cities eligible for membership from 50,000 to 30,000.

The Mayors Conference actively supported the Housing Act of 1937—the Wagner-Steagall Act—which, Betters told the mayors, would carry out a resolution on housing the Conference had adopted. The act established for the first time a United States Housing Authority to finance low-rent housing projects through loans to local housing authorities. Betters hailed the act as "one of the most important—if not *the* most important—pieces of federal legislation affecting the welfare of the cities that has ever been enacted in the history of our country."[3]

The champions of public housing advocated it not only as an emergency construction program to provide more jobs. They also honestly believed it would be a slum-clearance device that would improve cities, eliminate urban blight, and provide decent, safe, and sanitary housing, in the words of President Roosevelt, "for that one-third of the nation who are ill-fed, ill-clothed, and ill-housed." Even though the number of local housing authorities organized under provisions of the 1937 act had mounted to more than five hundred by the end of 1940, the public housing movement never achieved popular support, and it failed over the next generation to accomplish the social goals of its sponsors. In fact, some analysts, such as Professor Jay Forrester at MIT, can now make a good case that a city's decision to replace blighted areas with subsidized public housing can be counterproductive in its efforts to arrest urban decay and that a better solution is to clear blighted areas for job-producing industries.[4]

Meanwhile, a substantially larger American Municipal Association had begun to make the national impact that some of its founders had long envisioned. Clifford W. Ham, an aide to Betters, who succeeded his boss as executive director in 1935, had stepped up efforts to encourage the formation of new state leagues and to strengthen the existing ones through improved services. By the end of 1936, leagues were operating in thirty-eight states, combining a membership of approximately six thousand cities, towns, and villages.

Soon after the Public Works Administration was set up in 1933, Brownlow, who was consulting daily with PWA Administrator Harold Ickes, suggested that Ickes set up a planning committee to study public works and help the administration to allocate the $3.3 billion funds to the best possible advantage. He suggested as its members Frederic A. Delano, the President's uncle, with whom Ickes used to work when he was head of the Chicago Regional Planning Association; Dr. Charles E. Merriam, whose campaign Ickes managed when he ran for mayor of Chicago in 1911; and Dr. Wesley C. Mitchell, a distinguished economist of Columbia University. Merriam and Mitchell, as members of President Hoover's Commission on Recent Social and Economic Trends, had joined in a recommendation that a national planning board be established, an idea which Mr. Hoover approved but had never implemented.

On July 30, 1933, Ickes appointed those three as a National Planning Board to advise on preparation of a comprehensive program of public works through development of regional plans, surveys, and research, and correlation of effort among federal, state, and local agencies. Out of that came the presidential order of June 30, 1934, creating the National Resources Board and Advisory Committee to prepare and present to the President a program for development and use of land, water, and other natural resources. That agency, which a year later became the National Resources Committee, and four years later, the National Resources Planning Board, was set up in the Executive Office of the President. Through Brownlow and Merriam AMA had a good working relationship with the NRPB and its predecessors.

The growing city-federal ties in the 1930s and 1940s brought together mayors and presidents. Above, New York City Mayor La Guardia and President Roosevelt in 1940.

By making WPA funds available for staffing, the National Planning Board and its successors successfully persuaded many states to establish planning boards, a first for most of them. A national inventory of works projects conducted jointly by state boards and state PWA engineers in March 1935 provided an initial estimate of public works construction throughout the country. The following year the National Resources Committee undertook a second inventory, classifying projects by type, location, and priority. The committee expected that the program would be kept up to date by annual revision. Reporting of nonfederal projects was carried out through the state planning boards, which were all advised by a bulletin of the National Resources Committee to "take advantage of the existence of state leagues" to educate and secure the support of local public officials.

Stimulated by the availability of federal WPA funds, the number of state planning agencies increased from approximately three in 1933 to forty-five in 1935. The field and consultant service of the National Resources Planning Board gave further impetus to state planning. Other accomplishments of the board and its predecessors during its ten-year period of existence included a long list of research publications and policy recommendations on such vital but neglected subjects as river basin development, city governments, city planning, urban and rural land policy, technology and research, patterns of industry, energy resources, trends in population, income and spending habits of consumers, housing, and transportation. The board also had some success in coordinating the operations of federal, state, and local agencies in the development of river basin water resources.

Despite this lengthy list of accomplishments, the board was abolished by an act of Congress effective August 31, 1943, for several reasons which need not be reviewed here.[5] Most of its coordinative planning activities are now carried on in the Executive Office of the President and in the departments and agencies charged with specific program functions. There was, however, one important gap in substantive government-wide coordination that was not filled. The energy resources activities of the government continued to be divided among several agencies, with no overall program for conservation and use of energy resources. The lost opportunity in NRPB's national energy resources studies did not become obvious until thirty years later, with the surfacing of the energy crisis in late 1973.

Other federal concerns of the state leagues and AMA during the middle and late thirties included, of course, the financing of WPA and other public relief assistance, the expansion of vocational education to include public service training, amending of the Social Security Act to include public employees, federal aid for state highways within city limits, and federal aid for construction and improvement of municipal airports.

In a self-congratulatory resolution adopted at its 1938 convention, AMA commended its activities "in asserting leadership in the successful effort to head off discriminating highway legislation at the last session of Congress," adding that such leadership "demonstrates clearly what can be accomplished when the cities and villages of this country unite through their leagues of municipalities and their national organization." It directed its officers "to assume the same responsibility of leadership when other subjects arise in the future requiring united action by the cities and villages of the nation."

AMA's executive committee took the lead in December 1936 in calling on Congress to enact legislation for a national system of civil airways and airports and for a determination of federal aid. The association published a report that same month, which included a brief by John Stutz of the League of Kansas Municipalities showing the growing need for national airport planning and uniform development and ending with the statement that the federal government should pay "its proportionate share of the costs based on federal values." In the following year the Conference of Mayors likewise became involved with efforts to obtain federal aid for airports, but that was not to come about until October 1940, when the first federal appropriation was made—$40 million to be expended largely for defense instead of civil air requirements.

For all their efforts in behalf of the cities and their vigilance in protecting their interests, both AMA and the Mayors Conference seemed to miss the significance of the National Housing Act of 1934, which created the Federal Housing Administration for the insurance of mortgages and loans made by private lending institutions for the purchase, construction, rehabilitation, repair, and improvement of single-family and multifamily housing. The Federal National Mortgage Association was chartered in 1938 to provide a secondary market where lending institutions could sell their eligible FHA-insured residential mortgages, much as commercial banks can rediscount their short-term paper and replenish their reserves at the Federal Reserve Banks. The FHA program, backed by the FNMA, made it financially feasible for middle-income families to become home owners with only a 10 percent down payment, a highly commendable objective. It also enabled them to move from the cities to suburban developments that leapfrog over vacant lands being held off the market by speculators in a crazy-quilt pattern. That they did so in an ever-increasing tide was to help create the monstrous unplanned suburban sprawl that has been the fate of most metropolitan areas in the United States since the FHA was created. Yet its potential impact on the orderly growth of cities and on the urban environment apparently went unnoticed in the Depression thirties by the elected officials and appointed managers of governments at any level—city, county, state, or national—or by their state and national associations.

World War II and Its Aftermath

The Nazi invasion of Poland on September 1, 1939, followed two days later by declarations of war on Germany by Great Britain and France, signaled the start of World War II. On September 5 President Roosevelt issued a proclamation invoking the embargo on export of arms, ammunition, or implements of war from anywhere in the United States to any of the belligerents on either side, based on the Neutrality Act of 1937. Despite this neutral stance, and in the face of anxieties of the nation's strong isolationist bloc, the government launched a major mobilization of the armed forces.

Suddenly the manpower situation in cities reversed itself. Actually, the country was rebounding well from the recession of 1937–38 that had interrupted the progress of recovery from the deep Depression of the preceding years. But memories of lines of unemployed still lingered in the minds of mayors who had devoted so much time and energy to devising work-relief programs. As industry responded to defense orders from Washington, unemployment all but disappeared. In fact, shortages of workers began to develop in some cities. Army camps and hastily erected munitions factories changed some three hundred cities into boom towns. This put severe strains on facilities in those cities. Housing stocks, which had declined because of the economic stagnation of the Depression, were taxed to the limit as the unprecedented influx of workers from rural areas, especially the rural South, scrambled for shelter.

In truth, the heavy migration of workers to the cities was not just a phenomenon of World War II. The movement, particularly the migration of blacks from the South, had started by the turn of the century.

While the influx of blacks into Northern cities during the early 1900s was moderate, the outbreak of World War I in Europe sharply reduced the flow of European immigrants to the United States and prompted Northern industrialists to turn to the South for fresh labor recruits. A poor cotton crop in the South in 1915 put thousands of cotton pickers out of work, but plenty of jobs were waiting for them in packing houses, steel mills, and other industries in the Midwest and North that needed unskilled labor. By 1920 more than one-third of all American blacks were living in urban centers, both North and South, an increase of almost 900,000 in the decade.

Opportunities for blacks had expanded since a Howard University educator tried in 1902 to account for the attraction of industrial centers for Southern blacks. Kelly Miller, writing in the *Southern Workman,* asserted that "the Negro has little developed aptitude for the commercial and industrial requirements of city life." Miller concluded that lack of industrial opportunity for blacks enforced what he called unwholesome modes of living which, in turn, entail "physical and moral decay." He asked: "Why, then, do Negroes join in this mad rush to the cities in the face of the fate which almost certainly awaits them?"

He attributed the blacks' attraction to the city to three factors: (1) the general glare and glitter of city life; (2) poor compensation for agricultural industries and the dearth of rural social attractions; and (3) the better police protection and school facilities to be found at the centers of population.[1]

More precise answers to Miller's question emerged years later, however, after statistics on comparative levels of wages and relief began to be compiled. The average hourly wage in 1969 ranged from $1.01 in South Carolina to $1.78 in California. Disparities in relief were greater. In 1951 the average relief payment per person in the South was $14 a month, while all other regions had levels almost twice as high. At the extremes the disparities widened—a Mississippian got $5 a month, a California resident, $36. By 1969 payments had almost doubled everywhere; Mississippi paid $10 while Massachusetts paid $68. A Mississippi family of four with no income received $69; a comparable New Jersey family received $347.[2]

Whatever the attraction of the cities to American blacks and other rural migrants, it was a permanent attraction for most of them. After 1918, workers recruited to work in war industries stimulated by World War I were not inclined to return to the farm. Meanwhile, the flow of European immigrants increased from a low of 110,000 in 1918 to 805,000 in 1921. Most of them also settled in the big cities. However, the depression of 1920–21 and the "Red scare" that swept the country after the Bolshevik revolution combined to bring about a temporary immigration quota system in 1921, succeeded by congressional adoption of the Immigration Restriction Act of 1924. This reduced the number of immigrants to an average of 300,000 annually for the rest of the decade, but the cities continued to draw increased numbers of workers from rural America. During the 1920s some 1.5 million blacks left the rural districts of the South to live in Northern and Southern cities.

Federal policies inaugurated in the Depression years of the New Deal, which called for restrictions on agricultural production in order to create higher prices for smaller supplies, largely failed in their purpose when farmers resorted to increased use of fertilizers to produce higher yields per acre. This prompted quota restrictions and heavy federal subsidies to compensate for the restricted output. These policies supported agricultural prices at a tremendous cost to urban consumers and taxpayers. But they forced small farmers off the land and reduced the need for farm labor. Technological advances in farm machinery further reduced the need for manual labor at the same time that other federal policies eased the availability of farm credit to

Wide World

World War II's national mobilization burdened cities with extra problems. One of the worst was housing. Shelter shortages forced many workers to live in trailer camps or hastily assembled barracks-type structures

invest in these machines. But justification for the large investments required larger acreages for their economic use. Hence the modern phenomenon of consolidations resulting in fewer but bigger farms and industrialized farming methods with huge production per man-day. As Chapter 4 noted, these trends have resulted over the past fifty years in a drastic decline of farm population in the United States—from 32 million to 9.7 million, from 30 percent of the nation's total population to less than 5 percent.

During World War II, millions of these rural residents, black and white, moved to cities to take jobs in war industries or entered the armed forces. As their wartime predecessors twenty years earlier had done, they stayed in the cities.

Black leaders of the period were generally impressed by a concern exhibited by some Roosevelt administration officials for minority needs and rights, yet they were frustrated by FDR's reluctance to press for legislation that would lower racial barriers. His failure to publicly support antilynching legislation in 1935 in the face of a Southern filibuster in the Senate had been a particular sore point.[3] The wartime national emergency gave black leaders an opportunity to press the administration for executive action to relieve disparities. In the spring of 1941, A. Philip Randolph, president of the Brotherhood of Sleeping Car Porters, threatened to lead 50,000 blacks to Washington to present their demands for fair treatment in defense industries to Congress and the President. Randolph called off the demonstration after Roosevelt, perceiving the march as a threat to national unity, issued an executive order on fair employment practices on June 25, 1941. This required every company under contract with the United States and every federal agency to eliminate racial discrimination; violation of the order would result in contract cancellation. The Fair Employment Practices Commission was established to enforce the decree. Though the commission had limited funds and staff, the eventual consensus was that the action had given blacks a more secure place than the American urban world had ever before allowed them. One historian attributed an increase in tensions in many cities to what she identified as a new aggressiveness among Negroes who were now assured of legal rights during working hours.[4]

The antidiscrimination order did not extend to housing, but the mass movement of black families to teeming ghettos in city after city continued. Until about 1944 serious overcrowding was general in and around industrial centers. In 1941 privately financed residential building dropped to one-quarter of the 1940 volume. The Lanham Act of June 1941 made $150 million available for emergency defense housing, which provided only temporary relief. After the Japanese attack on Pearl Harbor on December 7, 1941, the Lanham Act was extended to provide another $150 million for temporary war housing and $300 million for permanent houses in areas containing factories and military establishments. Some 600,000 temporary and 200,000 permanent housing units were built for industrial workers and servicemen with those government funds before the war was over. Trailer parks, a new phenomenon, eased the congestion in some communities, prompting the American Municipal Association to publish a report and several state leagues of municipalities to prepare model ordinances on their regulation and control.

This was only one of scores of areas in which war activity and the prewar mobilization impinged on the activities of cities and the organizations that spoke for them.

Two weeks after President Roosevelt proclaimed America's neutrality in September 1939, Paul Betters, exercising his good sense of timing and flair for public relations, persuaded Mayor La Guardia, then president of the United States Conference of Mayors, to call a special meeting of the Conference in Washington. Its purpose, said La Guardia in his opening speech at the September 19 session, was to assure the President officially that the mayors of the cities would cooperate with him in the policy of neutrality. Appropriate resolutions were passed and presented to the President when he received the mayors at the White House that afternoon. In contrast to that well-publicized maneuver, the American Municipal Association remained publicly silent, although at a meeting the following month with its executive committee, its new executive director, Earl D. Mallery, did discuss the potential role of the association and its state league affiliates in federal plans for organization for national defense. Mallery, who had been manager of the association's Washington office for the preceding three years, was appointed executive director August 1, 1939, to succeed Clifford W. Ham, who had died of a heart attack on June 8.

Following the establishment of President Roosevelt's National Defense Advisory Commission in May 1940, an AMA staff memorandum was prepared on the role of municipalities and their state leagues in national defense, and the association sponsored the preparation of the report, *Local Government in the British*

Defense Program, published in July 1940. Concurrently its executive committee directed that the state league field service maintain effective liaison between the cities and the state and national agencies involved in the defense effort, including the newly created Division of State and Local Cooperation of the National Defense Advisory Commission. However, AMA's executive committee criticized that division the following January, charging that it had not conducted adequate information or service programs for local government. A committee was appointed to work with Mallery in formulating plans and programs for AMA and the state leagues in defense-impacted states.

Meanwhile, Paul Betters was working on a plan that led to the formation, on May 20, 1941, of the Office of Civilian Defense. The new office gave cities full responsibility, under federal direction, for civil defense. When La Guardia, still president of the Conference, presented the plan to the President, Roosevelt appointed the New York mayor director of the office.

The President's executive order establishing that office provided that it should include a Board of Civilian Protection, to be composed of the director of civilian defense as chairman, representatives of the War, Navy, and Justice departments, and one representative each from the Council of State Governments, the American Municipal Association, and the United States Conference of Mayors. The board was directed to help formulate measures "appropriate to the varying needs of each part of the nation." After establishing the principle that civil defense was a local government responsibility with federal support, La Guardia resigned the federal position to devote his full energies to the problems of New York, which, like many other cities, was experiencing a critical shortage of housing and an overcrowding of its schools, recreational facilities, and transportation system.

By 1943 city officials realized that the preparedness machinery they had been forced to establish in the face of a war threat could be useful during many kinds of disasters. Delegates to the American Municipal Association's convention that year instructed their executive director to draft a model plan for converting local civilian defense organizations into permanent auxiliary disaster preparedness agencies and to compile and publish a disaster preparedness manual. Before work on such a manual could be completed, however, the Office of Civilian Defense was abolished and the AMA executive committee decided to adopt the American Red Cross manual on disaster preparedness for use by state leagues and cities.

In the mid-1940s, AMA also concerned itself with congressional legislation providing federal aid for highways, including their urban connections inside city limits, and federal aid for airports. Along with other public interest groups, it also began to show concern for the World War II counterpart of the "peace dividend," the diversion of federal resources for domestic programs such groups anticipated in vain during the late 1960s before the close of the Vietnam War. The association advocated "a sound program of local participation in plans to cushion the shock of reconversion from war to peace and to assist in the prompt employment of returning veterans." It sought congressional legislation to make machinery and equipment owned by the federal government and leased to private producers by the federal government subject to local taxes. It proposed payment in lieu of taxes on all federal property not used exclusively for government functions, and urged continued opposition to any federal tax on income from municipal bonds.

The concern of AMA and the Conference of Mayors with the need for municipal planning for the postwar period was from somewhat different perspectives. This difference was evident in the approaches taken by the two organizations to the work of the National Resources Planning Board.

After his reelection in 1940, Roosevelt directed that the NRPB make postwar planning its major responsibility. In the spring of the following year the Conference of Mayors proposed to President Roosevelt through Mayor La Guardia that the federal government allot $3.5 million for the preparation of an inventory of postwar public works and for detailed plans for a vast program to cost $3 billion. Paul Betters, who shared with La Guardia a skepticism toward NRPB's approach to planning, wrote in *United States Municipal News:* "This is not a problem primarily for academic observers. In the main, it is an engineering job."[5]

On the other hand, AMA, no doubt stimulated by Louis Brownlow and Charles E. Merriam, vice-chairman of the NRPB, was more supportive of that agency's approach. At its October 1942 convention, AMA called for an immediate start on municipal planning for the postwar period. In January 1943 the executive committee named Mayor Wilson W. Wyatt of Louisville as chairman of a committee to stimulate local acceptance of the responsibility for postwar planning. It further charged the committee to encourage the channeling of assistance from all available sources for that purpose.

Norman Beckman, now director of the Legislative Reference Service of the Library of Congress, suggested in a 1960 review of the NRPB that the 1940 decision of the board to concentrate on postwar planning probably was a fatal error. The time was not ripe for public consideration of postwar problems, and the fact that the board was making no significant contribution to the immediate war effort was one of the factors that led Congress to kill it on August 31, 1943. Internal disagreements over agency objectives also contributed to its demise. Staff director Charles W. Elliott felt that planning should be quickly translatable into tangible results in the form of physical projects and public works planning. Influential individual board members, including Merriam, on the other hand, believed that economic and social planning should be the agency's dominant concern. Its rigid focus on long-range planning prevented it from contributing to immediate needs.[6] Central social and economic planning was already held in suspicion and distrust by many influential leaders in and out of Congress, a fact of which Paul Betters was well aware when he published the following comment:

It appears that federal authorities working on the general postwar problems have failed, insofar as a postwar public works program is concerned, to realize that we do not now need any more surveys, reports or inventories. What is needed is the actual preparation of detailed plans and specifications of needed public works which can be put "on ice." Then when the proper time comes, work can be prosecuted at once. In the early thirties we lost nearly two years in efforts to provide employment simply because working plans and specifications had to be prepared—with the result that we had to improvise work programs which cost billions of dollars. Let the federal government assist in the development of detailed plans instead of wasting funds on inventories and surveys.[7]

The death of the NRPB was imminent in June 1943, when Mayor Wyatt told the AMA executive committee that "the whole responsibility for a national planning movement seemed now to rest on the cities." He urged that AMA help cities plan to meet current conditions as well as impending postwar problems. The committee asked Walter Blucher, executive director of the American Society of Planning Officials, to serve on Wyatt's Special Committee on Planning and scheduled a series of statewide conferences on municipal planning, to be jointly funded by AMA and ASPO.

Mayor Wyatt that year was elected vice-president of AMA, and his elevation to president the following year began the uninterrupted tradition of electing mayors as presidents of AMA and the National League of Cities that has prevailed to this day.*

Wyatt showed foresight through a successful effort to persuade AMA in 1944 to establish a Joint Committee on Urban Rehabilitation to support legislation that apparently was the forerunner of urban renewal. Besides AMA, which Wyatt represented, the committee included ASPO, the National Housing Conference, the National Association of Housing Officials, the Conference of Mayors, and the Urban Land Institute. Wyatt reported to the AMA executive committee six months later that there were broad areas of agreement among committee members on provi-

---

*An intended break with that tradition took place in the 1972 election of City Councilman Tom Bradley of Los Angeles as vice-president of the National League of Cities, but before his elevation to the presidency a year later he was elected mayor.

sions of the Federal Urban Rehabilitation Act then pending in Congress. This prompted AMA at its November 1945 convention to endorse "the principle of sharing of state and federal credit with the political subdivisions of the states to assist them in acquiring and redeveloping blighted communities areas" and to urge Congress and state legislatures "to authorize grants-in-aid . . . to the political subdivisions to help absorb the losses which may be incident to the acquisition of blighted areas." This concept was embodied in the urban redevelopment legislation finally enacted in the Housing Act of 1949.

Louisville was then and still is one of those few unfortunate cities that limit by law the tenure of their mayors to one four-year term, undoubtedly a reaction to the corruption of the nineteenth century. Even though this system deprives Louisville citizens of the advantages inherent in continuity of outstanding leadership, some of her mayors have gone on to higher service for a wider public. Wyatt, for example, was appointed in 1946 by President Truman as Housing Expediter and Administrator of the National Housing Agency, which had been created in 1942 to incorporate into one agency the Federal Housing Administration, the Home Loan Bank Board, and the Public Housing Administration. He served until the following year, when President Truman by an executive reorganization plan created the Housing and Home Finance Agency with the same three units as its basic components.

The successful experience of Wyatt's leadership encouraged AMA to consider making its services directly available to the larger cities and involving their officials more actively in the affairs of the association. In 1943 the association adopted a proposal by Richard Graves, executive director of the League of California Cities, directing its executive committee to consider a specialized service for metropolitan areas. This struck a responsive chord in the Conference of Mayors, which proposed a joint effort for the provision of services to local governments that would include services to deal with metropolitan area problems. An AMA committee was authorized to meet with a Mayors Conference committee, but nothing resulted from the proposal. At its 1944 annual meeting, the association named a subcommittee headed by Herbert A. Olson, then director of the Michigan league, "to proceed with formulation of a definite proposal" for a Metropolitan Area Problems Division. However, Olson resigned his position with the Michigan league, and executive director Mallery apparently interpreted the metropolitan service directive to mean only the establishment of AMA services to large cities. Neither Mallery nor Wyatt could seem to cope with the idea of services on metropolitan area problems as such.

The organization was preoccupied during this period with finding ways to offset rapidly decreasing annual grants from the Spelman Fund, which was to be dissolved within the next three or four years. Early in 1945, Wyatt named a special committee on finance, chaired by Graves. That fall at its annual convention the association adopted the committee's recommendations that the dues schedule for member leagues be increased and that the same proposal advanced in 1943, to establish metropolitan area services, be put into effect.

At the executive committee's first postwar meeting, in February 1946, members approved a motion by Mayor Fletcher Bowron of Los Angeles to make available AMA services directly to cities on a subscription basis with a sliding schedule of fees. The schedule would apply to all cities, including those holding membership in state leagues affiliated with AMA. At that point the minutes of the meeting record the burial of the other half of the Graves committee's farsighted proposal: "The matter of Metropolitan Area Service was not discussed, as it was deemed disposed of by the above noted decision to inaugurate a special direct AMA service for cities of both league and non-league states."

A year and a half later, on recommendation of a special committee on AMA reorganization, the association's constitution was substantially revised. It provided for the first time that cities could become full-fledged members of the association, not merely service subscribers, although they had to have a popula-

tion of 100,000 or more and be members of their own state
leagues.

In its preoccupation with financial problems, the association
had lost an opportunity to get ahead of a trend that in less than
twenty years would assume overriding importance. It had
glimpsed the "real city" in its embryonic stage and failed to come
to terms with it. Worse, it apparently failed to recognize the scope
of metropolitanization.

It was not that metropolitan problems were considered unim-
portant. In fact, a plan for a possible major research project, a
comprehensive study on "Metropolitan Government in the
United States," was discussed by the AMA executive committee
in February 1946, but it was abandoned "because of a shortage
of staff and funds."

It is not surprising, perhaps, that Richard Graves was the un-
heralded prophet of metropolitan problems. His career was, to a
degree, shaped by those problems, which became visible in California in a more dramatic way than anywhere else in the country. He was one of the few local-government practitioners in the
country to recognize that the overcrowding of the cities and the
haphazard spread of population into suburban areas was causing serious problems—metropolitan problems.

Graves was an effective leader in the municipal affairs of California for twenty years until he resigned in 1954 in a fit of pique
at the incumbent governor, Goodwin Knight.* Although he had
long considered himself an Earl Warren Republican, he accepted a draft by the Democratic party leadership to head their
ticket when, at the last moment before filing deadline, the popular attorney general, Edmund ("Pat") Brown, decided not to seek
the governorship at that time. Graves and his promoters mistak-
enly believed that the thousands of city officials with whom he

---

*The tradition of brilliant and strong staff leadership of the League of
California Cities was carried on for another twenty years by Graves'
successor, Richard ("Bud") Carpenter, ably assisted by Howard Gardner
as associate director and an outstanding staff which included Don Ben-
ninghoven, the present executive director.

had had personal contacts over the years would form a solid base of political support. But they didn't reckon with the nonpartisan position of those officials. California had a long tradition of nonpartisan city government. So when it came to taking a partisan stance in a statewide election, many either did not wish to reveal their support publicly by campaigning for Graves or, if Republican in private, did not wish to support a Democratic gubernatorial candidate. With the rest of the voters, Graves was a political unknown, and the news media partisanly and studiously ignored him. He lost to the incumbent.

What prompted Graves' concern about metropolitan area problems in the forties is revealed in the demographic changes that were taking place during that decade, changes statistically revealed by the United States census of 1950. While the population of the nation as a whole increased only 14.5 percent, that of the metropolitan areas increased 22 percent. But most of the increase was taking place outside the central cities. Growth inside them was 13.9 percent, while in the metropolitan areas outside their boundaries it was 35.5 percent.

California's population during the same period increased 53.3 percent. While the nation had become 64 percent urban, California was 80.7 percent urban. More significant than the percentage increase was the fact that the effects of overspilling of incorporated boundaries were more visible sooner in California's burgeoning agglomerations of newborn towns and unincorporated clusters. The edges of cities that once told a motorist he was leaving "country" and entering "city" were growing fuzzy. Residents of some suburban areas on the fringes of cities found their sense of place diminished. No longer did urban services always come from a single source, managed by a single city hall. A multijurisdictional agency might supply water to a number of communities with no special allegiance to any of them. Police protection was often the responsibility of counties. Fire protection might be shared by several communities or purchased on a subscription basis. Over all these spreading areas was an umbrella that might be called Greater Los Angeles or the San Fran-

Charles E. Merriam (left) and Louis Brownlow (right) flank Earl D. Mallery, executive director of the American Municipal Association, 1939–1948.

cisco Bay Area, but nobody could precisely define the perimeters of these regions. Central cities retained their prominent positions in the area, but the centrifugal forces were gradually growing stronger than the centripetal one in many respects. Unfortunately, the implications of these changes were not identified in time so that the forces could be properly channeled.

The Intergovernmental Mix and Mess

I live in Garden Grove, work in Irvine, shop in Santa Ana, go to the dentist in Anaheim, my husband works in Long Beach, and I used to be president of the League of Women Voters in Fullerton.

A Southern California woman volunteered that response in 1971 to a team of *New York Times* correspondents exploring what they described as "broad, ballooning bands [of suburbs], interlinked as cities in their own right . . . the 'Outer City.' "[1] Her difficulty in identifying with a single place has its parallels among public officials who must deal with patterns of decision making and service delivery in today's metropolitan areas.

Long before 1971, however, perceptive municipal officials had become aware of the spread of metropolis with its multiplicity of political jurisdictions, overlapping service areas, and mismatches of public facilities and population. The spillover of population from city boundaries to surrounding suburban territory was accelerated dramatically in the immediate post–World War II period. In 1940 suburbs contained 27 million people, two of every ten Americans; 19 million fewer than the cities. Now they contain 76 million, almost four of every ten—12 million more than the cities they surround.

As we have seen, however, the outward movement of population started at least twenty years before the postwar exodus. It was during the 1920s that the population in metropolitan areas passed 50 percent of the national total for the first time. The movement of urban populations over city boundaries was becoming clearly evident in the development of mushrooming suburbs. Note the use of the phrase "movement over city boundaries," rather than "fleeing" from the cities or "flight" to the suburbs. Flight connotes a running away from danger or evil. It is too simplistic to apply the term to the growth of urban areas, and yet it is a popular phrase with many so-called urban experts.

There are probably as many different reasons why people move their place of residence as there are families who move. Each year about 40 million people change their address. Increasing academic interest in the topic of population migration, both into and within metropolitan areas, has produced numerous studies by scholars of various disciplines—economists, geographers, regional scientists, sociologists, and demographers—particularly since publication of the 1960 *Census of Population.* One recent study, for example, shows that contrary to popular belief, high welfare spending does not produce an expanded influx of nonwhites into the nation's largest metropolitan centers.[2]

City congestion itself is a lure for many. They like to be near the center of it. Without it there wouldn't be a city with all its work opportunities, conveniences, and diverse amenities. Others are satisfied to live within commuting distance of the congestion, preferring residence in detached homes surrounded by green lawns where their children can play and grow. Like our highly mobile Southern Californian, one-fourth of the nation's jobholders work in a county different from that in which they reside.[3]

The changing technology in transportation was the basic factor in the changing shape of cities. First came the streetcar suburbs beginning near the end of the last century, followed by commuter suburbs along rail lines. The mass production of automobiles, which came into full flower in the 1920s, was accompanied by the new phenomenon of installment credit for their purchase. This was an even stronger stimulus to suburban growth. Other changes in technology, in size of population, and in income increased the ability and mobility of people to make a variety of choices that affected the patterns of suburbanization.

Historically, as people moved out from the centers and settled in new homes at the edges, leaving their older houses behind to be filled by newly arriving immigrants or commercial enterprises, the city merely expanded its boundaries to annex the urbanized fringe. Until about the beginning of the twentieth century, central cities in metropolitan regions grew by annexation. This prevented the formation of numerous small cities of the kind that subsequently proliferated around urban centers. The annexations were usually accomplished through special acts of the state legislatures, many without a separate vote of approval in the annexed areas.

Use of the device began to decline around the turn of the century. By the 1920s its use for many central cities, especially in the more populous areas, ceased almost entirely. At the same time widespread new incorporations of suburbs took place as the automobile made it possible for people increasingly to settle farther beyond the limits of central cities. By the time of World War II, annexation was of little significance as a device to provide an orderly structure of government in most metropolitan areas. Changes in many state laws and constitutions had made the procedure highly complicated and difficult. For example, in some states the residents of outlying areas were given exclusive right to initiate annexation. In others they could veto it by having the right to vote on the proposal separately from the central-city voters. In such instances it was the state legislature, probably reflecting gains in suburban representation, that thwarted the integration of governmental organization of metropolitan areas.

One notable exception has been Texas, where cities adopting their own home rule charters can write into them rules for annexing adjacent territory. Sixty-five of the 120 home rule cities, including most of the big ones, permit annexation of unincorporated territory without consent of the voters or property owners of the land involved. Most of those can annex merely by council ordinance. A few require approval of the city's voters, which is similar to the procedure operating in home rule cities

The post–World War II demand for housing plus federal mortgage and transportation policies sparked suburban developments such as this one in San Jose, California.

Wide World

of Missouri. Another exception is Virginia, which since 1904 has provided for judicial determination of annexation proposals.[4] In recent years the state leagues of municipalities in Tennessee and North Carolina have successfully promoted state legislation liberalizing the ability of cities to expand their boundaries.

In 1963 the League of California Cities, in cooperation with the County Supervisors' Association, pioneered in the establishment of a Local Agency Formation Commission in each of the state's fifty-seven counties (all but the city-county of San Francisco). The commission reviews and controls annexation, consolidation, creation, and dissolution of municipal corporations and special districts. The procedure was recommended the following year to all states by the Advisory Commission on Intergovernmental Relations. Four states have followed suit.

Meanwhile, another factor entered into the growth of suburban settlements. Designed primarily as an antidepression measure to stimulate jobs in construction of houses and allied industries, the mortgage insurance program of the federal government was initiated in the mid-thirties. The Federal Housing Administration insured home loans made by private lenders at lower interest rates and longer terms than conventional mortgages. The impact of this policy was interrupted by World War II, which also brought the big rural migration that overcrowded housing facilities in many cities. However, immediately after the war the FHA, abetted by an even more liberal mortgage insurance program for war veterans, stimulated new suburban development with a rush. This period witnessed a revival of annexation activity; approximately one-half of all central cities of metropolitan areas annexed territory during the next ten years. The trend extended to many smaller cities inside and outside metropolitan areas. Despite these renewed expansions, cities were unable to keep pace with the rapid urban growth taking place at their edges.

Even before the war, the spreading population had stimulated the incorporation of hundreds of new general-purpose municipalities—cities, towns, villages, boroughs—to provide such basic needs as police and fire protection, sanitation, and public works. Incorporation gave the new municipality its own financial base and the power to levy taxes and other charges to pay for such services. Significantly, it also gave it the power to control land use within its borders through its own zoning ordinances. Another frequent motive for incorporation was to prevent the central city or even a nearby smaller city from annexing the territory.

An additional administrative device was adding to the governmental diffusion in urban areas in the early 1940s. The laws of most states made it easy to establish special districts to carry on specific functions such as the provision of cemeteries, fire protection, hospitals, libraries, flood control, parks and recreation, sewers, water supply, and electric power. They are limited-purpose governmental units which exist as separate corporate entities having considerable fiscal and administrative independence from general-purpose governments. They are governed by boards of directors, trustees, or commissioners who are selected by various processes. Because of their fiscal self-sufficiency, special districts are useful as a means of performing one or more special services that could not be performed by a county or municipality because of financial or legal limitations imposed by the state. Their jurisdictions frequently overlap existing local government boundaries, since a special district can serve an unincorporated area, a portion of an incorporated municipality, an entire municipality, an entire county, or any combination of these areas. There were 8,299 such districts in 1942, not counting school districts, which totaled 108,579.

The Bureau of the Census that year also counted 16,220 municipalities, 18,919 townships and New England towns, and 3,050 counties, a total of more than 155,000 governmental units.[5] While at least two-thirds of them were located outside metropolitan areas, the multiplicity of units inside the more heavily populated regions was causing increasing problems and growing awareness of the intergovernmental mix and mess. Literature on the subject was not yet extensive. The first comprehensive study of governmental problems caused by metropolitanization, a product of the reform-oriented National Municipal League's emerging concern, was not published until 1930.[6]

As we have seen, efforts had first been made in 1943 to get the American Municipal Association to inaugurate special metropolitan service and in 1946 to undertake a comprehensive study on metropolitan government in the United States. During the 1940s the population inside standard metropolitan statistical areas (SMSAs) increased 22.6 percent, compared to an increase of only 4.5 percent outside. Inside the SMSAs, however, an even more startling change was taking place. While the population of the central cities increased 14.7 percent, the areas outside their boundaries in the rest of the metropolitan areas gained nearly 36 percent! Failure of AMA to take serious note of the urban problems involved in these population shifts was possibly one reason some of its leaders determined that a complete reorganization was needed. Difficulty in financing the organization, of course, was a more immediate reason.

Reorganization really started with the decision to admit the larger cities to direct membership and to involve their chief executives more actively in the affairs of the association. Louisville Mayor Wilson W. Wyatt, the first of these mayors, was succeeded in late 1945 by Portland, Oregon, Mayor Earl E. Riley. Riley, with Mayors Woodall Rodgers and Fletcher Bowron of Dallas and Los Angeles, and Kansas City's City Manager L. P. Cookingham, formed a majority on the seven-member executive committee. A year later Rodgers and Bowron became president and vice-president, and Minneapolis Mayor Hubert Humphrey was added to the executive committee. Critics among the state league directors of Earl Mallery's leadership as AMA director were also elected to the committee, notably Mrs. Davetta L. Steed of North Carolina and John Huss of Michigan. A California-inspired convention motion authorized a seven-member committee on AMA reorganization chaired by John Huss and including Mayor Bowron and John G. Stutz. Their recommendations resulted in a completely revised constitution, effective September 1947, which provided, among other things, for direct membership in the association by cities of over 100,000.[7]

The broadening of membership to include individual big cities, as well as the state leagues of cities, was crucially important politically and financially. Of equal importance, and a necessary corollary, was a May 1948 decision to revise completely the association's activities. Thereafter they were to be based on a program that would provide the continuing direction and purpose which AMA had lacked in the past. Fletcher Bowron had become president six months earlier at the annual convention in New Orleans. Closely advised by Richard Graves, director of the League of California Cities, he exerted strong leadership in an executive committee that included Mayor deLesseps S. ("Chep") Morrison of New Orleans and Mayor Quigg Newton of Denver, two of a new crop of young, progressive postwar mayors. The committee, which had been expanded to nine members, also included four strong state league executives, including the veteran Frederick N. MacMillin of Wisconsin, John Huss of Michigan, Harold F. Alderfer of Pennsylvania, and Morgan Strong of New York.

That group decided at a meeting in December 1947, a month after the New Orleans convention, to employ an outside consultant, Carl H. Chatters, to develop a program of action and research for the association. It was his report, adopted by the committee at the May 1948 meeting, that set the American Municipal Association on a new course.

At the same meeting Earl D. Mallery's resignation was accepted, and Chatters was appointed to succeed him as executive director. And, not so incidentally, the Spelman Fund made a $100,000 terminal grant to the association to tide it over its next few years of transformation.

Carl Chatters was a well-known expert in municipal finance. After several years as city director of finance in Flint, Michigan, he became executive director of the Municipal Finance Officers' Association of the United States and Canada when that organization established its headquarters with the Public Administration

Clearing House at Chicago in the early thirties. He left to join the United States military government service with the occupation army in Germany, then accepted a lifetime tenure as comptroller of the Port of New York Authority until AMA beckoned him. He was brilliant, aggressive, and experienced.

Chatters' report envisioned the American Municipal Association as "the leader in the future development of municipal government in the United States." Such leadership, he said, must be based on programs beneficial not only to municipal governments but to their citizens. The association, he contended, should develop a "national municipal policy" to give it the continuing direction and purpose it had lacked in the past. He outlined his concept of such a policy as follows:

The elements of the National Municipal Policy will vary from time to time and initially may include twenty or twenty-five individual items such as the extension of home rule, the place of municipal government in a democratic society, metropolitan area government, relations between the federal, state and local governments, adequate municipal revenues, the allocation of activities between the various levels of government, citizen instruction in government, the structure of local government, and several other urgent matters such as housing, transportation, municipal credit, compensation of municipal employees, municipal airports, urban redevelopment, grants-in-aid, and urban decentralization.[8]

Chatters' recommendations were enthusiastically adopted by AMA's executive committee as the basis for the working program and general policy of the association, and these have guided it to a position of increasingly constructive influence to this day.

Many sections of Chatters' report explored special problems of metropolitan areas, including services, revenues, annexation, powers, special charges for special services, transportation, and highways. He urged voluntary cooperation among municipalities and between states and metropolitan areas to halt or slow the continued rapid growth of local special districts for limited functions. He suggested contractual arrangements to provide both centralization of services and decentralization of authority. Recognizing urban decentralization as a continuing phenomenon, he viewed urban redevelopment as one possible response to it. He wrote:

When people start moving to the suburbs, the central city loses assessed valuation, and the fringe areas assume a new obligation which they are not always ready to assume. How can the two communities cooperate to their mutual advantage? Urban redevelopment is frequently related to questions of urban decentralization. Why does the need for redevelopment exist? What are its causes and what are the procedures to bring about redevelopment? Where do public and private interests meet? What part in redevelopment should be played by the central city, the state, the nation? And what effect will urban development have on the trend toward decentralization? Finally, is it desirable in the public interest, from a national viewpoint, to discourage decentralization? These are questions of prime importance in whose solution AMA should take a leading role.

Chatters blamed the conglomeration of governmental units for thwarting efficient local government in almost every urban area in the United States. "There are so many governmental units that no one has been able to count them accurately," he said. Lamenting the fact that most of those units were too small, deficient in tax resources, and hampered by overlapping authority, he listed these detrimental consequences of glaring imbalances in the 140 metropolitan areas then containing 48 percent of the nation's population:

1. Tax burdens become inequitable; and taxes are not in proportion to services rendered.
2. It becomes impossible to make effective use of centralized purchasing, budgeting, and other measures of modern fiscal administration.
3. Political responsibility becomes dissipated; the citizen becomes confused or apathetic and is unable to exercise control over his local institutions.
4. The cost of governmental services becomes high, and there is no equal distribution of equally need services.

5. Community-wide action for the solution of community-wide problems is completely forestalled.

Chatters argued that metropolitan integration would result in stronger local governments, a larger measure of popular control over those governments, and more services per tax dollar. "Strong local governments can be achieved only through the enlargement of local units," he concluded. "And effective local democracy can be achieved only in strong government."

In his 1948 report and in subsequent statements Chatters urged the creation by Congress of a national commission on all phases of federal, state, and local government relations. Legislation to accomplish this was introduced the following year. Chatters and other AMA leaders recognized that metropolitan problems required the attention of a broadly constituted body. Not only was Chatters' inventory of problems not comprehensive, but it was apparent that solutions required actions by state and federal as well as local government.

It was not until 1952, however, that AMA expressed its strong support of an intergovernmental relations commission in a resolution. Congress created the Commission on Intergovernmental Relations the following year, and President Eisenhower appointed Meyer Kestnbaum, board chairman of Hart, Schaffner & Marx Company of Chicago, as its chairman. One of the earliest hearings of the Kestnbaum commission was held as part of the 1953 AMA convention in New Orleans and included testimony from association delegates.

In an address at the association's 1955 convention, after publication of the commission's report, Kestnbaum described the growth of metropolitan areas as "probably the most difficult of all the problems that we face, because we have not yet found the governmental structures that will permit us to manage these metropolitan areas in the most efficient manner."

Kestnbaum's speech was followed by an address by the governor of Oregon, Paul L. Patterson, one of the few governors in the country at that time known for his sympathetic understanding of local government problems and for his leadership in improving city-state relations. Later a lengthy session on "Metropolitan and Fringe Area Problems" took place, with Mayor Robert F. Wagner of New York as chairman of a panel that included the new mayor of Chicago, Richard J. Daley. Daley's speech showed unmistakable signs of input by Carl Chatters, whom Daley had recently appointed as city comptroller of Chicago. Chatters had resigned as executive director of AMA in June 1954; he had suffered a severe heart attack in the fall of 1951.[9]

This author succeeded him on July 1, 1954, and at the same time the association's Washington office was made its headquarters, the Chicago office remaining as a branch for research and information services under the direction of John R. Kerstetter. Randy H. Hamilton, who had been manager of the Washington office for the previous two years, continued for a short time as assistant director for federal relations.[10]

The association climaxed its 1955 convention with a lengthy resolution authorizing further study of the metropolitan area problem and pledging the resources of the organization to its early solution.

Earlier that year, representatives of several national organizations, including the executive director of AMA, met in New York with specialists in metropolitan affairs to try to define some of the problems associated with the fact that by then more than 60 percent of the people of the United States were residing in 174 metropolitan areas and to suggest what kinds of approaches might be made toward solving them.

The group had been assembled by Frank C. Moore, a former lieutenant governor of New York and president of the Government Affairs Foundation, which had been established by Nelson Rockefeller. The group considered the effects of rapid urban growth, migration of people and business, mushrooming of new suburbs, and deterioration of older sections and neighborhoods, all of which were complicating the daily living of people in the smaller urban communities as well as the great metropolitan centers.

These developments were creating or magnifying problems of transportation, water supply, sewers, housing, schools, public health, and other services and facilities. It was evident that resultant difficulties and proposals for overcoming them involved not only intergovernmental relations, governmental structure, planning, finance, community standards and values, politics, and citizen understanding and participation, but also sound application of basic democratic principles.

Recognizing that ills so extensive and so complex could not be successfully diagnosed and cured by the efforts of any one segment of society, the group decided to plan and organize a national conference on metropolitan problems, which the Government Affairs Foundation agreed to finance. Some twenty national organizations sponsored the conference the following spring at Michigan State University. It was the first time a cross section of groups directly concerned with metropolitan difficulties was brought together.

About 250 participants from all parts of the nation represented business, labor, universities, research agencies, professional and civic groups, and federal, state, and local governments.

Mayor Daley again defined the big city's place in the metropolitan area, as he had at AMA's convention in Miami five months earlier:

No one must have fears for the future of the central city. Its functions as the focal point of the metropolitan area are assured by its geography, by its long-term institutional development, by its great economic facilities, and by its role as a communication center as well as the center of transportation to and from other regions.

There may be a great deal of talk about the so-called flight to the suburbs. But the essential truth is that the central city remains as the main economic bulwark of most metropolitan areas and the focal point of their social, cultural, and recreational activities. The central city provides leadership for most of the great accomplishments for any metropolitan area. The leadership does not emanate from a place of residence but rather from the central city as the center of daily activities, of both city residents and suburbanites.

Daley concluded that "the metropolitan areas present the most complicated local problem America has ever seen." He urged those who wanted to change metropolitan government "to consult with the political leaders—let them know what you want to accomplish, ask them for their suggestions, keep them up-to-date in what you propose to do. They will support more progressive programs than you imagine they will." He pointed out that unless a reform program has strong political leadership, it will be subject to considerable objection, obstruction, and delay. It is necessary, he emphasized, "to keep your political leaders informed and sympathetic when you plan great, progressive steps."

Academic participants wrestled with such terms as "metropolitan complex" and "metropolitan area," but it took Dr. Luther Gulick, president of the Institute of Public Administration and long-time student and practitioner in the field of urban affairs, to give the clearest and most concise definition:

The North American metropolitan complex is a large aggregation of human beings packed together in a geographic area of considerable size, in an economic and social pattern of private enterprise and great fluidity, enjoying a large measure of local representative self-government, at present in a complex pattern of largely unrelated jurisdictions which do not coincide with the patterns of work and life. . . .

The essential elements in this definition of the metropolitan complex are: large size, high population density, interdependence, fluidity of movement, and fractionated governments.

Gulick went on to define broad areas of studies that should be made in order to arrive at any real understanding of metropolitan problems and how to solve them. One of these dealt with political institutions and behavior and, as part of that subject, the structure of political power. He placed even more emphasis than Mayor Daley on the role of political leaders. He said:

It would be dangerous to go very far in building a new theory of political institutions in metropolitan areas without a better understanding of the nature and function of political leadership, and the relations of this structure of power to the broader power structure of nation and state. ... And I believe that the most searching questions we must answer have to do with these political factors. Those who approach metropolitan problems from any other point of view are writing on water and building on sand.

The papers and discussions, the general findings and conclusions, and a list of sixty-three suggestions for needed research were published by the Government Affairs Foundation[11] in what was described eighteen years later by William N. Cassella, Jr., executive director of the National Municipal League, as "a landmark document in the attention to metropolitan problems."

The conferees adjourned the East Lansing meeting after persuading Frank Moore to establish a Continuing National Conference on Metropolitan Problems to cooperate with groups conducting research and preparing publications in this field. The Conference, based in New York and supported by the Government Affairs Foundation, operated a clearing house, prepared an extensive bibliography, and published a bimonthly bulletin, *Metropolitan Area Problems: News and Digest.* The Conference could have become an even more important and constructive resource had it remained in New York City. But Nelson Rockefeller, then serving his first term as New York governor, increasingly sought the advice of Moore. Moore moved to Albany in 1959 and continued to provide Conference services from there for a few months before relinquishing the chairmanship to Luther Gulick. The Continuing National Conference on Metropolitan Problems went out of existence in 1962, but the Graduate School of Public Affairs of the State University of New York at Albany continued publication of the bimonthly bulletin until 1972.

Sponsoring organizations of the Continuing Conference and other groups continued to seek solutions in the field. The American Municipal Association charged the special metropolitan area committee it established in 1955 to pursue "mutually beneficial relationships with other national recognized organizations ... concerned with metropolitan problems."

In 1956 the association asserted in a resolution "that adequate use of the annexation device is not possible under the existing laws in many jurisdictions and may not be practicable in others." It directed its staff to compile a report on state statutes pertaining to annexation and the incorporation of cities and towns for distribution to all state and municipal leagues and member cities.

The association that year also urged each state league to provide for mechanisms to monitor the changing needs in its state's metropolitan areas and other urban areas and to assist in effecting such changes. The resolution declared that "the existing metropolitan problem in large measure is due to archaic, inflexible, and even discriminatory state constitutional and statutory provisions which must be modified and supplemented. . . ."

Not many state leagues heeded that exhortation, but the American Municipal Association did employ George Washington University law professor Robert G. Dixon, Jr., to begin the report on annexation, which was completed by John R. Kerstetter and published in a limited quantity in 1959.[12] Published separately was a pamphlet, "Basic Principles for a Good Annexation Law," which received widespread distribution. Developed after nearly thirty hours of discussion in three sessions by a group of thirty-five governmental practitioners and scholars, the principles won the endorsement of a subcommittee of AMA's metropolitan areas committee and its executive committee.

Interest in that study and continued interest in annexation resulted in a 1966 decision to update and make generally available the Dixon-Kerstetter report. The revision, whose major contributor was Professor Charles A. Hollister of Bucknell University, was published under the direction of Andrew S. Bullis, then director of Urban Studies for the National League of Cities.[13]

One of the most useful documents in the field was a comprehensive bibliography published by the Government Affairs Foundation in 1958. It included an analytical digest of metropolitan surveys undertaken since 1924.[14] There was an abundance of such surveys in the 1950s, many of them encouraged by Paul Ylvisaker of the Ford Foundation. The most comprehensive was an analysis of efforts by twenty-one local business leaders to correct intergovernmental balance in Saint Louis. It was financed by grants of $250,000 from Ford and $50,000 from local business sources. The leaders of the movement formed a non-profit corporation known as Civic Progress Inc. Inspired by the successes that a similar group, the Allegheny Conference, was having by working with Mayor David Lawrence to improve conditions in Pittsburgh, it had been organized in 1953 at the initiative of Mayor Joseph M. Darst and received the encouragement of his successor, Raymond R. Tucker.

It was self-interest that prompted the businessmen to try to bring order out of what one of them called the "crazy quilt of communities of all sizes, shapes, and systems, growing without planning, [and] without reasonable relationship one to the other." In acknowledging this to fellow delegates to the 1956 National Conference on Metropolitan Problems, the Saint Louis executive said, ". . . such a wonderland of waste, paid for by tax dollars, is offensive to the tax-paying businessman."

Saint Louis was in the 1950s, and still is, the epitome of inter-governmental mix and mess. The Civic Progress activist gave the Conference delegates this analysis:

The population of metropolitan St. Louis approaches 2,000,000 people. The area includes three counties on the Illinois side of the Mississippi River, where most of the heavy industry is located, and then it includes St. Louis City and St. Louis County on the Missouri side. The so-called metropolitan problem is more pronounced on the Missouri side. The city itself has an area of 61.4 square miles, unchanged since 1876, and approximately 860,000 people. The county is a booming suburban area of 493 square miles, and now is attracting substantial business and industry. It has a population of about 600,000 people. About 165,000 people come into the downtown area every day from the suburbs to work, to play, or to shop.

Saint Louis, which, like cities in Virginia, is separate from and not overlapped by the county, was bearing a disproportionate share of the economic and social costs of the irregular and inequitable pattern of growth, the delegate said. He continued:

The county, on the other hand, has its full share of both parts of the metropolitan problem that relates to the inability of local government to adjust itself to tremendous growth. Its county-wide government, headed by a supervisor and seven-member council, is inadequate. It has neither the authority nor the manpower to manage the complex activities of a booming metropolitan area. Political disunity has almost reached the comic opera stage. There are ninety-six separate incorporated municipalities within St. Louis County, varying in population from 40,000 to a low of fifty-seven; from 5,875 acres in size to a low of eleven acres; from $1.08 tax rate for municipal purposes to a fifteen cent tax rate.

The inefficiency that results from disunity in government in St. Louis County is increased further by the existence of fourteen townships, by the presence of some unincorporated areas with more residents than most of the municipalities; by thirty separate school districts; and by eighteen fire districts.

In St. Louis City, the basic physical necessities of sewers, sidewalks, streetlights, etc., were brought close to the population requirements years and years ago. But St. Louis County has never caught up with its population. The duplication of so many governmental functions has led to indescribable confusion.

The survey of the problem was directed by a joint board created by Saint Louis and Washington universities. It involved both research and education and the preparation of alternative proposals for action, designed to remedy some or all of the major ills arising out of the existing pattern of government in metropolitan Saint Louis. Its research procedures, devised by Professor Henry J. Schmandt and his associates, as well as its report edited by John C. Bollens, became the models for other metropolitan surveys. The speaker at the 1956 Conference on Metropolitan Problems confidently predicted that "when the people are made aware of the problem and the proper solution to be taken, the people can be depended upon to take the correct action." When the new metropolitan district proposal came to a vote in 1959, the people in both the city and in the surrounding area overwhelmingly defeated it.

A similar effort in Cleveland met the same fate. The first moves for the organization of metropolitan governments at Seattle,

Louisville, and Nashville were defeated in their suburbs in 1958, and the next year similar measures lost in the same way at Knoxville and Albuquerque.

Proponents of these unsuccessful efforts at restructuring local government had perhaps been inspired by two successes. One was the consolidation of the city of Baton Rouge, Louisiana, and its parish (county), which became effective January 1, 1949. The plan was approved in a county-wide referendum by 307 votes only because a large majority for adoption was received within the central city. Had it required separate approval of the voters outside the city, it would have been defeated.[15] The other was the formation of a metropolitan government in Toronto in January 1954 by action of the provincial legislature without a referendum. (A third success came in 1957 when voters in the Miami area approved a home rule charter for Dade County in a county-wide referendum.)

These efforts, both the failures and successes, were not the only evidence of the considerable interest in the fifties in urban growth in general, metropolitan growth in particular, and intergovernmental relations. The January 1955 *Economic Report of the President* drew attention to the critical nature of specific weaknesses in metropolitan areas and called upon the states to study the problems so that "area-wide transit systems, sanitation systems, water supplies, or educational facilities may be provided with maximum returns from public funds expended." This appeal was reinforced in June by the report of the Kestnbaum Commission on Intergovernmental Relations, which exhorted the states "to assume the leadership in seeking solutions for the problems of metropolitan governments."

Even the states, which are legally responsible for local governments, began to wake up. In August the Governors' Conference adopted a resolution directing the Council of State Governments to study the metropolitan problem and make suggestions for improving the situation.[16] Although the approaches of the states to local government have generally been hesitant and piecemeal, the ten years between 1955 and 1965 have been described as "probably one of the few truly revolutionary periods in state history to better organize local government." The number of school districts was reduced by 67 percent during that decade, for example.[17]

Finally, additional impetus was given to a continuing study of urban growth and metropolitan problems by the creation in 1959 of the permanent Advisory Commission on Intergovernmental Relations. It was established by Public Law 380, passed by the first session of the Eighty-sixth Congress after hearings in both House and Senate committees in which the legislation was strongly supported by the American Municipal Association, the United States Conference of Mayors, and the National Association of Counties, among others. Effective floor leadership in the Senate by Senator Edmund S. Muskie of Maine and in the House by Representative L. H. Fountain of North Carolina assured its passage, but the bill almost suffered a presidential veto. As a routine procedure the United States Bureau of the Budget (now the Office of Management and Budget) reviews all congressional enactments and recommends approval or veto by the President. In this case the bureau recommended a veto, and the measure was saved only after Presidential Assistant Robert E. Merriam interceded with President Eisenhower and gained his approval on September 24, 1959.

The commission is composed of twenty-six members representing all levels of government.* It selects intergovernmental problems for analysis and for policy recommendations, and ever since its creation a growing number of these have related to urban areas. A commission subcommittee headed by Congressman Fountain and staffed by Delphis C. Goldberg, counsel to

---

* The act provides that the President appoint four mayors from a panel submitted jointly by the National League of Cities (then called American Municipal Association) and the United States Conference of Mayors, no more than two from the same political party. The first four mayors appointed to the original commission were: Anthony J. Celebrezze, Cleveland; Gordon S. Clinton, Seattle; Don Hummel, Tucson; and Norris Poulson, Los Angeles.

Fountain's House Subcommittee on Intergovernmental Relations, made a careful search for a highly qualified executive director for the commission. They made a fortunate choice when they selected William G. Colman, who assembled a highly competent staff and directed over the next ten years a massive program of research and publications.

Close observation of activities in metropolitan areas during the late 1950s led the staff leadership of the American Municipal Association and the National Association of Counties* to the joint conclusion that everybody seemed to approve metropolitan reorganization except the voters. Proof of that was seen in the defeats of proposals in Saint Louis, Cleveland, and many other places in 1958 and 1959 after long and expensive studies and elaborate citizen organization for support. Meanwhile, something was taking place which gave promise of progress because it could develop cooperation at the local level between existing counties and municipalities without imposing a new governmental structure. This was the development of metropolitan councils of governments (COGs).

The institutional beginning of this cooperative movement took place in the Detroit area in 1954, when Edward Connor, a Detroit city councilman and president of the Wayne County Board of Supervisors, became concerned about the lack of common understanding about southeastern Michigan's metropolitan problems. He invited his counterparts from neighboring counties to meet with him to discuss mutual problems and to find a way to meet them. Out of their search for a common framework for continuing cooperation within which local autonomy could be preserved, the Supervisors Inter-County Committee (SICC) was formed. Each county had equal representation, and each county's representatives were chosen by its board of supervisors. SICC

*Good relationship and close cooperation existed between the two staffs, particularly after Bernard F. Hillenbrand became executive director of NACO on May 1, 1957. He had been AMA's assistant director for federal affairs, beginning August 1, 1955, after this author had become AMA's executive director the preceding year.

began to meet regularly and to discuss ways of solving regional problems.

In 1956 Mayor Robert F. Wagner of New York City, then president of the American Municipal Association, invited the officials of neighboring jurisdictions to join him in establishing a metropolitan regional council for the New York area.

In 1957 Robert E. McLaughlin, then president of the Washington, D.C., Board of Commissioners, invited suburban local government officials and state legislators of Maryland and Virginia to consider forming a metropolitan conference to deal with urgent regional problems. This led to the formation of what is known now as the Metropolitan Washington Council of Governments.

In 1958, at the initiative of Salem, Oregon, City Manager Kent Mathewson, the local governments of the two-county area surrounding the Oregon capital formed the Mid-Willamette Valley Council of Governments, this one organized officially under a compact signed by each of the five governments of the region: the state of Oregon, the city of Salem, the two counties, and the major school district.

At the joint initiative of the League of California Cities and the California County Supervisors Association, local governments in the San Francisco Bay Area established in 1961 the Association of Bay Area Governments (ABAG). Much of the organizing staff work was done by John J. Garvey, Jr., then assistant city manager of Richmond, California. ABAG appointed as its first executive director Wilber E. Smith, then assistant director of the American Municipal Association. Garvey succeeded him in the AMA spot in Washington. Smith later became the first executive director of the Southern California Association of Governments (SCAG).

AMA and NACO viewed these developments of voluntary cooperation of local government officials on a regional basis as an exciting possibility for approaching solutions to metropolitan problems. As one way to encourage the movement, they invited members of the COGs to meet together in their own annual workshop, to be held alternately one year at the NACO convention, the next year at AMA's. The first such workshop took place at NACO's convention at Miami in 1960 and the next at AMA's convention the following year at Seattle. The theme of the Seattle convention, incidentally, was "intergovernment cooperation." Representatives of eight voluntary, multipurpose regional organizations came together at Seattle to discuss organizational and operation problems common to each. The two organizations jointly published minutes of the workshops and publicized the activities of the COGs. Yet by April 1965 only ten had been organized, and one of those, Baltimore's, had ceased to operate. It was slow going.

Staff members and some of the officers of NACO and the National League of Cities (the American Municipal Association changed its name in late 1964) continued to promote the concept, however. They strongly believed that the most promising way to get some area-wide solutions to area-wide problems was to develop understanding and cooperation by the elected policy officials of the counties and municipalities in an area. A metropolitan council of governments was a logical medium. At least it could bring these officials together face to face for discussions, probably for the first time. From these discussions would develop an agenda of topics for future meetings and consideration. This would require staff research. These discussions and studies would presumably be an educational process, leading hopefully to some agreements for area-wide actions. Representatives of the local governments involved in this process would ideally then return from the COG meetings and "sell" their policy colleagues in their own communities. But the idea was not catching on around the country because of the formidable prospect of financing the necessary capable staff.

At this point the federal government stepped in and provided the needed stimulants. In the spring of 1965 the Housing and Home Finance Agency was preparing amendments to the Housing Act of 1954 for consideration of Congress. Victor Fischer, executive director of the Alaska League of Cities, had left there for employment in Washington with the Housing and Home Finance Agency. Naturally, he worked closely with the staff of the National League of Cities, and in the drafting of amendments to the planning section of the act, Section 701, he was persuaded to include a subsection authorizing the administrator of HHFA "to make grants to organizations composed of public officials whom he finds to be representative of the political jurisdictions within a metropolitan area or urban region for the purpose of assisting such organizations to undertake studies, collect data, develop regional plans and programs, and engage in such other activities as the Administrator finds necessary or desirable for the solution of the metropolitan or regional problems in such areas or regions." The grants could be for an amount of up to two-thirds of the estimated cost of the work for which the grant was made.

Congress accepted that 1965 amendment, Section 701 (g) of the Housing Act. It instantly created a surge of interest in COGs as regional planning agencies in both metropolitan and rural areas. Passage the following year of the Model Cities Act, followed in late 1968 by Bureau of the Budget Circular A-95, required most federal aid applications from local governments for major development projects in a metropolitan area to be reviewed by a regional planning agency before submission to the appropriate federal agency. These measures created a rush to form COGs. There is now a council of governments in nearly all of the nation's 264 metropolitan areas.

Admittedly, political feasibility is the trademark of the COGs. They are considered inadequate by the metropolitan reformers, because COGs are not really new governmental structures; and with few exceptions COGs do not attempt to formulate metropolitan-wide policies that significantly alter existing social and economic functions or redistribute tax resources among existing localities. However, they do have the general authority to provide an impressive list of governmental functions and services, whether the services are provided or not. These include planning for transportation, sewers, water, comprehensive land use, and open space; and services for sewage and solid waste, data collection, air and water pollution control, communications, flood control, economic developments, codes and licensing, libraries, and fire protection programs.

They can also become involved in certain limited phases of law enforcement, recreation, education, and health where there are no social implications that could cause potential conflict between members of the COGs. However, five COGs have adopted a "fair share" plan which allocates lower-income housing throughout the metropolitan area, thus reducing concentrations of such housing in the central cities. The Miami Valley Regional Planning Commission of the Dayton, Ohio, area adopted the nation's first fair share plan in 1970, and as of January 1974 an additional twenty-five COGs were in some stage of developing a fair share plan.[18]

Meanwhile, what has been happening about the intergovernmental mix and mess? On the face of it, a dramatic change has

Carl H. Chatters set the American Municipal Association (National League of Cities) on a new course and served as its executive director from 1948 to 1954.

taken place since Carl H. Chatters cited in 1948 the 155,000 local units of government throughout the United States which had been identified by the United States Bureau of the Census in 1942. Thirty years later, the 1972 *Census of Governments* showed a reduction to 78,000 governmental units. The major portion of the change was due to consolidation of school districts during that period, leaving 15,781 of them in 1972 compared to 108,579 in 1942, a reduction of 92,798. Actually, the number of other local governments has increased from about 46,500 to 62,400, despite a decrease of nearly 2,000 in the number of townships. The latter was offset by a gain of 2,300 municipalities, which increased from 16,220 to 18,517. But the big increase came in the steady proliferation of special districts, from 8,300 in 1942 to 23,900 in 1972.

As noted earlier in this chapter, most special districts are established to perform a single function, although some are authorized by their enabling legislation to provide several kinds of services. Nearly 28 percent of all special districts today are concerned with natural resources: soil conservation, drainage, irrigation, flood control, and other resource purposes. Fire protection districts constitute one-sixth of the total number; and housing authorities and urban water supply districts 10 percent each. A total of more than 3,000 special districts are concerned with urban water supply either as the sole function or as one of a combination of functions.

It is interesting to note that two-thirds of all special districts had no full-time employees in 1971, while nearly one-fourth had only one to five. Most of them are not big-scale operations, as evidenced by the small number of employees and by the fact that nearly 60 percent had no debt and another 14 percent had a debt of less than $100,000.

Two-thirds of all the special districts were located outside the 264 areas classified by the Census Bureau as standard metropolitan statistical areas (SMSAs). However, *inside* those 264 SMSAs there were 8,000 special districts, 3,500 townships, 5,500 municipalities, and 444 counties—a total of 17,400 local governments other than school districts. There were nearly 4,800 of the latter, to make a total of some 22,200 local governments of all kinds in those 264 areas where more than 143 million people live, 70 percent of the nation's total population.

Efforts to correct this condition since World War II have, with few exceptions, succeeded only in the massive consolidation of school districts. The states must be given credit for that.

Annexation still offers possibilities as a form of governmental reorganization which is being used considerably outside the northeastern part of the United States. In many metropolitan areas, suburban cities as well as central cities are using annexation as a means by which they can expand to provide viable governance over the metropolitan growth.

Another method of arresting the trend toward too many local governments has been city-county consolidation. However, in a 1974 analysis Dr. Vincent L. Marando, associate professor of political science at the University of Georgia, has concluded that this method is not politically feasible. His study of voter support for city-county consolidation in forty-three referendums held between 1945 and 1973 shows that only twelve were approved.[19] This does not include the Indianapolis–Marion County consolidation, which was accomplished by act of the state legislature, not by voter referendum. With few exceptions, most of the successful voter-approved city-county consolidations have occurred in small and middle-sized (less than a million population) Southern metropolitan areas. Dr. Marando finds that "the impact of social differentiation and racial factors (both white and black resistance) between city and suburbs appears to be increasingly having a negative influence upon the adoption of consolidation." He also concludes that annexation is more politically feasible.

His contention is that the problems facing urban areas have not been severe enough to indicate that reorganization would be an obvious course of action—the public is not convinced that reorganization would make a significant difference in resolving the major problems in urban areas. Many voters are not interested in the possibility of additional services regardless of how "fair" the price might be, and yet arguments for efficiency, economy, equity, and better quality of services for less money are the prime reasons given for reorganization. All these reasons may be too abstract for the average voter and not enough to convince a majority that reorganization should be accepted. Between 1805 and 1907 all metropolitan reorganizations were mandated by state legislatures, without local referendums.[20] It appears that that century of experience may have to be relied upon again in order to bring about any significant change in today's intergovernmental mix and mess.

Modernizing City Hall

The increased urbanization of America during the past fifty years has put the management structures of the nation's cities under severe strain. Each new development in a variety of fields has helped shape the organization and management response of municipal government. As we have seen, the reform movement at the turn of the century spurred numerous cities to change their form of government. Since the movement set a high premium on efficiency, it is not surprising that many cities chose a structure designed to divorce administrative procedures entirely from political policy—the city-manager system. This meshed well with the Calvin Coolidge adage that "the business of America is business." What better way to bring improvement into city hall than to lift private business management techniques and cloak them in a new public mantle?

The basic logic of the idea could not be argued. Yet by the 1960s questions were being raised about whether city halls, no matter how efficiently managed, were responding adequately to the overlooked social needs of urban citizens, many of them newly arrived from rural settings. The national and social programs of the 1960s designed to meet these growing urban problems forced a number of cities to reconsider their organization arrangements, particularly when federal agencies were providing funds to establish what appeared to city officials to be "paragovernments."

The 1964 Economic Opportunity Act, which launched the "War on Poverty," mandated "maximum feasible participation" for residents of the areas the bill was designed to benefit. Though that phrase was subject to a wide range of interpretations, it was invoked in many cities to give a high degree of autonomy to Community Action Agencies. It was through the governing boards of the CAAs and their counterparts in the Model Cities program that the poor and their spokesmen often exerted a strong influence on local affairs. Some leaders in these programs began to build political support of their own. Elected mayors and councilmen quickly became concerned about what to them amounted to an end run around their local legal authority.

This aspect of the antipoverty legislation worried some municipal officials even while it was pending in Congress. Mayor John F. Collins of Boston made a special trip to Washington on the matter in the summer of 1964, shortly before the bill was reported out of the House Committee on Education and Labor. He was then president of the American Municipal Association, the name of which he was instrumental in changing later that year to the National League of Cities. At his request, a meeting was arranged in the association's offices with two of the administration's principal lobbyists for the bill, Sanford Kravitz of the Department of Health, Education and Welfare, and Jack T. Conway, former aide to Walter Reuther in the United Auto Workers.

Mayor Collins expressed his concern about the bill's provision authorizing federal funds to be channeled directly to nongovernmental, private groups in the cities. An observer at this encounter recalls the following exchange.

"If any federal money is coming into Boston for antipoverty programs," Collins said, "I want it to come through the elected mayor and city council, not to private agencies that are not responsible to the voters."

His threat to organize opposition to the whole bill by the National League of Cities prompted hasty reassurances by Conway and Kravitz.

"It's the only way we can get the bill out of committee," they said. "Representative Edith Green insists on that provision, and she wouldn't let it out of her subcommittee without it.

"But you can rest assured, Mr. Mayor, that when it actually comes to administering the program, we will see to it that everything is channeled through the mayors, that nothing will be done without their approval. They will not be by-passed."

Mayor Collins and the NLC staff made the mistake of accepting these assurances, albeit reluctantly. When the matter came up for a vote at NLC's Miami Beach convention in late July after an impassioned plea by Secretary of Labor Willard Wirtz for support, a resolution of approval was passed, but only after a roll call vote that barely gained the necessary two-thirds in favor. Telegrams reporting the action were promptly dispatched to President Johnson, to his chief lobbyist for the bill, Sargent Shriver, and to leaders of the House of Representatives, including the bill's sponsors. The bill was being debated on the floor of the House at the time. Individual mayors also telephoned or wired their own representatives, and the bill squeaked through the House by a narrow margin.

The mistake in accepting the assurances of Conway and Kravitz about the way the measure would be administered became evident immediately after the Office of Economic Opportunity was established, with Sargent Shriver as its director. He appointed Conway director of community action programs. Although Conway liked to characterize community action as a three-legged stool, resting equally upon public officials of the community, representatives of social agencies and other private organizations and interest groups, and the poor, the mayors were nevertheless effectively bypassed in the formation and funding of local Community Action Agencies.

Established institutions, including city hall, became targets of demonstrations, angry rhetoric, and sit-ins. Many city officials traced the impetus for such action to the direct federal administration of the local programs, and the mayors quickly became "turned off." Without their enthusiastic participation, based on responsibility, the program was doomed to falter.

Municipal information systems, with computers at their heart, play a large role in modern city-hall management. Here, former Dayton, Ohio, City Manager James E. Kunde (right) and James Cook (left), operations manager for the city's computer center, discuss data on a computer printout.

Congressman Edith Green began to realize her mistake in insisting on direct federal administration of a program that bypassed city hall. She made a 180-degree turn with the so-called Green amendment of 1967 to give local governments the option of assuming responsibility for administering the programs. But it was too late. Most mayors and councilmen by that time couldn't have cared less and were content not to have responsibility for the controversial activity. Moreover, the new Model Cities program introduced by the Johnson administration in 1966 seemed to offer a better approach to bring together urban renewal and social programs to meet the needs of slum residents and to recreate the cities' physical as well as social environment.

Today most of these programs, while fading because of federal fund cutbacks and phaseouts, are found within the organizational structures of city governments. The process of assimilation was not unlike the one that has taken place in Washington, in which component divisions of the Office of Economic Opportunity have been transferred in a series of reorganizations to cabinet agencies. At the local level, many community-action and Model Cities functions are now assigned to new Community Development or Human Resources departments organized in recognition of city hall's evolving role in the improvement of the quality of urban life for its residents. More importantly, these programs often served as incubators for testing new concepts in planning and management and citizen participation which have found their way into other, more traditional municipal government operations.

These organizational changes reflect the way city hall has been altered through the infusion of federal programs and funds and new laws. America's mayors and councilmen supported many of them and opposed others. One federal provision which was opposed by municipal government generally was the extension of federal wage and hour laws to cover local government employees. Despite determined opposition from the National League of Cities and the United States Conference of Mayors over the years and a presidential veto which Congress sustained in 1973, the law's extension was approved the following year by Congress, signed by President Nixon, and in force May 1, 1974. Its constitutionality is doubtful and will likely soon be tested in the courts. The opposition of NLC was based on the traditional concept of federalism that one level of government should not interfere with the internal operations of another. Citing the same principle, the league and the Conference of Mayors opposed a bill to provide a National Labor Relations Board for state and local government employees similar to one which has long overseen unionization in the private sector.

The influence of the federal government on city government started long before city hall's reactions to the agencies spawned by the antipoverty program. Categorical grant programs such as urban renewal, under way in hundreds of cities in the early 1950s, usually carried with them numerous requirements that the city government had to meet before federal money was forthcoming. These requirements, in turn, necessitated additional staff, matching local funds, and often organization adjustments. The "701" funds (grants made under Section 701 of the National Housing Act) have made possible expansion of comprehensive planning in thousands of jurisdictions. In recent years the Department of Housing and Urban Development, which administers the program, has revised the guidelines to permit the use of those moneys for management aspects of policy implementation. This has often paved the way for basic city management changes with wide impact in city hall and the entire community.

Now the thrust of federal assistance has shifted away from emphasis on specific program grants (although they are still important) to the block grant or general and special revenue-sharing approaches. These recent concepts aim at cutting the number of federal strings on program funds to a minimum in favor of letting the local governments set the goals and determine the best methods to be used to achieve them within broad national guidelines set by the Congress. Here again, the prospect is for significant internal municipal government structural and management changes in the years to come. At the center of determining which directions these changes take will be the mayor and city councilmen.

The compound of enthusiasm and anxiety with which many city officials view this prospect is reflected in a response by the president of the city council in a large Eastern city to a 1973 NLC attitude survey of elected city leaders:

> As long as federal programs continue along the lines of general revenue sharing and elimination of categorical grants, the entire responsibility for program development will shift from the Congress and federal administrators to local legislatures and local bureaucrats. This will, in effect, revamp the form of American government as we have known it for the last forty years. The tragedy is that none of the local legislative bodies is even remotely prepared for this challenge, including my own, which I think is better prepared than most.

A 1974 Census Bureau report showed the scope of the challenge of the influx of federal and state funds. The bureau's records revealed that city government revenues since 1971–72 from other levels of government surpass the money collected in municipal property taxes, traditionally the biggest revenue producer for city hall. Increasingly, cities are realizing that they need specialized help in dealing with this intergovernmental revenue system. Allen E. Pritchard, Jr., NLC's newly designated executive vice-president, took note of this evolution when he addressed the first graduating class of the Lyndon B. Johnson School of Public Affairs at the University of Texas in 1972. He said:

> The historic intergovernmental and public-private stratification of responsibilities no longer exists. As a result, applications for intergovernmental assistance are on the way out. The state or local government federal aid "bag-man" is fast becoming passé.
>
> On the other hand, the intergovernmental negotiators are on the way in.
>
> National goals and local objectives will be achieved more frequently in the future with greater reliance on a bargaining table agreement involving local, area-wide, state, and federal representatives and the related private sector interests designing a specific package to meet a defined set of needs and objectives.

Many cities now have intergovernmental coordinators on their staffs. In a growing number of cases, additional staff people have offices in Washington and the state capital to monitor developments of potentially great impact on the city and region. In the late 1960s the National League of Cities and the United States Conference of Mayors recognized the growing importance of federal aid programs and funds to municipal governments by establishing a Man in Washington Service. Through special contracts, cities and urban counties can employ a full- or part-time man or woman to be their eyes and ears in the nation's capital. Working out of offices in the NLC and USCM headquarters building two blocks from the White House, these city representatives keep close tabs on pending federal legislation of interest to their cities, monitor the actions (or inactions) of federal government agencies and departments, and help steer program applications through the bureaucratic maze. The program has grown significantly. Today some fifty cities ranging from Los Angeles and Detroit to Hoboken, New Jersey, and Oak Park, Illinois, employ the Man in Washington Service to assist them in staying on top of the evolving federal intergovernmental role in city hall operations.

Furthermore, some cities use special boards to coordinate the intergovernmental assistance programs from Washington and the state capital. Los Angeles, for example, has a Board of Grants Approval. In its first year, in spite of the declining number and dollar amount of federal grants available from Washington, the BGA increased the city's share of federal program funds from $143 million to $201 million.

In addition to the Section 701 program, a number of other federal programs are playing large roles in determining the direction of city government management and organizational thrusts. The Intergovernmental Personnel Act, the Emergency Public Employment Act, and the Comprehensive Employment and Training Act have significantly altered traditional city hall views of personnel and manpower policies. As a result, many innovations in personnel management and manpower training programs have been undertaken. State municipal leagues also are getting involved in these programs (by way of special grants funneled through NLC and USCM) to provide their member cities with technical assistance and information on setting up new personnel and manpower operations. To meet the federal government's affirmative action requirements, these programs are administered in ways that encourage increased representation of minorities in key management positions in city hall.

In the massive shifting of institutional gears that has moved local government to its present rapid rate of responsiveness to change, city hall has experimented with virtually the full range of modern management techniques, and adopted many of the successful ones. Here is a brief review of some of those in use:

The Mayor-Appointed Administrator: In an increasing number of cities of all sizes, especially those with a mayor-council form of government, topflight administrators have been given broad responsibilities for coordinating the work of city departments and carrying out special assignments by the mayor. In smaller cities such an administrator may have functions similar to those of a city manager.

Orin F. Nolting, former executive director of the International City Management Association, believes that more cities will seriously consider the mayor-appointed administrator as a way to attain better management and control over functions that heretofore have been the exclusive responsibility of elected officials. The part-time officials who serve some smaller cities are overburdened by the dual role of administrator and legislator.

Systems Analysis: The advent of the widespread use of computers in city hall and the adaptation of federal government systems analysis techniques have afforded a quantum jump forward for city hall in trying to master complex urban management systems. Much innovative work has been done through the federally sponsored USAC (Urban Information Systems Inter-Agency Commission) program, which is developing model municipal information systems in Charlotte, North Carolina, Wichita Falls, Texas, Long Beach, California, Dayton, Ohio, and

Reading, Pennsylvania. If the five-city demonstration is successful, the systems presumably will be made available to other municipalities. NLC and USCM have been intimately involved in this program.

The so-called PPBS (Planning, Programming, Budgeting System), widely tested in cities in the 1960s, has not produced the same kind of results in municipal government that it apparently did when former Secretary of Defense Robert S. McNamara introduced it at the Pentagon.

John N. Urie of Kansas City, president of the Municipal Finance Officers' Association of the United States and Canada, has found that some cities are turning away from the concept. He explained:

It took some time for us to recognize that what appeared to be good for the U.S. Department of Defense was not necessarily good or even applicable for municipal government. Cities operate under very different circumstances and cover a much more limited geographical area . . . and at the local level an empirical study of the cost-benefit ratio may not prove to be more influential than a local political alliance.

Urie said cities that tried to implement performance budgeting found they were doing a lot of additional work for limited results.

Measuring Municipal Service Effectiveness: Real progress is being made on techniques for measuring the effectiveness and quality of municipal government services. Pioneering work in this field by the Urban Institute and the International City Management Association has been directed toward selecting measures and data collection procedures for such vital municipal services as solid-waste collection and disposal, recreation opportunities, library services, police protection–crime control, fire protection, local transportation services, water supply, wastewater treatment (including storm drainage and the quality of bodies of water), and the handling of citizen complaints and requests for services and information.

A key aspect of this research is cities' widening interest in finding out what their citizens think about municipal services. Consumer-conscious cities consistently sample public attitudes through survey questionnaires and personal interview polling techniques. Important studies in this field have been done by the Urban Observatory Program of the National League of Cities and by the Urban Institute. Comparing the extent and quality of municipal programs in various cities is the goal of a relatively new private organization, the Council on Municipal Performance in New York City.

Labor-Management Relations: Professionalization in municipal labor-management relations has followed the rapid growth of organized labor in the public sector. Fewer mayors, councilmen, city managers, or department heads are negotiating directly with municipal union leaders. Increasingly, cities are hiring experienced labor-management specialists. This has improved the public management side of the labor-management equation and has brought innovations in bargaining, such as demands by the city for productivity clauses in contracts to encourage more output from municipal employees.

A leading role in the improvement of city hall labor-management techniques in recent years has been played by the Labor-Management Relations Service, headed by Sam Zagoria, a former member of the National Labor Relations Board. This service, established in 1970, is cosponsored by the National League of Cities, the United States Conference of Mayors, and the National Association of Counties. It has been funded by the Ford Foundation. The service provides extensive information and technical assistance to cities on collective bargaining techniques.

Municipal Purchasing Developments: Cities represent a multibillion-dollar annual market for goods and services. Helping cities buy better and get more for their taxpayers' money has been the goal of the growing ranks of municipal central purchasing officers, who have their own professional society, the National Institute of Governmental Purchasing. Borrowing ideas from private purchasing agents and buyers for state and federal governments, city purchasing agents today have found numerous ways to improve their purchasing power. Many cities pool their purchases to get volume discounts through joint contracts. Others ride piggyback on much larger state government or area-wide public purchasing contracts, thus saving significant sums annually on everything from plastic library covers to gasoline. Some of the largest cities—New York, Chicago, and Philadelphia are examples—operate their own laboratories for testing equipment and materials before they are certified for purchase.

City Government Reorganization: In recent years there have been dozens of city charter revision commissions, reorganization study teams, and citizen task forces appointed to examine minutely the ways our cities are run. The resulting reports and recommendations often produce striking changes in the city hall organization charts. Sometimes many departments are merged into a few or the entire governmental system changed, as in the case of Albuquerque, which in 1974 abolished its commission-manager form of government for a full-time mayor-council form. Other reorganization studies have led to demands for city-county consolidation. Such mergers as those in the Indianapolis, Nashville, Jacksonville, and Columbus, Georgia, areas draw many inquiries from other cities interested in consolidation and the more efficient governmental system it promises.

Citizen Participation: As we noted at the beginning of this chapter, when pressures started building in the early 1960s for more citizen representation in cities, the reactions of mayors ranged from skepticism to outright resistance. (After all, weren't they elected to represent the citizens' interests?) But rapid social change, the influx of new federal programs with their mandates for citizen involvement, and the growing consumer activism, which lapped over into governmental services, have led to the realization that citizen involvement is good business and good politics. Citizen advisory committees, neighborhood councils, and little city halls physically located in neighborhoods are all aspects of this movement which are not likely to disappear. New York City has experimented with paying citizen volunteers for their opinions regarding the effectiveness of city services. Such information could be fed back into the total city management process.

Public Information Programs: Although public relations sometimes has a bad connotation, city governments are turning to innovative public information programs to get their messages over to citizens. Improved public understanding of city hall operations is essential if a city is to have successful programs and the necessary resources to carry them out. Once almost entirely limited to dealing with daily newspapers, public information programs run by cities now encompass the broadcast media, motion pictures, slide shows, annual reports, citizen newsletters, and complaint handling. Special appearances by the mayor and other officials on radio and television are arranged. Some city halls are experimenting with cable television to communicate with residents.

Staff Assistance for Mayors and Councilmen: Often overlooked in the past, adequate professional staff help is now being provided in many cities to part-time mayors and councilmen. But a 1973 NLC survey showed that almost a quarter of the mayors and a third of the councilmen felt their professional assistance at city hall was inadequate. One councilman from a middle-sized city responded this way:

> I feel that part-time government is on the verge of either collapse or total incompetence. Legislators must learn to use both their staff and time much better. Staff must learn about the role of the elected official and learn what a "policy" is and how to present policy issues and alternatives to their elected officials. If we can't use legislators' time more effectively, the increased responsibilities will never be addressed, much less met. In which case, I foresee a shift away from local government back to state and national.

The National League of Cities and its state municipal leagues are addressing the needs of elected mayors and councilmen through orientation sessions for newly elected officials, conferences, seminars, publications, and research.

A Western city councilman, responding to the NLC survey, spelled out the management challenge to America's cities this way:

In order to justify itself in the future, municipal government must evolve. It must become both a catalyst for change and the interface for its citizens between them and the myriad county, regional, state, national, legislative, judicial, and administrative agencies that increasingly govern their lives. Also, in our space-age era of technological growth, the spirit and philosophy of the level of government closest to the people—municipal—must keep pace with technology.

There is no question that strengthening municipal government as an institution is the basic ingredient for responsive government and for successful democracy. The urban character of the nation dictates that any improvements in the quality of life in this country are inevitably tied to our ability to make the urban system function effectively. And its effectiveness *is* evolving. Although cities have been severely limited in their area jurisdiction, powers, and financial resources by state restrictions placed upon them beginning after the Civil War, their capacity to function more effectively has been improving over the past fifty years. The past ten years, especially, have witnessed an increase in management capacity and structural improvement, and yet their financial capacity is still restricted.

City Hall's Worsening Fiscal Dilemma

"An incredible and seemingly insoluble array of financial difficulties confront urban governments in America today," the Advisory Commission on Intergovernmental Relations reported in 1973.[1] In earlier studies the commission called for a massive rearrangement in the scale of fiscal resources available to the three levels of government—federal, state, and local—to strengthen our federal system.

In its voluminous reports on the disparities within that system, the ACIR has catalogued just a few of the problems city officials face as they try to direct the highly restricted flow of dollars to a constantly expanding list of needs. Some of the problems the commission cited include capital facilities that are outdated and lack sufficient capacity, rising demands for services for minorities and the poor, worn-out equipment, the inability to increase the tax base because of tax restrictions, the inability to exceed debt ceilings, citizen tax rebellions, competition with other governmental units for state and local revenue sources, and a general inability to make the revenue resources stretch to fit the expenditures mandated by the state and demanded by the people.

While these and other menacing problems cluster at the local level, municipalities have less access than the other two tiers of government to the revenues for dealing with them. Government practitioners and scholars are engaged in an ongoing pursuit of ways to distribute aggregate national resources equitably. Within the past ten years, the imbalance between resources and needs in cities became so acute that nationally prominent mayors began to make persistent appeals for a "reordering of national priorities."

To understand the sense of urgency behind their demands, it is necessary to examine the historical roots of the contemporary financial crisis of American cities. Much of the current dilemma lies in the clash between a changing society and the persistence of a local government system rooted in the past.

The increasing concentration of poor people in the central cities has been accompanied by a relocation of higher-income families, and ultimately jobs, in the suburbs. The poor require more public services than higher-earning families, and more densely populated areas require more police and fire protection. At the same time, the revolution of rising expectations that swept America in the sixties taught the poor how to be more effective in pressuring their local governments for public services. Thus cities, at the center of urban sprawl, caught in the web of an archaic governmental system, must supply services in ever-increasing scope and depth at a time when their ability to raise funds is seriously diminished.

The beginning of the urban financial dilemma can be traced back to the Depression of the 1930s. This was followed by two more decades of civilian scarcities caused by World War II, the Korean War, and postwar readjustments. Thus, there was a tremendous backlog of unmet needs by the end of the 1950s. The enormous fiscal effort required by World War II began the imbalance of national resource allocation which has reached critical proportions today. From 1940 to 1944, federal spending exploded, rising from $10 billion to $100 billion, pushing the federal bite of the total government tax take to an overwhelming 70 percent. State and local spending dropped from $11.2 billion to $10.5 billion during the same period.

After the war spending priorities were regeared, with the expectation that state and local governments would resume a greater share of the expenditures, as well as the revenues. The cold war ended the prospect for such sharing. State and local governments, instead of taking over sources of revenue vacated by the federal government, found themselves competing head to head with Washington for every tax dollar. At the same time, there was no letup in the demand for public services. By 1963 the percentage expenditure for these needs equaled those that reflected the major social programs of the 1930s. In addition, the relative levels of expenditure by state and local governments were sustained, despite the major encroachment of the federal government in the national tax pool.

City officials are severely handicapped in coping with their basic problems by the concentration of critical financial resources outside their control. These include private capital controlled by industry, which, when located inside or outside the city, has profound effects on job opportunities, private housing conditions, and the city's tax base. They have only limited influence over distribution of state and federal funds, which comprise a crucial share of municipal revenues.

Throughout the United States the demand for and cost of public services have outpaced the ability of cities to raise additional funds from sources under their own control. Among the multitude of contributing factors, the most obvious are restrictions on local taxing powers, the inelasticity of the traditional local tax base (the property tax), and, simultaneously, the concentration of financial powers at the national level. An immediate solution would seem to be the provision of a more diversified local tax base and increased local tax powers. In Sweden and Germany, which have similar urban problems, such reforms have been beneficial but not a panacea.

Thus, the solution to municipal fiscal problems is not simply broadening local taxation powers; rather, it lies in the consideration of many factors at both local and national levels. Studies in the United States and in other countries with similar urban problems have unearthed two fundamental issues—the shift from private to public expenditures and local autonomy versus central control.

The major thrust toward change in the mix of modern goods and services has come in education, health, and welfare, as well as community facilities, urban amenities, and environmental protection. The ground swell of activity in these areas has been stimulated by continuing urban development, combined with a heightened degree of social consciousness in the society as a whole. The impact of urbanization cannot be overestimated. During the twentieth century the United States has exploded from a rural to an urban society, with nearly 70 percent of the population living in metropolitan areas by 1970.

These greater concentrations of people and resources have led to higher levels of expenditures for such items as police and fire protection, highways and other public transportation, and public buildings. Parks and recreation areas, which are amenities in rural settings, become necessities in cities. Furthermore, urbanization has transformed the rural system of family and community security into a system of social security, requiring large public expenditures for aid for the elderly and the handicapped, and other forms of public welfare. With a shriveling tax base, but a surge in demand for services, cities have turned to the federal government for funds. Allocations of such funds are made within the context of national considerations regarding economic growth, employment, inflation, and income distribution.

Such economic considerations have led to increased federal control of the national economy, essentially within the public sector. Since revenues and expenditures of all levels of government—federal, state, and local—have a profound effect on national economic policies, the federal government has attempted to extend its control over state and local decisionmaking. This is evidenced by the fact that the Nixon administration has impounded funds for many grant programs in a move to curb inflation. For a similar reason the Johnson administration tried a different approach.

After Lyndon Johnson stepped up the tempo of U.S. involvement in the Vietnam War, he attempted to cool the overheating national economy by curtailing and postponing domestic public works spending and by appealing to state and local governments

Wide World

President Nixon signs the historic general revenue-sharing program into law October 20, 1972, at Independence Hall in Philadelphia as representatives of the national organizations of state, city, and county governments look on. From left: Mayors Pete Wilson of San Diego and Louie Welch of Houston, representing the National League of Cities and U.S. Conference of Mayors; Vice-President Spiro Agnew; Governor Nelson Rockefeller of New York, representing the National Governors' Conference; and Councilwoman Gladys Spellman of Prince George's County, Maryland, representing the National Association of Counties.

to do the same. In an address to the National League of Cities' 1966 Congressional-City Conference in Washington, he urged the mayors to cancel or postpone their plans for capital improvements, and he held similar "jawboning" sessions with governors and with industry leaders.

A few days later, Vice-President Hubert Humphrey, whom

Johnson had designated as the administration's liaison with local governments, assembled executive directors of their national associations in his office to explore ways for implementing the President's appeal. Also present were the chairman of the Council of Economic Advisors, the Undersecretary of the Treasury, the Director of the Budget, Presidential Assistant Joseph Califano, and others. After administration spokesmen emphasized the threat of inflation and the serious need to cool the economy, the Vice-President asked the association directors for their views on how the states and local governments could be persuaded to cooperate. Turning to this author, he said, "Pat, why don't you start it off?"

"I think it is completely unrealistic to expect that mayors and city councils are voluntarily going to cut back or postpone their public works projects," was the response. "In the first place, there is still a huge backlog of unmet needs that accumulated in the forties and fifties. In the second place, a mayor who has stuck out his neck to campaign for voter approval of a bond issue is not about to turn around and tell the voters that, after all, the project isn't all that urgent and can wait until the Vietnam War is over. If you really want to restrict state and local public works, you might impose a system of rationing and priorities such as was in effect in World War II. You already have the machinery for it set up in your Office of Emergency Planning in the Executive Office of the President. But a better way to control inflation, balance the federal budget, and cool the economy is to raise the federal income tax. You wouldn't have to overhaul the whole Internal Revenue Act—just put a surtax, like 10 percent, on everybody's tax bill after he computes it under existing law. Call it a war tax if that will help explain it to the public."

Bernard F. Hillenbrand, executive director of the National Association of Counties, agreed. So, too, he said privately, did Vice-President Humphrey. Yet two more years were to pass before President Johnson finally asked for, and got, a 10 percent surtax on the income tax, which, as is obvious today, was too soon repealed.

The point of that anecdote is that in the United States the local governments are to a considerable extent fiscally autonomous. It is the strength of our federal system. The root cause of the loss of local autonomy is the loss of local fiscal independence. You only have to look at some countries in Latin America, at Russia, Spain, Portugal, and other dictatorships to recognize that truth. There can be no democracy without local government autonomy. That is part of city hall's worsening fiscal dilemma in the United States, and that is why local governments here press for revenue sharing from state and federal governments *without strings attached.*

Though the federal government has responded to cities' needs with innumerable grant programs, it has attached conditions that the funds be used to implement national policies at the local level. Local considerations prompt city officials to establish their own administrative and budgetary priorities, which in many cases are at variance with national objectives. Proper integration of all governmental efforts toward national goals is threatened by a potential imbalance of control at either end of our governmental system—totally locally oriented spending priorities or excessive inhibition of local autonomy by an all-powerful federal state. In Sweden, in which both local and national governments are powerful, the system relies heavily on consultation to balance local and national perspectives.

Cities undertake a broad range of expenditures, from building and maintaining airports to educating children, from operating libraries to maintaining highways. The major items in the expenditure pie of modern cities, as shown in the graph on page 178, are education, which represents 14.5 percent of the total; police and fire protection, 14 percent; and the utilities, 14.5 percent. The utility expenditures, of course, are largely self-financed by users' fees. Sanitation and highways also require major expenditures. Over 40 percent of the total is comprised of a variety of activities, ranging from public welfare to interest on the general debt, as shown in the detailed portion of the graph.

The "all other" category has been one of the fastest-growing divisions of the municipal budget. Welfare, for example, represented 1.8 percent of the 1924 budget, as compared to 6.8 percent of the 1971 budget. Housing and urban renewal and health and hospital expenditures also have shown proportionate increases during the forty-seven years. Education, on the other hand, has shown a marked decline in the city budgets, dropping from 29.9 percent in 1924 to 14.5 percent in 1971, due to the greater state role in financing local school activities. The most dramatic change, however, has been in the magnitude of the budget—in 1924 America's cities spent about $2 billion on all activities; by 1971 their spending had ballooned to over $44 billion. This expenditure growth has been particularly dramatic in recent years, as shown in this table for 1967–71:

City Expenditures vs. Gross National Product: 1967–71
(in billions)

Item	1967	1971	% Change
GNP	$864.2	$1,054.4	22.0
City Expenditure	24.4	44.2	81.1
City as % GNP	2.8	4.2	—

Faced with expenditures rising more rapidly than the nation's productivity, cities have been forced to expand their sources of revenues beyond their traditional property tax base. In 1924 property taxes accounted for over 60 percent of net revenues, compared to about 25.6 percent in 1971. The slack has been taken up in a variety of ways, as shown by the graph on page 180. Intergovernmental revenues, primarily from the federal and state governments, now represent 27.3 percent of municipal revenues, while other taxes, charges and miscellaneous, and utility revenues provide important sources of funds.

The increased reliance on nonproperty tax revenues is certain to continue. The growing intensification of central city problems and increasing urbanization mean increasing needs for public services. And as urban life becomes more complex, so will the

EXPENDITURE OF MUNICIPAL GOVERNMENTS BY FUNCTION: 1971-72

TOTAL EXPENDITURE $44.2 BILLION

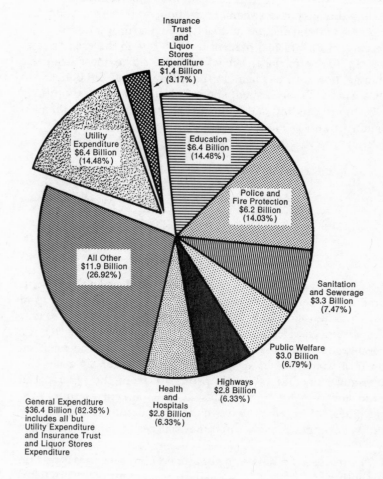

Insurance Trust and Liquor Stores Expenditure $1.4 Billion (3.17%)

Utility Expenditure $6.4 Billion (14.48%)

Education $6.4 Billion (14.48%)

Police and Fire Protection $6.2 Billion (14.03%)

All Other $11.9 Billion (26.92%)

Sanitation and Sewerage $3.3 Billion (7.47%)

Public Welfare $3.0 Billion (6.79%)

Highways $2.8 Billion (6.33%)

Health and Hospitals $2.8 Billion (6.33%)

General Expenditure $36.4 Billion (82.35%) includes all but Utility Expenditure and Insurance Trust and Liquor Stores Expenditure

U.S. Department of Commerce, Bureau of the Census

DETAIL OF "ALL OTHER"
EXPENDITURE OF MUNICIPAL GOVERNMENTS

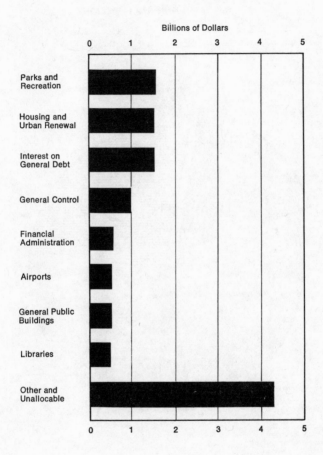

Billions of Dollars

Parks and Recreation

Housing and Urban Renewal

Interest on General Debt

General Control

Financial Administration

Airports

General Public Buildings

Libraries

Other and Unallocable

U.S. Department of Commerce, Bureau of the Census

REVENUE OF MUNICIPAL GOVERNMENTS
BY SOURCE: 1971-72

TOTAL REVENUE $42.1 BILLION

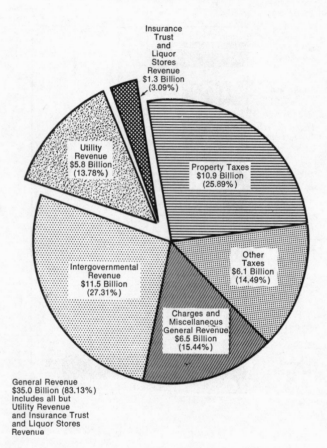

Insurance
Trust
and
Liquor
Stores
Revenue
$1.3 Billion
(3.09%)

Utility
Revenue
$5.8 Billion
(13.78%)

Property Taxes
$10.9 Billion
(25.89%)

Other
Taxes
$6.1 Billion
(14.49%)

Intergovernmental
Revenue
$11.5 Billion
(27.31%)

Charges and
Miscellaneous
General Revenue
$6.5 Billion
(15.44%)

General Revenue
$35.0 Billion (83.13%)
includes all but
Utility Revenue
and Insurance Trust
and Liquor Stores
Revenue

U.S. Department of Commerce, Bureau of the Census

DETAIL OF "OTHER TAXES" AND
"CHARGES AND MISCELLANEOUS GENERAL REVENUE"

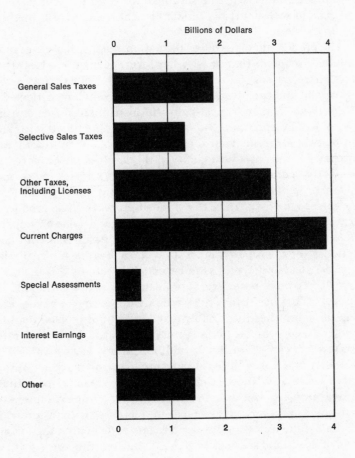

Billions of Dollars

U.S. Department of Commerce, Bureau of the Census

needs of the citizens, resulting in expansion of the scope and depth of city services. The scramble for revenues will lead city officials to seek to modify or supplement their present methods of financing.

The property tax is as old as the nation, but it still arouses more public discontent than most other forms of taxation. Nevertheless, there are several reasons for retaining it. Though it is controversial and can often be inequitably assessed and collected, it is local government's most powerful instrument for generating revenue. The apparatus for assessing and collecting it is already in place and in the control of local officials. Furthermore, real property is the chief beneficiary of the services the property tax supports—police, fire protection, sanitation, streets, and sewers.

The property tax has a reasonable degree of income elasticity. As the economy expands, the value of property rises, producing a greater tax yield for the municipality. Yet the value of property does not fluctuate sharply with sudden changes in economic conditions; thus, property taxes provide a degree of insulation against sudden downturns in revenue collections.

Property taxes pose several problems, however. Ownership of property does not always reflect the wealth of the taxpayer, leaving some families inequitably taxed in light of their annual incomes. In general, the tax is regressive, creating higher tax rates for lower-income families. In addition, many services funded by property taxes bear little relationship to the ownership of property, especially those that redistribute income—education, health services, welfare, and public housing, for example.

Though property taxes tend to increase with a growing economy, the inflow to the city treasury falls behind the expansion of goods and services in general. Accelerating the growth of property tax revenues would require an increase in the tax rate, which is always politically difficult. Federal income taxes, in contrast, contain a powerful acceleration feature. As family incomes rise, the taxpayer moves into higher brackets with automatic increases in his tax rates, allowing the federal tax take to keep pace with national growth. Finally, exemptions for such properties as educational and religious institutions, government facilities, and industry erode the local tax base.

Major municipal headaches can grow out of the assessment process. Perhaps the most frequent one is caused by the widespread practice of evaluating property at some percentage of its full value. This reduces the tax base and creates a number of inequities, because the percentage of value assessed varies from locality to locality. Cities with low percentages often receive larger shares of state taxes corresponding with their lower yields. Citizens in the other cities not only pay a higher local tax, but see a portion of their state income tax diverted to the neighboring city where the residents enjoy a lower property tax. Because assessments are made infrequently, these inequalities are perpetuated along with inequities among different classes of property. Even when state laws require full valuation, there is little implementation of the concept and tremendous political pressures on local assessors to continue partial valuation.

The most vigorous critics of the property tax recognize the realities of its existence. It is unlikely that cities and other local governments would accept much tampering with so vital a source of revenues. Some experts argue that the tax is not as regressive as it appears. Nevertheless, three approaches to reform have been advocated:

First, property taxation should be based on a full assessment of property values in order to wipe the slate clean of inequities and to establish a realistic assessable tax base. The present system is well entrenched, however, and such reform will be slow and painful.

Second, there should be some form of relief (such as the rapidly increasing use of "circuit breaker" rebates) for poor and elderly families.

Finally, cities are forced to look to other revenue sources to supplement what their ordinary property tax base provides. This can reduce the inequities that arise from saddling property with income distribution functions. Furthermore, prudent city officials recognize that the property tax base is neither great enough nor expanding rapidly enough to sustain the increasing public needs of the future.

Local nonproperty taxes have become increasingly important since their initiation in the 1930s. By far the most important is the local sales tax. These alternative revenue sources are primarily the invention of large cities. New York City was the first to establish sales taxes in 1934; Philadelphia inaugurated the payroll tax in 1939. The taxes are used predominantly in urban areas in a limited number of states.

Sales taxes provide substantial alternative funds without increasing burdens on property. But they have a number of handicaps. Sales taxes, like income taxes, are most efficient when applied over a wide geographic area, broader than the area of most cities. This tends to even out the local differences in types of industry and levels of income. Besides considering the possibility of uneven tax distribution within the city limits, cities must be concerned about what a sales tax would do to their position among other localities in the competition for new industry and new residents. Moreover, the cost of administering a local tax can be high unless it is collected as a "piggyback" on a state tax.

Intergovernmental revenues have become indispensable in the finances of American cities. The federal grant-in-aid, a concept nearly as old as the Union itself, has been the predominant method of federal assistance. Some federal grants are made to the states for distribution to cities; others directly to the cities themselves.

As noted earlier, widespread use of federal grants began during the Great Depression. Federal assistance took a further dramatic surge after World War II, and reached its peak in the late 1960s. Most grants available to cities are not for operating programs, but are "one-shot" allocations to aid in the installation of capital improvements, such as airports, hospitals, water and sewer line extensions, sewage disposal, urban renewal, and the acquisition of open space. Cities, however, derive benefits from grants to states for education, health services, medical care for the indigent, and other functions.

Despite the steady expansion in the growth of federal funds to local government, it became apparent to some local officials in the early 1960s that such spending was significantly out of proportion with funds going for other national purposes, particularly defense and the space program. Mayor Henry W. Maier of Milwaukee became the first of a succession of municipal leaders to call for a "reordering of national priorities to meet the needs of America's cities."

Elected president of the National League of Cities in 1964, Maier carried that message around the country in addresses to annual conventions of state leagues of municipalities and other gatherings during the following year, climaxed with his speech to NLC's 1965 Congress of Cities, in which he said:

There is no question now but that the city problem is a national problem and that to solve it there must be a re-allocation of our national priorities. The nation must be as committed to saving our cities, to promoting their growth and orderly development, as it was committed to saving the farmlands in the 1930s.

In some respects, the central city is the dustbowl of the sixties. Here we find a loss of fiscal topsoil with the flight of wealth and talent to the suburbs. Here we find an erosion of human resources, a long drought of tax revenues and the deep gullies of poverty.

Yet, while we live in this most urban of urban ages, at a time when there are probably more slum dwellers than farmers, it's estimated that we allocate to our cities only one-thirteenth the amount of federal aid that is allocated to saving the farms.

We spend about as much in developing a single space shot as we spend in federal assistance to urban renewal. Yet in many cases we have not found a way to get a man from his home to his place of work in less time than it takes him to orbit the earth.[2]

Later in the 1960s, city officials had become as concerned with *how* federal funds could be spent as they were with *how much* their cities were receiving. In 1964 there were some 190 separate categories of federal grants. Congress had begun to create so many federal grant-in-aid programs that city officials could not keep up with them. The National League of Cities found it necessary to publish a summary of them for its members in a *Federal Aids Manual.* Because it became obsolete soon after publication, a revision was issued. Finally, it had to be changed to a loose-leaf format in order to keep pace with the proliferating programs and their amendments. By the end of Lyndon Johnson's tenure in the White House, the number had increased to 430, and approximately a hundred more have been added since. More than 20 percent of the federal domestic budget is distributed through grants, most of them made by the Department of Health, Education and Welfare. Grants now account for about 27 percent of the revenues of local governments.

Legislation authorizing most federal grants specifies the purpose for which the funds are to be used. Local officials welcome the additional revenues for city treasuries but are often bewildered by the maze of overlapping and duplicating programs offered by government agencies and spelled out in a number of public laws. Application procedures are cumbersome, and reporting requirements and federal control features have proved troublesome. With so many "strings" attached, local officials struggle under Washington's thumb while trying to shape their own fiscal policies. Furthermore, such conditional grants encourage a program-oriented rather than policy-oriented approach at the local level, resulting in piecemeal efforts rather than integrated and priority-oriented budgets.

Elimination of the strings attached to the federal largess has long been attractive to local governments. As early as 1934, delegates to the National League of Cities annual conference were discussing the issue. At a session with Dr. James W. Martin, on leave from the University of Kentucky to work with the Commission on Conflicting Taxation, a suggestion of sharing federal income taxes with the states led Paul V. Betters, NLC's executive director, to ask: "What can the local governments of the United States do to eliminate what apparently is the ingrained opinion of the federal officials and state officials that the agency which collects the taxes is entitled to control expenditure of the tax?"

Dr. Martin's response was that the only thing that could be done "in the light of the historical background is just to continue to hammer at it exactly as the state municipal leagues and American Municipal Association and some other agencies have been doing."[3]

It took more than thirty years of "hammering," however, before the idea was taken seriously at the national level. In 1967 more than half a dozen bills emerged in Congress proposing that the federal government distribute a percentage of the taxes it gathers with such efficiency to state and local governments. These bills bore signatures of scores of senators and representatives on both sides of the aisles. The concept apparently had substantial popular support as well. Seventy percent of the population sampled by a Gallup poll approved of giving 3 percent of federal taxes back to the states.

Though municipal officials liked the idea of having federal dollars shorn of entangling red tape, many of them were highly skeptical of a plan that would leave redistribution of the money solely to the states. They had little cause for concern on that score during the remainder of the 1960s because revenue sharing did not appeal to President Johnson. He had rejected a revenue sharing proposal drafted by Walter W. Heller, chairman of the Council of Economic Advisers under Kennedy, and other members of a secret task force headed by Joseph Pechman of the Brookings Institution. The proposal had leaked to the press, a sure way to lose the support of Lyndon Johnson. When he had a task force appointed to study a specific problem, he wanted its recommendations kept secret until he could propose them himself as his own program to Congress and the public. Its premature release in November 1964 plus a strong letter of protest to the President from the National League of Cities were enough to convince Johnson that he would not make it a part of his program during his remaining tenure in the White House.

The NLC protest focused on the proposal to distribute federal tax revenue to the states rather than directly to municipal governments. League president Maier transmitted to Johnson on

January 8, 1965, an executive committee resolution adopted the previous month declaring that the distribution of unrestricted federal block grants to the states "would compound existing inequities within the states in the allocation of financial resources as between state and local governments for the operation of municipal government services for the urban population." If such federal assistance was to be given, the committee said, it should be in the form of unrestricted block grants direct to incorporated municipal governments "for such general purposes as may be determined by the officials duly elected by the people of each community to establish local policies."

In his letter of transmittal Mayor Maier described the acceleration of pressures on city governments and their limited fiscal resources. In spite of the mounting urban crisis, he said, local governments received approximately the same percentage of payment from state governments as was the case thirty years earlier. "In addition, state aid distribution formulas have traditionally favored rural areas at the expense of the urban population. . . . Any redistribution of national resources should be specifically directed to the source of the problem—our urban areas."

The governors of the states, of course, became enthusiastic about the proposal to share federal revenues. A committee of the National Governors Conference, headed by Governor George Romney of Michigan, began a study and suggested joint discussions with representatives of the National League of Cities. The latter, however, felt that before such discussions should be held, an economic analysis of the fiscal needs of local government in relation to the state and federal governments should be made. The association in 1966 therefore contracted with the Center for Advanced Studies, at Santa Barbara, a subsidiary of General Electric Company. Its report, *Options for Meeting the Revenue Needs of Local Governments,* published in March 1967, built a strong case for the needs of local governments. It estimated that during the succeeding ten years, local governments would need $125 billion total increased support from the federal government, over and above all existing grant-in-aid programs, which in themselves would increase an estimated additional $60 billion.

After that, NLC's executive director met with Romney's committee of governors, and later meetings took place between mayors and the governors committee. Although both sides realized that there would be no possible chance of gaining congressional approval of a revenue sharing measure without complete agreement and support of the states and their local governments, no such agreement was reached until July 8, 1969. On that day Arthur F. Burns, then Counselor to the President, assembled representatives of the governors, mayors, and county officials in the White House, assuring us that President Nixon would adopt as his own proposal to Congress whatever the group agreed upon. After two hours of discussion, consensus was reached and the group so informed the President.

A new coalition was then formed to lobby the program through Congress. The National Governors Conference, the National Association of Counties, the National League of Cities, and the United States Conference of Mayors joined forces. To facilitate communication between and among their staffs on this and other matters of mutual interest, a joint State-County-City Service Center was established the following January with a full-time coordinator, John J. Garvey, Jr., who had been deputy director of the National League of Cities. The Council of State Governments and the International City Management Association joined the group supporting the center.

President Nixon made revenue sharing the keystone of his domestic policy. His first proposal died in the Ninety-first Congress. But a proposal to share with states and localities $5 billion annually with no strings was at the top of his legislative proposals in 1971. In addition, he proposed to provide an additional $1 billion for special revenue sharing through six broadly defined categories with far fewer strings than were attached to existing domestic programs.

Congress has been slow to accept President Nixon's special revenue sharing plans; the first one—for manpower—finally became effective July 1, 1974. The block grants for law-enforcement assistance under the Safe Streets Act of 1969, however, closely approximate revenue sharing. With these exceptions, revenue sharing has been restricted to general revenues, and the level of effort is only marginally important, amounting to less than 3.5 percent of annual local expenditures. The cuts in ongoing grant programs, in fact, have more than offset the additional revenues provided in the revenue sharing program. Furthermore, state and local governments have not been involved in the revisions of existing grant programs nor in the further development of the revenue sharing system. The restrictions tied to revenue sharing funds—that they are not to be used for matching funds, for example—plus the requirements for reporting the purposes for which the funds were used have thwarted the integrative budgeting process that revenue sharing was supposed to enhance.

Municipalities are not limited to taxes, intergovernmental revenues, and service charges for funds. Borrowing is a prime source. Prior to 1900, municipalities suffered a stormy history in the bond markets. Some heavily financed projects proved less fruitful than expected, and defaults were frequent. The 1930s Depression was also a disastrous period because of defaults, as noted in Chapter 7.

The experiences of the post–Civil War period resulted in state legislation placing strict limitations on municipal borrowing, usually expressed in terms of a fixed percentage of the aggregate assessable tax base. Though in many cases unduly restrictive, these limitations have not precluded a substantial expansion in the use of municipal debt. The tax-exempt status of municipal bonds, which allows cities to escape the higher interest rates on their debt instruments, has been a favorable factor.

Since World War II, the stable and growing national economy has been the springboard for the major growth in municipal debt. Municipals have a record of performance nearly equal to the best private bonds. Cities use debt to finance capital improvements, paying principal and interest out of current revenues.

The magnitude of the capital improvement effort has made the use of long-term debt a necessity. In the same postwar period, all state and local governments financed about $300 billion in capital improvements with the help of $100 billion in bonds, the rest coming from current resources. From 1924 through 1972, the outstanding debt of municipalities increased from $6.1 billion to $49 billion.

It has not been possible in this analysis of revenues and expenditures to emphasize the diversity that abounds among American cities and towns. There are wide differences throughout the country in local practices and in the relationships between states and municipalities. In the final analysis, the merits of proposals for fiscal reform cannot be fully determined until they have been tested in Peoria, or Eau Claire, or San Bernardino.

To correct the general fiscal problems faced by cities, however, the Advisory Commission on Intergovernmental Relations has recommended the following specific policies:

1. Sharing of a percentage of the federal personal income tax with states and major localities.

2. Assumption by the federal government of all costs of public welfare and Medicaid.

3. Assumption by the state government of substantially all local costs of elementary and secondary education.

4. Encouragement of a high-quality, high-yield state tax system through a federal income tax credit for state income taxes paid.

5. An active state role in the administration of the local property tax.

To the extent that these recommendations are now in the process of being fulfilled, they represent a cause for hope in alleviating part of the fiscal pressures on cities.

Mayors on the National Stage

In the nation, and particularly in the cities, the pent-up demand for housing that had grown rapidly during World War II had reached acute proportions by 1949. Congress recognized the shortage in the Housing Act of 1949, declaring in the eloquent and oft-quoted preamble that national policy included "realization as soon as feasible the goal of a decent home and suitable living environment for every American family."

That act, which included the first step in federal aid for urban renewal and the authorization of 810,000 units of public housing, required five years of effort concentrated on Congress by all the major urban groups. The successful campaign in behalf of the highly controversial measure over intense opposition of private interest groups was a classic performance by the "urban lobby" —an urban policy network with the "municipal lobby" as its nucleus.

Allied in a coalition favoring the bill were the National League of Cities, the United States Conference of Mayors, the National Association of Housing and Redevelopment Officials (NAHRO), the National Housing Conference, and organized labor. The phalanx of those opposing critical parts of it included the National Association of Real Estate Boards, the Chamber of Commerce of the United States, the National Association of Home Builders, the United States Building and Loan League, the Mortgage Bankers Association, and the American Bankers Association.

The housing groups in the coalition were fighting for survival of public housing. The first public housing bill had been passed in 1937 over the protests of congressmen who saw it as a springboard to socialism. President Truman had supported a bill containing a public housing measure in 1945, but Republican leaders in Congress were unsympathetic to the concept until Senator Robert Taft of Ohio turned them around in 1949. His name (along with those of Democratic Senators Allen Ellender of Louisiana and Robert Wagner of New York) gave public housing a legitimacy it had never enjoyed in Congress.

Although the Conference of Mayors supported the public housing provisions, it was primarily interested in Title I, which authorized federal aid for urban renewal. The proposal authorized a city to assemble and clear slum land, then write down the price and resell it on the open market for redevelopment. The federal government would pay the difference between the cost of assembling and clearing and the price paid for the land by a private developer—a radical concept at the time. Probably the main reason the program was enacted without heated debate was because it became lost in the larger controversy over public housing. Following a strategy shaped chiefly by Paul Betters, executive director of the Conference of Mayors, the urban network was able to picture private enterprise as the major participant in urban renewal. Hence the idea of eliminating slums did not create the same hostile outcries of "socialism" as did public housing. All of the groups that participated in that urban policy network still consider the urban renewal concept as among their best achievements. The public interest groups won on almost every issue, as they continue to do whenever an issue of municipal concern arises.

The National League of Cities and the United States Conference of Mayors have been described as "the two organizations that appear to come the closest to representing urban interests across the board" in a collection of case studies on urban legislative efforts published by the Brookings Institution. Titled *Congress and Urban Problems,* this generally sound analysis of urban legislative activity, by Frederic N. Cleaveland, contains an error that should be corrected and a statement that can be disputed. Cleaveland is in error in asserting that "the Conference of Mayors speaks particularly for large cities and the League of Municipalities [*sic*] for towns and small and middle-size cities." Actually, the National League of Cities speaks for municipal governments of all sizes, large and small, some fifteen thousand of them that maintain membership in the affiliated state leagues of municipalities, and directly for the more than five hundred large cities that maintain direct membership in NLC. Most of these same large cities are members of the United States Conference of Mayors, so that both organizations speak for large cities, and NLC represents the others as well. While the two organizations maintain separate identities, hold separate annual conventions, and elect separate officers, there is some overlap in their boards of directors, and their policy objectives are almost identical.

Cleaveland, who is chairman of the Department of Political Science at the University of North Carolina, also says that both organizations are "spokesmen for local governments rather than direct representatives of city dwellers."

"Their priorities," he says, "reflect the agenda of problems defined by city hall as targets for governmental action—and even at that high policy level of municipal government the perspective on urban problems is less than a whole view."[1] He claims that their orientation appears more like that of a producer interest than a consumer interest. This is what is open to dispute. As noted in Chapter 9, the National League of Cities since 1948 has structured its entire program and policy on the premise that the municipal governments of America represent the "public interest" in matters of national policy affecting the lives of the citizens. It is apparent that private interests make their impact in national affairs through their associations. It may be said that the Congress and the state legislatures represent the public interest—yet they also represent the private interests as well since they were selected by the private citizens and not by some other public body. Therefore, a national organization of municipal governments may appropriately represent the "public interest" at the national level in matters which are generally the local responsibility of municipal officials. This is also the premise upon which the United States Conference of Mayors operates.

Cleaveland correctly credits the efforts of both organizations for "the increasing commitment of federal resources to the solution of urban problems." These efforts began with the leadership of the Conference of Mayors in the 1930s and were continued thereafter by both organizations, sometimes working separately, sometimes cooperatively in varying consortiums of other public interest groups.

Previous chapters have reviewed the entry of the mayors on the national stage in 1932 and their organization in 1933 of a permanent United States Conference of Mayors, using the National League of Cities as its secretariat and Paul V. Betters as executive director of both organizations for three years until they separated at the end of 1935. They have told how, with Mayor Fiorello La Guardia of New York City as president of the Conference for ten years, the mayors helped shape national policies that provided direct aid to cities for the first time in the nation's history. This assistance took the form of loans and grants for emergency public works, work relief, public housing, and for expenditures for highways, airports, hospitals—all designed to bring the country out of the Great Depression. These efforts continued up to World War II. Then, with La Guardia still the dominant figure, the mayors turned their attention to federal measures for civil defense, priorities for the purchase of essential supplies to relieve wartime shortages, emergency housing for war workers, and postwar planning.

The overall policy objective of the Conference of Mayors was to involve the federal government directly in urban affairs and, above all, to establish the principle that the welfare of the cities was a national problem. This meant a major policy innovation. USCM wanted the city and its problems to be considered as a distinct and separate point of view in arriving at political decisions, rather than simply as a subdivision of a state. Its participation in the shaping of federal programs prodded the federal government to take a new look, to acquire an urban perspective, giving special attention to cities as independent entities in terms of policy, legislation, and administration.

USCM's policy objectives were shaped during those years and still remain its guiding principles. They can be summarized as follows: (1) to press for a larger percentage of the federal contribution to federal-city matching fund programs; (2) to strengthen direct federal-city relations and programs; (3) to obtain outright grants as opposed to loans; (4) to bring about an assumption of federal responsibility for national problems such as relief, poverty, air and water pollution, and adequate housing for low-income families; (5) to bring about federal policies that would

Harry R. Betters succeeded his brother, Paul, as executive director of the U.S. Conference of Mayors in 1956 and served until his death in 1961.

International News Photos

expand help to municipalities in their financial problems; and (6) to press for programs that would leave the cities maximum autonomy.

As the National League of Cities began in 1948 to define more clearly its own objectives based on a national municipal policy, it agreed with USCM. What would be more vital to the cities and of greater long-range value than any other set of programs, it concluded, would be these broad objectives: more money (from practically any source but especially from the federal government); control and authority for city governments over programs commensurate with their responsibility; grants given to cities directly rather than through states. Commenting on these goals in an examination of the intergovernmental pressure group in urban lobbying, the late Dr. Suzanne Farkas wrote: "The primacy of these preferences for unearmarked funds, political autonomy, and municipal home rule distinguishes the core of the general and the 'governmental' urban interests from the more limited program-oriented objectives of more specialized and regular membership urban interest groups."[2]

The effectiveness of mayors as an urban interest pressure group is based on at least three factors: (1) they are *organized* to cooperate together to seek mutually agreeable objectives, at the national level through their National League of Cities and their United States Conference of Mayors, at the state level through their leagues of municipalities; (2) they have a political base, being recognized by Presidents, members of Congress, governors, and state legislators as the elected political spokesmen for city-wide constitituencies; (3) executive and legislative branches of national and state governments recognize that the cities do, indeed, share problems that are national in scope and require national and state government attention and aid, a recognition increasingly shared by the general public beginning in the early 1960s.

Sometimes elected city councilmen resent what some of them consider an undue amount of attention given to mayors by both USCM and NLC. In some cities the mayor is merely another member of the governing body, particularly in those having the council-manager or commission form of government. Even though he may be elected at large, he may have no more authority than the councilmen or commissioners. Other cities may have a "weak-mayor" form, where the mayor has no real executive authority, and the city is actually run by the city council. In "strong-mayor" cities the mayor is the elected chief executive. Whatever the form of government, however, the mayor is at least the ceremonial head of the city, and the general public and the press regard him as the city's spokesman. He is the one, therefore, who gets the attention of the national and state governments, and the one most likely to receive the attention of the news media. It follows, then, that the national and state organizations of cities maintain close contact with mayors and call upon them as spokesmen for the cities.

Nationally, it is the mayors who do the "lobbying" for the municipal pressure group, not the staff of the association. The latter serve more as "brokers," drafting bills, evaluating new ideas, consulting with legislative committees, arranging hearings, screening testimony, and structuring lobbying coalitions. The staff keep the members informed of new legislation and administrative rulings and advise them of the significance of changes. Through a communications network they alert the mayors when the timing is right to let their views be known to members of Congress. When a senator or representative hears from mayors in his state or district by letter, telegram, telephone, or personal visit, it has great influence on him, especially if backed by a resolution of the city governing body that is reported in the hometown press. They get his attention. He knows that the mayors are the spokesmen for their communities and that they consider their requests to be in the public interest. Tacitly understood is the fact that a mayor's political support in future elections could be important.

That is how the "municipal lobby" works. Unlike lobbying in the private sector, no lawyer-lobbyists are retained or necessary. Neither NLC nor USCM makes political campaign contributions, nor do any of the state leagues of municipalities. The municipal lobby could be called an "urban lobby" when it becomes part of a coalition of other groups, which can be governmental, private, or both, depending upon the objective for which the coalition is formed.

Much of the success of the urban lobby in the thirties and forties must be attributed to Paul Betters, executive director of the Conference of Mayors. But after the major triumph by the urban forces on the 1949 housing bill, Betters seemed to begin to "coast" and to rest on his laurels. Meanwhile, the National League of Cities was coming on strong as a result of its new emphasis on formulating national municipal policy. Big-city mayors increasingly chose to identify themselves with NLC and to participate actively in its expanding activities. Bowron of Los Angeles, Wyatt of Louisville, Riley of Portland, Rodgers of Dallas, Morrison of New Orleans, Newton of Denver, and others who were active in the immediate postwar period had been joined in leadership of the association in the early fifties by Devin of Seattle, Rishell of Oakland, Cobo of Detroit, Hartsfield of Atlanta, Golder of Utica, Hynes of Boston, Darst of Saint Louis, Zeidler of Milwaukee, Kemp of Kansas City, Thompson of Jackson, and Clark of Philadelphia. Finally, the mayor of the nation's largest city, Robert F. Wagner of New York, was NLC president in 1956. The 1952 appointment of the energetic, resourceful, and innovative Randy Hamilton* as manager of NLC's Washington office had greatly enhanced the league's effectiveness in dealing with Congress and executive agencies. His groundwork made the league even more effective when it moved its headquarters to the capital in 1954. The number of big cities that joined NLC as direct members increased from half a dozen or so when Carl Chatters became executive director in 1948 to forty-one when he left in 1954. By the end of 1956 the number had grown to 145. It

*To Davetta L. Steed, executive director of the North Carolina League of Municipalities, should go the credit for discovering Randy Hamilton, then an obscure manager of a resort town on the Carolina coast.

was in March of that year that Paul Betters approached his counterpart in NLC with a proposal that the two organizations should merge.

"It was necessary to organize the Conference of Mayors back in 1933," he explained. "The old American Municipal Association simply wasn't structured to represent the cities in national policy issues. Now that it has been restructured to be a policy spokesman for the big cities directly as well as their state leagues, it is no longer necessary to have a separate Conference of Mayors. Having two separate organizations speaking for the cities not only confuses the mayors themselves but also members of Congress and the Administration. I propose that we cut out all this [expletive deleted], that the Conference of Mayors be dissolved and turn over all its materials, files, and assets to your association."

He expressed a desire to be retained only as a consultant at a nominal salary while he wrote a book "about the mayors I have known." Two months passed, during which further discussions took place and Betters drafted a memorandum of understanding, when he suddenly died of a heart attack at the age of fifty. That ended the possibility of merger. Although further attempts were made, including efforts by Mayor Richardson Dilworth of Philadelphia when he was president of the conference in 1960–61 and by Mayor Jerome P. Cavanagh of Detroit when he was president of both organizations simultaneously in 1966, only Paul Betters could have brought it about. There were always a few influential mayors in the power structure of the conference who preferred to retain a separate organization to preserve the identity of mayors as such. A similar attitude prevails among governors, who maintain a National Governors Conference as an entity separate from the Council of State Governments.

Actually, there is no longer any compelling reason for a complete merger of the two associations of cities. Harry Betters, who succeeded his brother as director of the conference, was not in good health, and the effectiveness of the organization continued its downhill slide until he died five years later. However, he had the good judgment in 1958 to retain as his assistant and general counsel a smart young lawyer, John J. Gunther, who succeeded Harry as executive director of the Conference in 1961. Gunther had had training and experience as a member of Senator Flanders' staff on Capitol Hill and had good contacts with other congressional staff and with many federal agencies. He maintains, and he is probably right, that if the two organizations were merged into one, there would inevitably be a movement in the future to start still another Conference of Mayors.

Gunther employed as his principal assistant Hugh Mields, Jr., who earlier had served as NLC's assistant director for federal affairs, added other qualified people to the staff of the Conference, and led in expanding the scope and depth of the group's activities. Relations with the National League of Cities became closer, and the two groups began to cooperate closely in joint endeavors. In 1969 they consolidated their offices and staffs into one headquarters, a move that has eliminated most of the confusion as to who was serving and speaking for the cities. The effectiveness of the city governments' presence in Washington immediately accelerated.

After the National League of Cities moved to center stage in the 1950s, it assumed the leadership of the urban interests on a number of important matters. One was the Housing Act of 1954. The debate preceding the 1949 housing act began a period of intensive "urban-oriented" activities by several strategically placed national legislators with whom NLC, USCM, and their allies were able to establish close relationships over the years. For example, Paul Douglas of Illinois was beginning his long leadership in the field of housing and urban development legislation as a freshman senator on the Housing Subcommittee of the Senate Banking and Currency Committee, a strategic group for urban programs. He shared responsibility for managing the 1954 bill with Senator John Sparkman of Alabama, whose involvement with urban legislation spans a period from 1946 through 1974. Sparkman became chairman of the Housing Subcommittee and later of the full Senate Banking and Currency

Committee. In the latter role he headed the Senate conferees appointed to meet with conferees from the House of Representatives to work out differences between Senate and House versions of housing bills. His counterpart in the House, until he retired as chairman of the House Banking and Currency Committee in 1966, was Albert Rains, also of Alabama. Sparkman and Rains between them had very little difficulty working out the differences and producing the kind of legislation they wanted, often with the advice of the late Ed E. Reid, executive director of the Alabama League of Municipalities. Jacob Javits, who, as a representative from New York, introduced the House version of the Taft-Ellender-Wagner bill in 1947, later moved to the Senate and became a member of the Banking and Currency Committee. Albert Cole, a Republican congressman from Kansas, was active in the original urban redevelopment legislation of 1949. Later he became administrator of the Housing and Home Finance Administration and chairman of the Eisenhower Task Force on Housing Policies in 1953. Senator Hubert Humphrey, former mayor of Minneapolis, was another active supporter of the 1949 bill. John Barriere was chief of staff of the Housing Subcommittee of the House from 1949 to 1965, during which time he developed close working relations with the staff of the urban interest groups, as did Casey Ireland, minority counsel on the same subcommittee.

These and others helped to fashion the housing legislation in 1954, which made significant modifications in the urban renewal program and established a separate Urban Renewal Administration in the HHFA. It provided, also, that 10 percent of federal grants could be used for commercial renewal. The 1949 act had required that a renewal project area be either predominantly residential in character to begin with or redeveloped primarily for residential use. The 1954 bill also provided that cities submit to HHFA and have approved a "workable program for community development" in order to be eligible for renewal funds.

Not every legislative gain requires hours of vote counting and telephoning to mobilize pressure from hometowns. Early in 1955

Senator Russell B. Long of Louisiana telephoned the National League of Cities to request that its executive director come to his office to discuss a proposed bill. At the meeting the senator explained that he proposed to introduce a bill to set up an agency in the Housing and Home Finance Administration with authority to borrow to $100 million from the United States Treasury for the purpose of making loans to municipalities for the construction of public self-liquidating facilities when such municipalities were unable to obtain such loans on reasonable terms in the private market. Priority would be given to municipalities under 10,000. He requested the support of the National League of Cities for such legislation. He was told that the association had no policy on the matter but that a quick nationwide survey would be made to determine the views of municipal governments on whether it would be helpful. The survey showed that such a measure was not particularly needed in the Northeast but that in the South and West it would be highly useful. NLC's executive committee endorsed the bill on February 13. At a subsequent public hearing before Senator Sparkman's committee, the only witnesses testifying for the bill were Senator Long and NLC's executive director. Spokesmen for the administration and for investment bankers opposed it. Senator Sparkman announced that rather than report it as a separate bill to the Senate, he would include it in the Omnibus Housing bill that year, which had already been passed by the House. After Senate approval of the Sparkman committee's amended Housing bill, including Senator Long's measure, the Senate-House conference committee accepted it, the House approved the conference committee report, and it was signed into law by the President—a new $100 million revolving loan fund for municipalities, just like that!

A somewhat similar experience occurred in 1956, but enactment this time was more difficult. Congressman John Blatnik of Minnesota, chairman of the Subcommittee on Rivers and Harbors of the House Committee on Public Works, telephoned NLC's executive director to say that he proposed to draft and introduce a water pollution control bill that would provide federal grants to municipalities for construction of sewage treatment plants. He asked whether NLC would be interested. It happened this time that the organization had at its 1954 convention adopted a policy calling for such a program, but its officers and staff frankly felt that it would take several years to build up sufficient interest and support to get congressional approval of such a radical new program of federal aid. Bernard F. Hillenbrand, then the association's assistant director for federal affairs, was dispatched to consult with Congressman Blatnik and his aide, Jerome Sonosky. They developed a strategy that resulted in the formation of a coalition of several groups, notably national associations of sportsmen and conservationists. This coalition exchanged information, developed strategy, and coordinated its tactics at weekly breakfast meetings—dubbed "sewer breakfasts" by Hillenbrand.

Blatnik's bill was actually a substitute for a measure passed by the Senate the previous year, an administration bill that had been considerably weakened by Senator Robert S. Kerr of Oklahoma, chairman of the Public Works Committee's Subcommittee on Flood Control, Rivers and Harbors, who was skeptical about an extensive federal commitment.

At the 1955 hearings on air and water pollution control bills before Senator Kerr's subcommittee, Mayor Joseph S. Clark of Philadelphia represented the National League of Cities in support of the Air Pollution Control Bill. There was not much controversy about the need for federal involvement in that field. However, when this author, then NLC's executive director, presented the association's position calling for federal grants to cover at least 50 percent of the cost of constructing sewage treatment projects to control water pollution, Senator Kerr gave me a rough time. Kerr was extremely hostile to the idea. The following is part of the exchange:

Senator Kerr: Do I understand that to mean that you recommend that the Federal Government make a grant-in-aid to a municipality, and pay up to half of the total cost of that municipality's disposing of sewage which it itself created?

Mr. Healy: Yes, sir.

Senator Kerr: In other words, then you would impose upon every community in the Nation that was taking care of its own problem, the penalty of helping pay half of the cost of any other community in meeting its requirements where it had made no provision to do so on its own initiative and with its own resources?

Mr. Healy: That is one way of putting it, Senator.

Senator Kerr: Is that an inaccurate statement?

Mr. Healy: That is substantially accurate and relates to the same type of activities that the Federal Government engages in in slum clearance, subsidization of public housing, and other types of health and welfare activities.

Senator Kerr: Are there communities in the Nation which on their own initiative and at their own expense have cleared their own slums?

Mr. Healy: I would say "No."

Senator Kerr: Then it is not a similar situation, is it?

Mr. Healy: What I am driving at, Senator, is—

Senator Kerr: Is not the program of slum clearance one of loans and not grants?

Mr. Healy: There are substantial Federal grants in the Federal redevelopment program. . . .

Senator Kerr: I would like to have some examples of where the Federal Government is making a grant-in-aid for a project as purely local as the sewage disposal of a municipality. . . .

Mr. Healy: I will be glad to try to dig up some such examples, Senator, for the record.

Senator Kerr: Do you not think that the enactment of a law doing what you set forth there in your third item would actually encourage municipalities to fail to meet their own responsibilities?

Mr. Healy: What we are talking about here is to get the job done, this whole thing.

Senator Kerr: I understand the job has got to be done of feeding my family, but you are not concerned with it.

Mr. Healy: This whole approach that we are suggesting here is to get the job done on the matter of controlling water pollution and one way we feel will accelerate—

Senator Kerr: Is not the prevention of pollution quite an item in the control of pollution?

Mr. Healy: That is true, Senator. Yes, sir.

Senator Kerr: What theory of government can you give this committee that would justify the Federal Government on a nonreimbursable basis paying for the building of the facility, the sole purpose of which was to handle sewage produced by the citizens of a community and which they either fail or refuse to adequately dispose of?

Mr. Healy: I will start from the other end. The benefits are interstate in character. They benefit the people downstream from that city.

You say that does not excuse the city from taking care of the people downstream, but the point I am trying to make is that a great many cities will never, within the next many years, be able to construct those facilities without some such program as this.

They cannot do it financially, and you can order them to do it by a court order, and they still cannot do it, and so if you want to get the job done, we are suggesting this course.

Senator Kerr: I must say I have an interest in getting the job done, but I also am aware of such a thing as basic and organic law, which sets up certain principles and certain identities with certain responsibilities and certain limitations and one of which is the Constitution of the United States.

Mr. Healy: If this were strictly a local effort, I could certainly agree with you.

Senator Kerr: It is strictly a local cause, is it not?

Mr. Healy: You might also say that building an airport is strictly a local cause, too.[3]

Blatnik's major innovation was a provision for federal grants to help local communities build sewage disposal plants. He viewed the Senate bill as little more than a slight expansion of the 1948 act, which had provided only for the Public Health Service to coordinate research and provide technical information. It did provide for individual project loans of up to $250,000 at 2 percent interest to cover up to one-third of the total cost of a project, but this had been inoperative for lack of appropriations. Blatnik's proposal to provide $50 million annually in grants with a $500 million total for ten years was branded by conservative Republicans as another step down the road to socialism. Opposition to grants also came from members of the national organization of state public health officers who were fearful that some municipalities, while waiting for federal grant funds, might delay projects that otherwise would go ahead.

At hearings before Blatnik's subcommittee, two small-city mayors presented testimony in behalf of the National League of Cities: R. P. Weatherford, Jr., Independence, Missouri, and George W. Dill, Jr., Morehead City, North Carolina. After a favorable committee report and House approval, the bill went to a Senate-House conference committee, where Senator Kerr reluctantly agreed to the conference report that contained most of the House provisions. Nobody could ever figure out why he changed his position. Conjecture has it that he must have made a trade for support of one of his own pet bills.

An incident took place the following year which demonstrated the municipal muscle that can be brought to bear when local municipal officials act in concert. The House of Representatives was sitting as a Committee of the Whole House to consider appropriations for the Department of Health, Education and Welfare. As such, their decisions were made without a record vote of the members. A motion was approved to delete the $50 million authorization for construction grants to municipalities for sewage treatment plants for the coming fiscal year. Action completed on the bill, the Committee of the Whole was dissolved, and the House adjourned to convene again at noon the next day to formally adopt the bill as amended in the Committee of the Whole.

When the National League of Cities learned of the deletion in the middle of the afternoon, its executive director sent the following telegram to each of the forty-eight state leagues of municipalities:

House sitting as Committee of the Whole today deleted $50 million appropriation for sewage treatment construction grants to municipalities. Will reconvene tomorrow noon for record vote. Urgent you advise municipalities in your state planning to apply for these grants next fiscal year or thereafter and urge them to wire or telephone their Congressional representatives before tomorrow noon urging their vote to restore appropriation.

Next day on the roll call vote the $50 million appropriation was restored by a substantial margin of 231 to 185. In reporting the reversal the following day, a *New York Times* article stated that "House members apparently had been hearing from their constitutents back home." Some state league directors worked until midnight after receiving the NLC telegram, telephoning mayors and other local officials throughout their state. It was a dramatic illustration of how effective the network of state leagues of municipalities can be.

The Highway Act of 1956 was also one in which NLC was actively involved to protect the interests of cities. President Eisenhower chose the National Governors Conference in June 1954 as the forum for announcing his "grand plan" for federal aid to the states to construct a complete nationwide system of interstate and defense highways to connect all state capital cities and most other cities over 50,000 population, including major ports of entry on the coasts and on the borders with Canada and Mexico. It would be built simultaneously by all states with major funding by the federal government to design standards that would accommodate anticipated traffic needs of the 1980s. Unable at the last moment to attend the conference himself, the President designated Vice-President Richard Nixon to deliver the message to the governors.

The President appointed a task force headed by General Lucius Clay to develop details of the plan for presentation to Congress. Representatives of federal, state, county, and city governments were designated as unofficial advisers to the Clay committee—Frank Turner and other engineers from the United States Bureau of Public Roads, Alf Johnson, executive director of the American Association of State Highway Officials, a representative of the National Association of Counties, and two representatives of the National League of Cities. The latter were Glenn Richards, Detroit's Commissioner of Public Works, and Randy Hamilton, NLC's assistant director for federal affairs. The principal interest of the cities was to see to it that the plan included the urban connecting links as part of the new system, to be financed by federal and state funds on the same basis as in rural areas. In the past most states had required cities to bear the cost of the connecting links to state highway systems, while state-collected revenues from highway users were spent mostly outside municipal boundaries. Cities also looked on these new freeway connecting links as a means of relieving congestion caused by through traffic on existing streets that were not designed for such purposes.

General Clay made the first public announcement of the elements of his committee report at NLC's annual convention in Philadelphia that fall, and the association enthusiastically endorsed it. The President submitted the plan to Congress early in 1955. However, the powerful Senator Harry Byrd of Virginia, chairman of the Senate's Finance Committee, delayed action on the bill because he objected to its financing provisions, particularly to a provision for issuance of federal highway bonds to be repaid from future earnings of an increased federal tax on motor fuels and tires. This delayed the bill until the following year, when a plan acceptable to Senator Byrd was adopted to establish a Highway Trust Fund, into which would go the federal motor vehicle user taxes and from which would be paid all federal aid for highways on a pay-as-you-go basis, including the new Interstate System.

After the Clay committee made its report and was dissolved, an informal coalition was formed to support the legislation. Known as the Highway Information Group, it was chaired by Pyke Johnson, retired president of the Automotive Safety Foundation. In addition to the executive directors of AASHO, NACO, and NLC, it was composed of representatives of various associations of highway users, such as the American Automobile Association; the National Grange, representing farmers; truckers' associations, tire manufacturers, the National Retail Merchants Association, and road builders. The petroleum industry was not invited to participate, because it selfishly opposed any highway program that called for an increase in motor fuel taxes. Representatives of this coalition held luncheon meetings almost weekly for the same purpose that the water pollution control coalition held their "sewer breakfasts"—to pool information and develop strategy and tactics. The organizations represented broad-based constituencies and could generate widespread support nationwide. Mayors who testified in behalf of the legislation before congressional committees included Cobo of Detroit, Ben West of Nashville, and Wagner of New York.

A planned administrative move a couple of years after passage of the Interstate Highway Act almost stopped the program as it was getting under way. The House Ways and Means Committee was meeting in executive session with Secretary of the Treasury Humphrey, who, unknown to the White House, was proposing a transfer of the Highway Trust Fund to the general fund in order to balance the federal budget. When NLC's executive director was tipped off to this, he telephoned Presidential Assistant Robert E. Merriam to inquire whether the White House was aware that the President's "grand plan" for an Interstate Highway System was about to be scuttled by his own Secretary of the Treasury. Merriam went into action. Late that evening he telephoned to report that the matter had been taken care of and that the highway program would proceed on schedule.

Airports are uniquely a city problem and are particularly visible and expensive. The National League of Cities has long been a strong advocate of federal aid for construction and improvement of airports. Interest stirred by the 1936 brief on the subject by John Stutz, executive director of the League of Kansas Municipalities, was expressed for many years through an active committee on airports. NLC and the Conference of Mayors cooperated in another coalition that was coordinated by E. Thomas Burnard, executive director of the Airport Operators Council. A complete case history of their role in behalf of airport legislation, centering on the clash between congressional proponents and Eisenhower administration opponents of federal aid, has been written by Randall B. Ripley.[4] He cites the organization by the National League of Cities (then called American Municipal Association) of an "Airport Crusade" after an Eisenhower budget eliminated federal aid for airports authorized in earlier legislation. The coalition in support of congressional advocates of an expanded program was successful through the legislative struggle of 1958–59 and again when Congress extended the program in both 1961 and 1963–64. However, an exception will have to be taken to one of Ripley's concluding comments: "The interest groups here did not speak too loudly for urban interests. The Conference of Mayors and Municipal Association framed their arguments in terms of city needs but were not willing to devote much political muscle to the airport program."

On the contrary, it was the political muscle of the mayors that was an absolute necessity for the success of congressional champions of legislation opposed by the executive branch. With Mayor William B. Hartsfield of Atlanta as spokesman for both NLC and USCM, organized support by hundreds of mayors throughout the country was generated at crucial points in the legislative battle. Without that support there would have been no airport aid legislation enacted during the 1950s.

Mayors took the lead in still another aspect of national transportation policy. This was the five-year struggle to obtain a federal commitment to the solution of the mass-transportation problems of America's cities. Mayor Richardson Dilworth of Philadelphia started it in early 1959 when he requested NLC's executive director to set up a meeting in Chicago between the mayors of a dozen large cities that had mass-transit problems and presidents of seventeen railroads that had commuter rail service. Dilworth earlier had negotiated an agreement with the Pennsylvania Railroad to increase service on its commuter lines in the Philadelphia area and cut rates on experimental routes with the help of a city subsidy. He and the board chairman of the railroad hoped that at the Chicago meeting they would get the support of the mayors and railroad executives for a federal subsidy for commuter lines.

But the Western railroads would not go along. Ben Heineman, board chairman of the Northwestern Railroad, said that his commuter service in Chicago was good and was making a profit. He didn't need, or want, a government subsidy, emphasizing that good management was the key to success. The implication was clear that with better management the Eastern lines could have similar success. The Southern Pacific, which operated commuter lines in San Francisco, wanted no part of a government subsidy scheme because it felt this would be a foot in the door for eventual government takeover of the railroads. Thus thwarted in their hope for unanimous support through the Association of American Railroads, the Eastern lines decided, nevertheless, to go it alone with the help of the mayors. They met again with the mayors later in the summer at Philadelphia, where they decided to ask the National League of Cities to prepare an analysis of transit problems in five major cities that relied heavily on commuter rail service.

NLC's report, *The Collapse of Commuter Service,* was prepared under the direction of Patrick McLaughlin, a member of NLC's staff serving as Philadelphia's "Man in Washington," and was published that fall. It estimated that if New York, Chicago, Boston, Philadelphia, and Cleveland, the five cities surveyed, were to lose their rail commuter service, then a highway program adequate to handle motor vehicle traffic as a replacement for the rail service would cost $31 billion.

The Eastern railroad executives and the mayors met again as a joint committee at NLC's annual convention in Denver in November, and Dilworth gained the association's endorsement of a long-term low-interest federal loan program for maintenance and extension of all types of mass-transportation systems and for a study of the desirability of federal grants to improve mass transit. He also got the endorsement of the executive committee of the Conference of Mayors at its meeting the following January.

McLaughlin arranged to have a bill drafted to that effect early in 1960. It would have created a corporation in the Department of Commerce authorized to purchase bonds or make loans at 1 percent interest to public bodies for the acquisition, maintenance, and improvement of mass-transit facilities and equipment in metropolitan areas. Because it involved the Department of Commerce, such legislation would be referred for consideration to the Commerce Committees in both House and Senate. A number of representatives from urban areas introduced the bill in the House, but the chairman of the Senate Commerce Committee, Warren G. Magnuson of Washington, was uninterested.

Mayor Raymond R. Tucker of Saint Louis had been elected president of NLC at its Denver meeting, and in February 1960 he led a one-day "blitz" in Washington to acquaint the leadership of both legislative and executive branches of the federal government with the plight of mass-transit service in metropolitan areas and to seek their support of the program proposed by the Dilworth committee. Tucker, Dilworth, Wagner of New York, Celebrezze of Cleveland, and Governor David L. Lawrence of Pennsylvania, accompanied by several railroad presidents, held a series of joint meetings around the capital. At the White House they met with top presidential assistants and officials of the Bureau of the Budget; at the Department of Commerce they met with the Secretary; at the Capitol they met successively with Speaker of the House Sam Rayburn, House Minority Leader Charles Halleck, Senate Majority Leader Lyndon Johnson, and Minority Leader Everett Dirksen. Then they appeared as a group before the full House Commerce Committee at a special meeting called for the purpose.

This all generated considerable understanding and press attention, but after a month of further unsuccessful efforts to obtain the support of Senator Magnuson, a new strategy was devised to bypass the Commerce Committees and have the matter considered as an urban issue by the Housing Subcommittees of the Banking and Currency Committees. Senator Harrison Williams of New Jersey, a member of the Senate Subcommittee on Housing, took the lead. His legislative assistant, ArDee Ames, working closely with McLaughlin and others, drafted a new bill, which gave emphasis to the impact of transportation on urban development and the need for its consideration in urban planning. Williams introduced it in late March, and Senator Sparkman held hearings in May. Although the bill passed the Senate with little opposition, it died in the House committee. The following year, however, the Williams measure did become law as part of the Housing Act of 1961, and federal aid for mass transit became a reality. An administration bill to expand the program in 1962 passed the Senate and was approved by the House Committee on Banking and Currency but died in the House Rules Committee, which refused to report it for a vote by members of the House.

A new effort in 1963 was again successful in the Senate but was again thwarted in the House by refusal of the Rules Committee to report it for floor action. At this point the coalition that had been assembled by the National League of Cities and the Conference of Mayors in support of these measures decided to employ a coordinator to assist their efforts to move the bill out of the Rules Committee. In addition to the railroads, this coalition included the American Transit Association, the Rapid Transit Institute, and supplier industries. They created the Urban Passenger Transportation Association and retained Laurence Henderson as the coordinator for the group. With important help from Republican Congressman William Widnall of New Jersey, Congressman Albert Rains prevailed on Speaker McCormack to request a rule, the Rules Committee finally reported the bill in May, the House passed it in late June, the Senate approved the House version, and President Johnson signed it into law on July 9. With a strong supporting cast of actors from both inside and outside Congress, the mayors had given another sterling performance on the national stage. Royce Hanson has written a splendid account of the whole story in an excellent case history, "Congress Copes with Mass Transit, 1960–64."[5]

While the mass-transit drama was proceeding, another act was being written. This dealt with the creation of a cabinet Department of Urban Affairs. A case history by Judith Heimlich Parris[6] credits the first written proposal for such an agency to Philip Kates, who in a 1912 article for *American City* called for a federal department of municipalities. Reflecting the concerns of the muckrakers, he declared: "Municipal government has been our national failure." Kates urged Congress to create a department that would study municipal conditions in the United States and abroad. Apparently there was no response to the suggestion for another twenty-five years, not until the President's Committee on Administrative Management of 1937, headed by Louis Brownlow, recommended that the Bureau of the Budget assume responsibility for coordinating urban affairs programs. The same year, the National Resources Committee called for an urban policy coordinator. In 1942 Charles E. Merriam, who sat on both committees, urged the creation of a federal bureau, or department, to deal with urban affairs. Judith Parris cites the National Housing Conference as the first "interest group" to propose a department along the lines ultimately considered by Congress. In 1952 the NHC advocated a department as an institutional mechanism for coordinating community development in its broadest aspects. For a different reason, Thomas P. Coogan, former president of the National Association of Home Builders, in 1953 called for the elevation of the Housing and Home Finance Administration to cabinet status. He said it would help assure adequate housing for all Americans and make home ownership possible for more people.

The mayors did not get into this act until the 1955 annual congress of the National League of Cities, where Richardson Dilworth, newly elected to succeed Joseph Clark as mayor of Philadelphia, urged the delegates to endorse the idea of a Department of Urban Affairs, but it was not until 1958 that the league adopted the proposal as part of its official National Municipal Policy.

The first such bill in Congress, introduced in 1955 by Representative J. Arthur Younger, Republican from California, called for a Department of Urbiculture. Along with three other similar bills introduced in that Congress, it died in committee.

In 1957 the President's Advisory Committee on Government Operations, headed by Nelson Rockefeller, reported that a Department of Urban Affairs was greatly needed and suggested that

HHFA be the basis for it. That same year Albert Rains of Alabama introduced a bill on the subject.

The Eisenhower administration was not receptive to the idea of a cabinet Department of Urban Affairs. One of the arguments used in its favor by its advocates, including the National Housing Conference, was that such a department could "coordinate" all federal activities having an impact on urban development. It was not a good argument. As Presidential Assistant Robert E. Merriam said in a speech to the National League of Cities' annual congress in New York in 1960, only the President can "coordinate" activities scattered in different agencies and departments—a line department cannot coordinate activities of other operating agencies. Merriam advised the league not to spend its energies in that direction. But the mayors were not to be put off. They wanted a voice for the cities at the cabinet table.

However, presidential support came with the election of John F. Kennedy in 1960. Although he had not been a particularly urban-oriented member of Congress while serving in either the House or the Senate, he became very much urban-oriented as a presidential candidate and then as President. He knew that beginning with the New Deal, Democratic Presidents had been elected because of large pluralities among big-city voters. During his campaign he publicly committed himself to support the creation of a Department of Urban Affairs.

In December 1960 Richardson Dilworth and Mayor Don Hummel of Tucson, presidents respectively of the Conference of Mayors and the National League of Cities, met with President-elect Kennedy in New York to urge that he give high priority to the establishment of a department. Again in January they met with White House staff members to press that point. However, there were other important items on the new President's agenda of objectives, and the urban department was not high on the list. Likewise, considerable apathy about the proposal developed in Congress after Dr. Robert Weaver was appointed administrator of HHFA. Some Southern members did not relish the idea of voting for what in effect would be the elevation of a Negro to the cabinet. And in spite of resolutions of support by state leagues of municipalities across the country and direct testimony by Alabama League director Ed E. Reid that the bill would be of more benefit to small and medium-sized cities than it would to the big ones, the measure became tagged as a "big-city" bill. Even so, the administration bills were approved by the committees in both House and Senate, but the Rules Committee effectively bottled it up in the House, and the measure was as good as dead.

Nor did Congress pass matters of higher priority to the Kennedy administration in 1961, such as medical care for the aged through Social Security and federal aid to education. The following year saw no improvement in White House dealings with Congress. An attempt to bypass the House Rules Committee by submitting an executive reorganization plan to upgrade HHFA to cabinet status met with a decisive defeat. The administration lost for reasons of procedure, partisanship, racial antagonism, and rural opposition. In addition, there was no significant grass-roots support for the proposed cabinet unit. In her detailed account Judith Parris states: "The nation's mayors were perhaps the foremost allies of the Administration." But they could take no bows for that performance.

Early in 1963, Boston's Mayor John F. Collins, then vice-president of the National League of Cities, asked NLC's executive director to request an appointment with President Kennedy— just a courtesy call to have his picture taken with the President. The arrangement was made, and the President received the two NLC officers in the Oval Office. After the picture-taking and an exchange of pleasantries, the conversation turned to the Department of Urban Affairs. Kennedy assured the visitors that he was going to keep trying. At this point NLC's director suggested that the President establish an urban affairs coordinator in the White House or an office of urban affairs in the Executive Office of the President that would rank equally with the Bureau of the Budget. A new department, he suggested, could not coordinate urban affairs activities throughout the government—only the President could do that—and such an office would be valuable even if Congress should eventually approve a department. The President reflected a moment and then said, "I think we'll try the department route again first, and if it fails again, then we may try your idea."

Kennedy's assassination that fall ended the effort for the time being. But after the election of 1964 brought new faces to the House and Senate, President Johnson came on strong. Passage of the 1964 Civil Rights Act made the naming of Robert Weaver as secretary of a new department seem a less important race relations matter. Furthermore, there was a growing public consensus in 1965 supporting federal responsibility for the alleviation of urban problems. The climate was better, and Congress approved a proposal for an urban department that was almost identical to one defeated in 1961 and 1962. President Johnson signed the bill on September 9, 1965, and appointed Robert Weaver as the first Secretary of Housing and Urban Development on January 13, 1966. He named Robert C. Wood undersecretary.

In 1959 Ed E. Reid, the politically minded executive director of the Alabama League of Municipalities, suggested that NLC should present an identical urban plank to the platform committees of both parties, at the Democratic National Convention by Democratic mayors and at the Republican National Convention by Republican mayors. NLC's executive committee approved the proposal early in 1960 and invited the United States Conference of Mayors to join NLC in making it a joint effort. Many of the mayors' proposals were written into the Democratic platform that year, due in no small measure to the fact that James L. Sundquist, the urban-oriented assistant to Senator Joseph Clark of Pennsylvania, was secretary of the platform committee. However, there was no such strategically located personnel in the Republican platform committee, and the Republican mayors left its meetings thoroughly frustrated. The year 1964 was no better for the Republicans. In 1968, however, the Republican party adopted a complete urban plank, and both parties have been showing increasing attention to urban problems, largely as a result of better advance staff work by NLC and USCM in preparation for the mayors' appearances before platform committees.

The role of the National League of Cities in the enactment of the antipoverty legislation and of other measures has been described in previous chapters. There have been many other instances of the flexing of municipal muscle in Washington. The records abound in examples of the growing city hall lobbying efforts, the importance of elected city officials in working for the goals of cities, and the changing role of the federal government in urban affairs. Enough have been described here to corroborate the observation of Professor Frederic N. Cleaveland: "The change in federal policy on urban development accomplished between 1954 and 1964 was dramatic, even revolutionary."[7]

Performing on the national stage, Mayors Don Hummel of Tucson (left) and Richardson Dilworth of Philadelphia (right), presidents, respectively, of the National League of Cities and the U.S. Conference of Mayors, conferred with President-elect John F. Kennedy in December 1960 to urge his support of establishing a cabinet department of urban affairs.

The Long, Hot Sixties—Innovation and Turmoil

Financial analysts at the turn of the decade were heralding the advent of the "Soaring Sixties." National magazine cover stories sought to set the stage for an impending boom. The boom came, but not on schedule, and the economy did not really soar, in the hindsight judgment of some analysts, until after escalation of the Vietnam War in 1965.

As John F. Kennedy was inaugurated in 1961, "more men and women were out of work than at any previous time since World War II," wrote James L. Sundquist, reflecting as a scholar at the Brookings Institution on a period in which he was an active practitioner.[1] By February 1961, unemployment reached 5.4 million—the highest total in twenty years. And the national mood, as reflected in the writings of such widely read opinion-shapers as Henry R. Luce, John W. Gardner, Walter Lippmann, and Adlai Stevenson, mirrored the economic gloom.

In Pennsylvania, one worker out of ten was out of work, and in some coal counties the ratio was twice that high. It is not surprising that Pennsylvania Senator Joseph S. Clark, facing a hard reelection campaign, yearned for a presidential blessing for two pending bills: one which would provide retraining for the unemployed and a public works bill offered originally as a standby measure to be used in event of recession.[2] Early in 1961, Clark, a former mayor of Philadelphia, introduced revised versions of both bills and held hearings in seven cities. He found a substantial area of bipartisan support for assistance for the retraining of workers who had been thrown out of jobs because of the economic dip, automation, or some other kind of industrial dislocation. It took Clark slightly more than a year to resolve differences between those who advocated on-the-job training and those who favored vocational school training and to muster support from an administration more inclined to rely on fiscal remedies to end the slump. The Senate passed the measure, the Manpower Development and Training Act, in August 1961, and the House passed an almost identical version shortly after Congress reconvened in 1962. In signing it, President Kennedy called it "perhaps the most significant legislation in the area of employment since the historic Employment Act of 1946."

Though industrial cities benefited from the retraining provisions of the act from the outset, it was not until 1974 that mayors were able to exert much influence on what was by then a substantial cluster of manpower programs. A reorganization by the Nixon administration that year made mayors of cities over 100,-000 population the prime coordinators for regional manpower programs.

On February 20, 1961, in introducing a public works bill patterned after the Public Works Administration of the Depression era, Senator Clark said: "There is hardly a community in the country that does not have a backlog of public works."[3] The nation's mayors, growing somewhat impatient at what many regarded as undue insistence by Kennedy on fiscal prudence, couldn't have agreed more. A $1 billion community facilities lending measure had won the support of mayors and governors during the 1957–58 recession and had passed the Senate but died in the House. Hugh Mields, then assistant director for federal affairs of the National League of Cities, persuaded Clark that loans, which cities could obtain privately, would likely not generate much enthusiasm from the cities in 1961. He convinced Clark to include in the bill grants to allow cities to step up their public works programs.

NLC stimulated strong support for the bill among mayors and

leagues of municipalities, but the President again had to be persuaded. With recovery from the winter economic doldrums sluggish at best, Kennedy yielded to pressure and asked Congress to authorize $600 million for public works expenditures in areas of heavy unemployment. The House increased the authorization to $900 million and passed the bill, which was quickly accepted by the Senate. The President approved, and the Accelerated Public Works Act became law on September 14, 1962.

But it was a tax cut enacted in Congress in 1964 that began to pull the nation out of its economic slump. The measure was regarded as a major economic turning point. The government took in $4 billion more in fiscal 1965 than in the previous year. The stimulus provided by the tax cut continued through its fifth year without a downturn. Unemployment declined to 4.5 percent of the labor force, the lowest rate since October 1957. Economists predicted that the upward trend in the economy would provide continued increases in revenue, starting at $7 billion annually and rising, provided Congress disposed of the increase through pump-priming expenditures or further tax cuts.

In retrospect, the economic dips of the late 1950s and early 1960s were just ripples in the steady postwar rise of the economy since the end of World War II. The nation became so obsessed with abundance in the late 1950s and early 1960s that it was easy for many to misinterpret the title of John Kenneth Galbraith's critique of unbridled production of consumer goods and to trumpet the ascendency of "the affluent society." The publication in 1962 of *The Other America* by Michael Harrington focused the attention of the nation on an area of severe underconsumption in an otherwise comfortable society. Harrington attacked what he termed "an implicit assumption that the basic grinding economic problems had been solved in the United States." Not only are the poor neglected and forgotten, they are invisible, Harrington argued. "In short," he wrote, "the very development of the American city has removed poverty from the living, emotional experience of millions upon millions of middle-class Americans. Living out in the suburbs, it is easy to assume that ours is, indeed, an affluent society."[4] Harrington's treatise and others in a similar vein that were soon to follow struck a responsive chord in John Kennedy, whose own sense of outrage over poverty has repeatedly been traced to his impressions while campaigning in depressed areas of West Virginia. What he would have done about it had he not been assassinated will remain a matter of conjecture.

Accounts of the mobilization of the War on Poverty abound among Washington insiders of the early 1960s. Walter W. Heller, chairman of the Council of Economic Advisers, told a Pennsylvania audience some time later that the President gave the "green light" for his aides to pull together a set of proposals to counteract poverty a month before his fateful trip to Dallas in November 1963. The concept was eagerly embraced by Lyndon Johnson soon after his hasty inauguration as President. Among the participants in the planning at that time were David Hackett of the President's Committee on Juvenile Delinquency, officials of the Bureau of the Budget, and Richard W. Boone, a representative of the Ford Foundation's "gray areas" program. That program had already spawned some early models for what became Community Action Agencies, the local administrative vehicle conceived to carry out the major thrust of antipoverty efforts. A proposal for a few carefully chosen demonstrations was abandoned as not compatible with the President's call for an "unconditional" war on poverty.

A later phase of planning was conducted by a task force headed by Sargent Shriver, John F. Kennedy's brother-in-law, who headed the Peace Corps. Shriver had been tapped by Johnson to head the poverty war. As the legislation took shape, titles were added to authorize a Job Corps, a Neighborhood Youth Corps, and Volunteers in Service to America, the latter a domestic counterpart of the Peace Corps. President Johnson won a significant victory for the bill in both House and Senate, but many legislators expressed concern about the speed with which the bill was moved through both houses. The National League of Cities' role has been told in Chapter 10. Nevertheless, the poverty war was under way. "But it was, as it had been declared, the Administration's war, not a national war behind which the country was united," Sundquist wrote.[5]

Two years later, it still had not become a part of the national consensus. One of the functions of the Community Action Agencies, as envisioned by the national strategists, was to make established institutions, including city halls, more responsive to the needs of the poor. In many cities, however, as we have seen in Chapter 10, CAA leaders and municipal officials coexisted in an atmosphere of mutual hostility, communicating only during confrontations.

In 1967 Mayor William G. Walsh of Syracuse, New York, told a Senate subcommittee that the program of a Syracuse University training center for community action workers, funded directly from Washington, was "a horrible example of how not to handle federal-local relations." Instead of teaching people how to combat poverty, Walsh said, the program's directors taught them "how to agitate and attack city hall, and Albany, and Washington."[6]

However, Mayor Richard C. Lee of New Haven, whose city had a Community Action Agency two years before the Economic Opportunity Act was passed, and Detroit Mayor Jerome P. Cavanagh supported the concept in testimony before another Senate subcommittee. Cavanagh, then president of both the National League of Cities and the United States Conference of Mayors, strongly endorsed participation of the poor in the program.[7]

In retrospect, clashes between some city halls and Community Action Agencies were inevitable. Howard W. Hallman, who helped shape Community Progress Inc. under Lee in New Haven, has noted that the organization of CAAs and their emphasis on citizen participation came during a period of transition in the civil rights movement—between the Civil Rights Act of 1964 and the first significant use of the term "black power." In a paper given at a 1969 conference he wrote:

In many places civil rights leaders were gearing up to gain a larger role in local programs. Along came the Community Action Program tailor-made for their desires. Moreover, the key OEO staff within the Commu-

nity Action Program and the Office of Inspection were more than sympathetic, for they possessed deep suspicion of municipal government and
other parts of local "establishments." They were talking about power of
the poor.[8]

Thus was the stage set in many communities for confrontations that led to passage by Congress of the Green Amendment
in 1967, giving local governments the option of becoming the
Community Action Agency or designating a private body to run
the program. Ultimately, as Chapter 10 also notes, many municipal governments assimilated OEO-funded functions that they
found useful or that they could not avoid supporting for political
reasons.

The antipoverty program was just one of the more complex of
the programs that were part of the outpouring of legislation that
formed the administrative structure of what President Johnson
proclaimed as the Great Society.

The Model Cities program, authorized by the Demonstration
Cities and Metropolitan Development Act of 1966, required an
even more sophisticated administrative structure than the OEO
programs. Like the antipoverty act, however, it was a product of
a White House task force. Formed in 1965, the group was chaired
by MIT political scientist Robert Wood, soon to become undersecretary of the newly formed Department of Housing and Urban Development. Mayor Cavanagh was the spokesman for local
government on the nine-man panel that included business, labor, and civil rights representatives and other urban academi-
cians.

Mayor Cavanagh envisioned a demonstration by a single city,
and other panelists thought in terms of demonstrations in a
dozen or less cities. Records showing what kind of consensus the
task force reached on that point are not available. But whatever
the group's recommendations may have been, they were translated into expansive language by President Johnson in his January 1966 special message on cities, the first one an American
President had devoted to urban problems as distinct from housing.

The Demonstration Cities programs,* he said, "would set in motion forces of change in great urban areas that will make them the masterpieces of our civilization." He proposed a "massive demonstration program." In the bill he sent to Congress, "massive" turned out to be sixty or seventy.

The bill generated little enthusiasm in or out of Congress until the executive directors of the National League of Cities and the United States Conference of Mayors called on Senator Edmund S. Muskie and persuaded him to manage it on the Senate floor.

The League of Cities and Mayors Conference had been cool to the original bill, mainly because it was regarded as competition for federal funding of urban renewal. Though Cavanagh sat on the task force, the two groups had not been involved collectively in its deliberations. Neither group had any organizational policy in support of the measure, and their congressional relations staffs wanted to oppose the bill, as did NLC's executive committee. They were restrained from doing so only by the persuasion of NLC's executive director that the concept was a good one and that more time should be given to develop a better understanding of the proposal. Their support warmed somewhat when HUD Secretary Robert Weaver told a Dallas meeting of the Conference that he would press for exclusive funds for urban renewal to preclude a drain-off of such funds by the selected Model Cities. The League and Conference again formed a coalition of Washington-based interest groups with strong stakes in urban legislation to coordinate support for the revamped bill. This loosely knit coalition met periodically to count votes on key issues and hear administration status reports. The bill coasted through the Senate, then was passed by the House with a comfortable margin after narrowly surviving a motion to delete most of its funds.

Then the urban alliance turned to the much tougher task of securing appropriations for the program. By May the House and Senate had compromised on a figure of $312 million. Three weeks later, HUD named sixty-three cities (twelve were added

*The term Model Cities was chosen later to avoid the connotation the word "demonstration" gained as a result of urban unrest.

later) to get grants for planning, the first phase of a five-year cycle in the comprehensive improvement programs the legislation authorized.

The watchword for the Model Cities program was coordination. Its conceptualizers envisioned careful coordination among the federal agencies administering it at the national level, to be matched by coordination of functions by municipal governments and private sector groups in the cities.

Actually, coordination was the watchword for the basic strategy behind what President Johnson called "creative federalism." Many programs were designed to be implemented in stages after relatively long periods of planning. In some, efforts were made, sometimes belatedly, to encourage state governments to make greater commitments to urban problem-solving.

Because of these complex requirements, and because Congress was lavish with authorizations but, by comparison, parsimonious with appropriations, implementation often moved slowly. There was widespread impatience on Capitol Hill and among the public. The feeling grew that the executive branch, armed with an arsenal of programs, lacked the sense of urgency to deal with what had become known as the "urban crisis." Federal bureaucrats were not the only officials asked to account for their performance.

Beginning in 1966, the whole complex of urban problems—and the national response or lack of it—was flashed before the American people as Senator Abraham Ribicoff of Connecticut opened a long series of hearings on the urban crisis.[9] Mayors, addicts, cabinet officers, and social scientists were among the seventy-seven witnesses who looked into the cameras and revealed their efforts to relieve the pains of the cities.

It was the explosion on the streets of Watts, no doubt, that prodded the networks into airing those unusual hearings and shocked the nation into watching them. Thirty-four persons had been killed, more than one thousand injured, and almost four thousand arrested in six days of burning and looting in that low-density Los Angeles ghetto. It had begun August 11 when a highway patrolman halted a young Negro driver in Los Angeles. There was a crowd, rising tempers, arrests, retaliation, rock throwing, torching, overturning of cars, attacks on motorists. These grim ingredients were to be stirred over and over again in cities for the next five years.

The civil disorders of the sixties actually started at least two years before Watts. Police battled civil rights demonstrators with fire hoses and cattle prods in 1963 in Birmingham, where a bomb in a Negro church killed four young girls in a Sunday school class.

In 1964, four persons were killed and 350 injured in two days of rioting in Rochester, New York. A New York City riot killed one person and injured 144, and disorders were recorded in five other cities.

Forcible interruption of nonviolent civil rights demonstrations in Selma, Alabama, shifted the focus of the nation back to the South in the spring of 1965. Elsewhere in the nation there had been few disturbances until the Watts riots, the worst in the United States since federal troops quelled a disturbance in Detroit in 1943.

By 1966 the country had come to await the approach of the warm weather with anxiety. Pulse-taking to determine the prospects for a "long, hot summer" had become routine for the media. There were also numerous press accounts about the accumulation of antiriot weaponry by police forces. The Lemberg Center for the Study of Violence was established at Brandeis University to conduct systematic research on urban disorders and other forms of violence.

The "long, hot summers" continued. A skirmish on July 12, 1966, between police and Negro youngsters over the illegal opening of a fire hydrant touched off several days and nights of rioting in Chicago. Stray bullets killed three blacks, including a thirteen-year-old boy and a fourteen-year-old pregnant girl, before police and National Guard troops restored order. Less than a week later, rioting in Cleveland's Hough area left four dead and many injured.

Urban disorders swelled to their most intensive level in 1967 and occurred in more than eighty cities. Beginning early in June, rioting flared in Tampa, Cincinnati, Atlanta, Newark, and Detroit. These were among the twenty-four disorders in twenty-three cities surveyed by the National Advisory Commission on Civil Disorders, named by President Johnson at the height of the disturbances.[10]

In Newark twenty-three persons were killed and damages totaled $10.2 million, four-fifths of it attributed to loss of merchandise. In Detroit, where forty-three persons were killed, the city assessor's office estimated damage at $22 million. Cities fortunate enough to escape actual disorder were never free of the tension that usually prevailed from May through September.

Nobody was prepared for the intensity of the violence that swept through the cities in 1967. But the mayors and those who sought solutions to urban problems had recognized the rising levels of tension. They were very much aware that the mayors alone could not solve the underlying social, racial, and economic problems and that the leadership of business and other private-sector groups should be solicited to join an effort that should be coordinated outside the National League of Cities and United States Conference of Mayors. An ideal coordinating agency could be the newly organized Urban America, Inc., successor to ACTION (American Council to Improve Our Neighborhoods), whose purpose was to stimulate involvement of business leaders to improve housing conditions in the inner cities. Late in 1966, a series of meetings took place among the staffs of the three organizations. In January, the mayors of Atlanta, Baltimore, Boston, Denver, Detroit, Miami, Milwaukee, New York, Philadelphia, Pittsburgh, and Tacoma met in Washington, D.C., with Andrew Heiskell, publisher of *Life*, and other leaders at the invitation of the late Stephen R. Currier, founder and president of Urban America, Inc. They discussed the problems that faced them and concluded that it was time for all those who shared a stake in the well-being of cities to join a coalition to alert the nation about the critical nature of urban problems. Such a coalition, they agreed, should include all major segments of society— business, civil rights groups, labor, and religion—as well as municipal government. A series of meetings was begun with representatives of these groups, and a timetable called for formation of the coalition in the fall.

Only a few of those meetings had been held by the time Newark and Detroit started burning. Clearly the methodical approach to formation of the alliance would be too slow. Mayors Joseph Barr of Pittsburgh and John V. Lindsay of New York, acting as cochairmen of the dozen mayors who met in January, asked leaders in the five fields chosen as the components of a coalition to meet on July 31 in the Washington offices of Urban America. Thirty-four attended or conveyed their support. They became the steering committee of the Urban Coalition.

Because of a malfunctioning air-conditioning system, these men, some of the most powerful in America, assembled in shirtsleeves amid rumors of violence in the streets of the capital.

A special supplement to *City,* Urban America's bimonthly review, gave this account of the conference scene:

> There was tension in the room, too, at the outset: some of the participants—business and labor, mayors and civil rights leaders—were used to sitting opposite the table from each other, rather than side by side. But there was also a tangible sense of urgency, commonly felt. It was this sense of urgency that held the Urban Coalition together, that night and in the weeks thereafter.[11]

The Urban Coalition's first formal statement was a product of high-level draftsmanship. It was a composite of notes scribbled at the conference table by such representatives as David Rockefeller, Walter Reuther, and John Lindsay. It called for a reordering of national priorities, a theme that had been at the top of the agendas of the National League of Cities and Conference of Mayors for three years. It called on Congress to enact immediately a federal work and training program for the poor while pledging expansion of private-sector employment efforts.

The statement stressed the need for physical and social reconstruction of American cities. Finally, the founders called for an emergency convocation in Washington, before the end of August, of a thousand leaders in the five segments of society represented in the July 31 meeting.

The convocation, held August 24, ratified a "declaration of principles" which embodied the basic proposals of the July 31 statement. The language of the proposals had been made more forceful and the goals more specific.

The declaration called for "one million new jobs in socially useful work for the now-unemployed," "loan funds to establish Negro business enterprise," and "annual production of at least a million housing units for low-income families."

The convocation heard speeches by Lindsay; Whitney Young, director of the National Urban League; AFL-CIO President George Meany; UAW President Walter Reuther, and other steering committee members. Unsolicited suggestions, abrasive but not hostile, came from Rufus ("Catfish") Mayfield, a twenty-year-old organizer of a federally financed summer work program, and Marion Barry, a community organizer who later became a successful candidate for District of Columbia elective offices. The assembly adjourned after calling for the creation of "counterpart local coalitions."

Seven months later, John Gardner, who had resigned as Secretary of Health, Education and Welfare, was persuaded to become chairman of the Urban Coalition. The new organization's original budget of $1.4 million was provided primarily by the Ford Foundation; its 1969 budget of $3.5 million was drawn from multiple sources. Gardner built a highly diversified staff which began to conduct research, publish documents, and monitor the implementation of urban programs by federal agencies. Meanwhile, Coalition field workers began to organize local coalitions. More than forty were in existence at one point.

The Advisory Commission on Civil Disorders had been at work for nearly two months when the Urban Coalition was formally organized. Called the Kerner Commission after its chairman, Illinois Governor Otto Kerner, it was charged by President Johnson to find answers to three basic questions: What happened? Why did it happen? What can be done to prevent it from happening again? New York's Mayor Lindsay was named vice-chairman.

The commission, delivering its report on March 1, 1968, said it had reached this basic conclusion: "Our nation is moving toward two societies, one black, one white—separate and unequal."[12] The commissioners rankled many of their countrymen with the judgment that "white society is deeply implicated in the ghetto. White institutions created it, white institutions maintain it, and white society condones it."

The report suggested that the nation has three choices: (1) to continue the existing level of allocation of resources to the unemployed and disadvantaged and what it called "inadequate and failing" efforts toward an integrated society; (2) to adopt a policy of "enrichment" for ghetto areas, "while abandoning integration as a goal;" or (3) to pursue integration by combining ghetto "enrichment" with a policy that will encourage Negro movement out of central cities. "We believe," the report added, "that the only possible choice for America is the third."

The report included these other recommendations:

To relieve unemployment, it urged the federal government to take steps to create 2 million jobs—a million each in the public and private sectors—and tax incentives for jobs in poverty areas.

To correct disparities in education in impoverished areas, it recommended sharply increased efforts to eliminate de facto segregation in schools and a range of steps to enrich education for disadvantaged children.

To remedy deficiencies in the welfare system, the report urged uniform national standards of assistance and assumption by the federal government of at least 90 percent of total payments. As a long-range goal, the commission recommended development of a national system of income supplementation.

For the improvement of housing, the commission advocated a federal open housing law to cover the sale and rental of all housing. It called for increases in housing subsidies for low- and

FURNITURE
WILLIAMS
APPLIANCES
NCELLATION
SHOES
THE ENTIRE FAMILY
ENS SHOES TO SIZE 12
CANCELLATION
SHOES

Detroit's Twelfth Street burns in 1967 during the black rioting that struck many cities throughout the nation.

Wide World

moderate-income families and for expansion of public housing, Model Cities, and urban renewal programs. The aim of those efforts, it said, was to bring within the reach of low- and moder-ate-income families within five years 6 million units of decent housing, beginning with 600,000 units in the next year.

Measured by the usual level of readership of government docu-ments, the report was a runaway best seller. Almost 2 million copies of the government and private paperback editions have been sold. It generated an unusual amount of commentary in the press and in the flood of election-year rhetoric getting under way just as it came off the press. It is impossible to characterize atti-tudes toward the report. For those who accepted the commis-sion's analysis of the riots as the predictable (though not justifi-able) reaction by blacks to insurmountable odds, the report was embraced as a basic document of social reform. Others felt that the commission's concern about the "root causes" of disorders unwisely diverted the attention of the nation from the lamenta-ble consequences of the riots. Still others, regardless of their view about the commission's findings and recommendations, rejected its indictment of "white racism."

President Johnson chose to give the report no official recogni-tion. He felt, an aide said later, that it "over-dramatized the white racism theme" and was "counter-productive in terms of pro-grams for society as a whole."[13]

Scarcely more than a month after the release of the commis-sion's report, violence erupted again in the cities, touched off by the assassination of civil rights leader Dr. Martin Luther King at a Memphis hotel. This time there was burning and looting in the streets of Washington, a city many had considered immune to rioting. Columns of smoke were visible from the White House, and some of the 12,000 troops sent into the District of Columbia to bolster the police patrolled the Capitol grounds as the House of Representatives met to vote on the Civil Rights Act of 1968.

The act contained a fair-housing section which, with staged enforcement, would ultimately ban nearly all discrimination in the sale and rental of housing. When Johnson insisted on including that broad prohibition in the civil rights bill he sent to Congress in January, there were warnings it would be deleted and that it might even doom the bill. But on a crucial April 10 roll call the House voted, 229 to 195, to accept a Senate version of the bill containing an open-housing provision. It was that vote, many believe, that assured final passage. Press accounts attributed the bill's passage to reaction by congressmen and their constituents to the assassination of Dr. King and to the atmosphere in the capital in the wake of events that followed it.

In Washington and in the other cities in which post-assassination rioting took place, the fires burned with the same ferocity as in 1967. Police in those cities were reinforced by some 68,000 National Guard and Army troops. Curfews were enforced and there were massive arrests, but little use was made of antiriot arsenals that had been widely described in the press. The troops were not responsible for a single fatality.

The low death rate was attributed in part, at least, to a series of closed meetings in January and February at a conference center near Washington, attended by police chiefs and other officials of 120 cities. In the meetings, sponsored by the Justice Department, representatives of the International Association of Chiefs of Police briefed the officials on a new strategy of stopping violence with a large display of force and mass arrests instead of shooting.

Before the troops were deployed, looters and arsonists in Washington had already inflicted much of the $19 million damage caused in nearly four days of rioting. Some affected businessmen, black and white, questioned the policy of restraint, but the president of the Board of Trade defended it. Noting a debate that the new strategy had generated among city officials around the country, *City* magazine commented that it "took from black extremists the argument that white society is bent on genocide [and] ... gave the cities a way to survive limited and sporadic civil disorder without raising it to the level of civil war."[14]

Disorders continued into the early 1970s, but they declined in frequency and intensity after 1968.

It became clear during the presidential campaign of 1968 that Richard Nixon had concluded that the Great Society programs of the Johnson administration were too complex, too costly, and required too much administration from Washington. Soon after his inauguration he called for the return of "power to the people." What this meant in terms of federal-state-local relationships was spelled out more clearly in his 1971 State of the Union message: "The time has come to reverse the flow of power and resources from the states and communities to Washington, and start power and resources flowing back from Washington to the states and communities and, more important, to the people, all across America."

Despite the new administration's aversion for narrowly defined categorical grants, the transition from the Great Society to Nixon's New Federalism was more gradual than many in the capital and in the cities expected. The Model Cities program, which perhaps provided for the fullest indulgence of President Johnson's penchant for coordination from Washington, was subjected to close evaluation. It was examined by two task forces—a pre-inaugural group headed by Richard Nathan, a veteran Washington administrator now on the staff of the Brookings Institution, and another chaired by Harvard professor Edward Banfield.

The Nathan group said the Model Cities structure should be made "the accepted instrument for the entire federal government—not just HUD—for coordinating assistance to designated model neighborhoods." The Banfield team urged radical decentralization and extensive changes in funding. Fears that the program would be dismantled soon dissipated, although it took concerted action by mayors of cities containing target neighborhoods, plus the League of Cities and Conference of Mayors, to avert a major diversion of funds early in 1970.

Coordination was prized no less in the Nixon administration than in Johnson's. The styles, however, were significantly different. Johnson sought to mandate coordination within the federal bureaucracy through legislative mandate and program guidelines. The new administration seemed more inclined to coordinate programs from the Office of the President. To operate out of that office, Nixon appointed a Council of Urban Affairs, describing it as the counterpart of the National Security Council. The purpose of the new council, then-Transportation Secretary John Volpe told a "Meet the Press" panel of newsmen, was to permit "an interdisciplinary approach to these complex problems in the urban field."[15]

The President surprised many Washington observers by naming as head of the Urban Affairs Council Daniel Patrick Moynihan. Long identified as a liberal Democrat, Moynihan came to the White House from the Harvard-MIT Joint Center for Urban Studies, of which he was director. As an assistant secretary of the Department of Labor in the Johnson administration, he became embroiled in a controversy with civil rights leaders over a report he wrote on the Negro family. His presidential appointment almost coincided with the publication of his latest book, *Maximum Feasible Misunderstanding,* a critical analysis of the concept of citizen participation.

Accompanying the President to Indianapolis in April 1970 for a meeting with nine mayors, Moynihan presented a ten-point urban policy he had drafted. It described "poverty and social isolation of minority groups in central cities as the single most serious problem of the American city today" and called for "a greater commitment of resources [to that problem] than has heretofore been the case, and with programs designed especially for this purpose." Another point called for restoration of "fiscal vitality of urban government." It was never clear to what degree that draft represented the thinking of the President or other White House advisers.

Shortly after the Indianapolis trip, Moynihan was again the target of sharp criticism from black leaders after publication of memoranda he wrote the President. In one he used the term "benign neglect" to describe the policy he advised the administration to take toward racial issues. The memorandum cited a special Census Bureau study indicating that young, non-Southern Negro couples had attained income parity with whites. He described this and other economic gains by blacks as examples of "extraordinary progress." Reacting to the disclosure, a number of minority-group spokesmen declared that the gains minorities have made "were not won by benign neglect, but by courageous and aggressive action."

Moynihan was the chief architect of the President's family assistance plan, which would have guaranteed to every family, even if it included a wage earner, a basic annual income. It was through such aid to the working poor that the President hoped to fulfill his campaign pledge to "take people off welfare rolls and put them on payrolls." The administration tried unsuccessfully to get the plan through two sessions of Congress. On both occasions it failed to overcome the opposition of economy-minded legislators, competition from alternate plans offered by congressmen, and adamant resistance from groups representing welfare recipients, who said the proposed allowance was too low. After the second defeat of the plan, Moynihan resigned from the White House staff and shortly thereafter was named ambassador to India.

In the view of most municipal officials, no appointment by President Nixon was more significant than that of Floyd H. Hyde as an assistant secretary of the Department of Housing and Urban Development. Hyde, then vice-president of the National League of Cities, had been mayor of Fresno, California, for four years.

He and other mayors of both political parties, spearheaded by Milwaukee Mayor Henry W. Maier, had led an unsuccessful nationwide campaign to persuade President-elect Nixon to appoint this author to his cabinet as Secretary of HUD. It almost happened. According to one source close to Nixon, he had decided to make that appointment. George Romney was to be Secretary of Commerce. When Maurice Stans, Nixon's chief campaign fund raiser, discovered that he was not to be included in the cabinet, he and his friends raised such a storm of protest that Nixon decided he must accommodate him by naming him Secretary of

Commerce. Romney was moved to the HUD spot, and the candidate of the mayors was dropped.

Shortly after the new cabinet was announced, Moynihan called this author to relay a request of the President-elect for a meeting with a few city leaders of both parties, geographically scattered. He specifically asked that they include Carl B. Stokes of Cleveland, as a black mayor, and accepted the other suggestions: Mayors C. Beverly Briley of Nashville and Floyd Hyde of Fresno, respectively president and vice-president of the National League of Cities, Mayor Milton Graham of Phoenix, and the executive directors of NLC and the Conference of Mayors.

Nixon received the group on December 20 at the Hotel Pierre in New York, where he explained that his appointment of Moynihan indicated his interest in urban problems, that Moynihan would be the point of contact in the White House for the mayors and their two national organizations. After each of his visitors spoke briefly on previously assigned areas of city concern, emphasizing the need for federal revenue sharing, the President-elect said something like this:

"I want you to know that the problems of the cities will receive priority attention in my administration. Don't be concerned if it sometimes appears that other matters are distracting, such as possible trouble in the Middle East. Your problems will continue to stay on the front burner."

Awaiting his return plane to California at the New York airport, Floyd Hyde ran into his old friend Robert Finch, newly designated Secretary of HEW and close adviser of Nixon. It was that chance encounter that led to Finch's suggestion that Hyde be appointed assistant secretary of HUD, a suggestion readily approved by Nixon, who had been favorably impressed by Hyde at the Hotel Pierre meeting. When George Romney offered Hyde his choice of positions in the department, he chose the Model Cities program as the area where he could make the most constructive contribution based on his own successful experience in Fresno. The Model Cities program in most cities was in trouble. The previous administration had started it off wrong. Instead of a citywide coordination of all federal, state, and local programs under the direction of the city's chief executive and city council, it took the approach of the antipoverty program, with some of the same people administering it, focusing narrowly on only one or more blighted neighborhoods. Mayors were inclined to appoint a Model Cities director to run it like a Community Action Agency and then forget it. Hyde and Romney over the next four years turned it around, got the mayors personally briefed on objectives and methods in a series of regional conferences arranged by the League of Cities and Conference of Mayors, and contracted with the latter organizations to administer a Model Cities Service Center.

One of the many appraisals of the tumultuous sixties came from one of its most active practitioners. Back in the academic world whence he came, Robert C. Wood, who served as undersecretary and briefly as secretary of HUD, put many of his reflections on that decade into a series of lectures he delivered at Columbia University in 1970. They were published in a book, *The Necessary Majority: Middle America and the Urban Crisis,* in 1972.

Dr. Wood, now president of the University of Massachusetts, believes he has identified the basic flaw in the complex of programs he and his colleagues administered. In the absence of a majority committed to helping the cities, he declares, the Johnson administration achieved legislation through what he calls the "politics of innovation"—that is, the quiet collaboration of bureaucrats, legislators, and special interests to accomplish goals in a relatively isolated atmosphere. Majority backing for major urban innovations may yet be possible, Dr. Wood suggests, through policies that would bring order and justice into urban growth. These could include incentives for optimal industrial location, equalization of school expenditures, and tax policies that would recapture increased land values from public investments. "The final condition," he insists, "is that the majority as well as the minority be engaged."

A Look at the Future—Challenge!

The Watergate affair caused a temporary slowdown of what was emerging in the early 1970s as federal initiative to strengthen local government. President Nixon, through his New Federalism concept, was trying to reverse the traditional methods of centralizing all money distribution and decisionmaking powers in Washington. He was attempting to give local governments the discretion to define their problems, set their own priorities, and develop their own solutions.

He proposed to achieve this in four ways: First, by sharing a portion of the federal income tax with the states and local general-purpose governments to increase their general fiscal capacity —general revenue sharing. Second, by consolidating the numerous categories of federal grants in a given program area, such as community development, into one block grant to be distributed annually by formula for use in accordance with priorities established locally—special revenue sharing. Third, by strengthening the public welfare program through an income maintenance plan that would further ease the fiscal pressure on state and local governments. Fourth, by reorganizing and decentralizing the executive branch of the federal government.

This approach has been severely critized by some and greeted with latent hostility by others who have little confidence in local and state government and prefer to have stronger, nationally centralized controls. However, the New Federalism concept was enthusiastically approved by many state governors and legislators, mayors and city councilmen, and county officials. In fact, some Democratic mayors forsook their party's candidate in the 1972 presidential election to support, sometimes publicly, Nixon's reelection.

Fortunately, Nixon was able to make a good start on his program during his first term. With bipartisan support, Congress approved general revenue sharing. That was due in no small measure to the active support of Representative Wilbur D. Mills, Democrat of Arkansas and chairman of the House Ways and Means Committee, who made a complete 180-degree about-face on the issue from the position he expressed to this author at lunch in early 1967. "Congress will never approve taking the blame for federal taxes levied for governors and mayors to spend," he said flatly. "A bill like that will never get out of the Ways and Means Committee as long as I am chairman." Four years later he was its champion.

Mr. Nixon's proposal to consolidate seven domestic cabinet departments into four, each to be organized according to major purposes of government, did not progress beyond hearings in congressional committees. But he did succeed in restructuring by executive order the federal administrative regions of the country. Ten regions were defined, and the regional boundaries and headquarters cities of seventy-five of the most significant federal agencies and bureaus were made coterminous. He also decentralized the decisionmaking authority from Washington to these ten regions on ninety-nine federal assistance programs. To further improve the responsiveness of the federal government, he established the Federal Assistance Review (FAR), a systematic program conducted by fourteen major departments and agencies to streamline, simplify, and speed up the flow of federal assistance. An interagency steering group chaired by the Office of Management and Budget's Dwight A. Ink reduced processing time, cut red tape, and integrated the administration of grants-in-aid. The FAR program has also experimented with transferring to state and local governments the entire responsibility for carrying out all or parts of some federal assistance programs, especially where those governments already have had technical and administrative experience in providing similar services. To help upgrade their management capabilities, the Department of Housing and Urban Development has more than doubled funds for comprehensive planning and management assistance to states and cities, and in 1970 Congress passed the Intergovernmental Personnel Act to strengthen state and local personnel resources.

Congress made a beginning toward grant consolidation into special revenue sharing programs and was continuing the process even after Watergate weakened the President's influence. However, welfare reform remains for the future.

City government leaders will continue optimistically to press for reforms that strengthen local government and thereby buttress our federal system, a fact that is especially timely in these days of so much cynical pessimism. The basic institution for ensuring a strong democracy is strong general local government. Nobody challenges that. Yet the American people have a tendency to weaken general-purpose government in several ways. One is to restrict its powers to cope with change. Another is to impose tax and debt limitations. A third is to inhibit internal administrative reorganization. And still another is to bypass it in the assignment of some important local functions.

The best way to begin the strengthening of local government is to make it more responsible and responsive to the local voters. Even the most extreme right-wing anti-metro partisans ought to agree with that. They and others who oppose a "supergovernment" over a metropolitan area want control of local functions to be at the community level. But how can you control local functions if you take them out of the hands of the elected city or county officials and give them to independent agencies? That becomes "supergovernment" in its worst form, because responsibility is remote and diffused, and you weaken general local government.

The proliferation of special districts decreases local officials' ability to respond to public needs and removes incentives for

Allen E. Pritchard, Jr. became executive
vice-president of the National League of
Cities July 1, 1972.

John J. Gunther has been executive director of the United States Conference of
Mayors since 1961.

Chase Ltd.—Washington

accountability to the voters. Such districts bypass elected officials or strip them of local functions. The continued formation of single-purpose agencies to deal with problems as they arise diminishes the responsibilities of general local government, thereby diminishing its effectiveness.

Unfortunately, state-imposed restrictions often keep local governments from being responsive and, as a result, special districts are formed. Counties in particular are bound by state restrictions that make most of them inadequate as general units. With the exception of those few states that now permit counties to frame and adopt home rule charters, most states impose an antiquated governmental structure on them that does not permit executive responsibility and leadership or legislative flexibility. They should be granted legal means for internal administrative reorganization. Even more of an impediment is the requirement imposed on most of them to give uniform service throughout the county uniformly financed by a county-wide tax levy. If they were granted authorization to establish service and financing differentials, they could then provide more intensive services to the portions of the area that need them, and collect additional taxes or special charges from the people receiving them. Why incorporate separate, special districts to do the same thing?

Rigid tax and debt limitations imposed by some states on general local governments, both counties and cities, are another cause of the increasing number of special districts. These districts are often devices to get around such limitations. Hence, we get special districts with authority to undertake a self-financing facility such as an electric utility, a water system, or a toll bridge.

The federal government is responsible for the creation of many special districts by advocating or even requiring their formation as a prerequisite to federal grants for such programs as public housing and urban renewal in cities. During the 1930s, when the New Deal was anxious to start a public housing program, most cities did not have state statutory authority to construct and manage public housing. So legislation prepared in Washington was transmitted to state governors for introduction in the legislatures to provide a method for establishing special districts, in this case housing authorities. Each city council usually had to take affirmative action to establish the housing authority and the mayor appointed its corporate board of directors, but after that the city government had no operating responsibility. Perhaps many mayors and councilmen were just as glad to avoid the politically sensitive activity. Furthermore, the advocates of public housing argued that the function should be kept "out of politics," an argument frequently used to justify the formation of other types of special districts, including school districts.

Why shouldn't city government establish housing policy and operate housing programs? A regular city department of housing and urban development, responsible to the city's chief executive and to the elected city governing body, would likely have produced a much higher quality and quantity of subsidized low-rent housing in this country over the past forty years and with greater public understanding and support.

It is granted that the quality of housing projects suffered because of congressional policies that restricted their occupancy exclusively to low-income families or individuals, segregating tenants into ghettos for the poor and evicting those whose incomes increased above the poverty level. Among other bad effects, this often resulted in the breakup of families as the breadwinner deserted to allow his family to remain.

New support is gradually evolving for a change in this policy, and housing management is being improved under a program initiated by HUD during President Nixon's first term.

Yet public housing programs of whatever kind touch practically every phase of municipal government, including health, safety, recreation, public works, finance, and planning. As run by independent authorities, they produce substantial changes in the city pattern without adequate guidance and control by the city government. As long ago as 1952, an analysis of housing and redevelopment in Chicago by the Public Administration Service, a long-established independent consulting organization, found that local autonomous and semiautonomous agencies do not necessarily mean independence from political influence. Its report strongly supported the conviction that a municipal government does not progress toward responsible, honest, and efficient government by removing important functions from its elected chief executive and governing body. The same view was expressed the same year by the deputy administrator and general counsel of the United States Housing and Home Finance Agency, B. T. Fitzpatrick, a veteran in federal housing affairs. He attributed the sharp decline in public knowledge and acceptance of public housing in the three preceding years, since enactment of the Taft-Ellender-Wagner Housing Act of 1949, to the independence of local housing authorities. Local housing programs, he concluded, should be in city governmental politics in the sense of being a part of the city government, which is responsible and directly accountable to all its citizens for civic welfare.[1]

Somehow, when it comes to local government matters, Americans seem to believe they have to reinvent the wheel. They don't take enough advantage of experience in older, developed countries—not even from the mother country, Great Britain, from which America inherited so many local government traditions. There the town or city council has the primary authority for housing. It is run in the United Kingdom just like any other service, such as the fire service. The local government has a statutory duty to review the housing needs of its area from time to time and to provide housing to meet the needs that are not being met by private enterprise. It has a statutory duty to clear its slums and to rehouse the persons displaced. It is required to study the need for rehabilitation in other areas and to ensure that all houses will be brought up to minimum standards whether they are owner occupied, owned by a nonprofit association, or privately owned and rented.[2]

A few local general governments in the United States, both cities and counties, began in the 1970s to play a role in meeting some of the housing needs existing in their communities. These include Howard and Montgomery Counties and the city of Baltimore in Maryland; Fairfax County and Norfolk in Virginia;

Wilmington, Delaware; Hoboken, New Jersey; Boulder, Colorado Springs, and Denver, Colorado; and Eugene, Oregon.[3]

Although a 1974 congressional measure instituted a program of grant consolidation for several categories of community development, it is unfortunate that it did not also include making block grants for housing directly to local jurisdictions. Opposition pressure by special interests defeated that and similar proposals made earlier in the 1970s. When block grants to local general-purpose governments for housing do come in the next few years, they will permit greater flexibility and creativity in meeting local housing needs and will increase dramatically the role of general local governments in housing. However, it is to be hoped that before making decisions in this new field, local governments will engage in a thorough policy planning process, utilizing a systems approach (policy analysis) to develop various alternatives and their potential consequences. Without such an approach to decisionmaking, an intuitive action taken to alleviate the difficulties of a city could actually make matters worse.

Another opportunity for strengthening general local government has received too little attention from scholars and practitioners. That is the thoroughly sound proposal for placing public school systems directly under the local government's chief executive and its governing body. The bypassing of counties and cities by the creation of independent school districts in most states could be blamed as one cause of many of the educational deficiencies which the nation has experienced in recent decades, particularly in the deteriorating quality of primary and secondary school education in the inner cities and in some rural areas.

In twenty-eight states, independent school districts are the only governmental units performing the educational function below college level. In five others there are no independent school districts—Hawaii, Maryland, North Carolina, Rhode Island, Virginia. The system varies in the remainder, with independent districts the most prevalent in at least ten.

The school district system is so deeply rooted in many sections of the United States that people just take it for granted. It is a function of government for which most city and county officials have no responsibility whatsoever. To them it is somebody else's problem, and most of them seem glad to let it stay that way. Their main concern is that they do not get the political blame for the high property tax rate levied by the independent school board, usually higher than that levied for all other city and county purposes combined. The average taxpayer, however, does not differentiate. All he looks at is the total tax bill on his property, and when he grumbles about its size, he blames it all on city hall. Rarely does he stop to consider that 60 percent of it may be the levy of the independent school board, combined with those of the city and county into one tax bill. If city hall is going to get the blame for total property tax cost anyway, why not make the elected mayor and council really responsible and accountable? At least, better explanations might be made to justify the costs than is usually the case now.

Greater public understanding and support of the schools would result from having issues debated and results decided in city elections for mayor and council or, in case of a county school system, in elections for county council. Voter turnouts for separately held independent school board elections are notoriously small, which is the way most professional educators like it—they can more easily marshal their own forces to perpetuate themselves and their policies. And the news media rarely give anywhere near the same degree of attention to school board elections and meetings that they do to the elections and deliberations of the city council.

Like those who favor independent housing authorities, advocates of keeping the school function independent and separate from general local government argue that it should be kept "out of politics." The history of improvement of municipal efficiency and responsibility over the past fifty years has brought new public respect for city government in most areas of the nation, particularly where its structure has been simplified by establishing an accountable chief executive and a responsible governing body. In more recent years, many counties, too, are moving in this direction, encouraged by the "new counties" program of the National Association of Counties. Making the school system an integral and dependent part of general local government where that does not now exist, therefore, might arouse less opposition today than it would have fifty years ago.

Analysts found in a study of thirty-three cities of 50,000 or more population that school systems dependent on a general local government are not subject to greater political pressure than those that are independent, and that under a dependent system both school and municipal services have been improved much more often than either has been impaired.[4] This study was the composite work of a professor of education and a professor of political science, two scholars whose professional disciplines are generally on opposite sides of the question. Several arguments which the authors give in support of dependent schools include the fact that governmental simplification is an important result, with less service duplication and cost.

In a later study, Professor Roscoe C. Martin asserted that the professional schoolman's value system rests upon the bedrock proposition that public education is a unique function of government and that it must therefore have its own separate and independent administrative structure, resting "securely and serenely on a pedestal above the din of normal living." From this lofty perspective, Martin maintains, it is easy for educators to conclude that all other governments must be held at arm's length, and that the schools must be kept free to pursue their solitary way without significant involvement with government in the larger sense.

"Thus," Martin said, "the concern of the school and that of the city for the problems of juvenile delinquency (to name a single illustration) are completely divorced, with the school treating of the problem from one point of view, the city from another."[5] His devastating criticisms of the separation of public schools from other local government activities, unfortunately, have not received the public attention they deserve.

The massive report prepared for the United States Office of

Education in 1966 by James Coleman and his colleagues, *Equality of Educational Opportunity,* shook up the education establishment by its conclusion that the major reasons for unequal academic achievement must lie outside the school, not always for lack of money spent per pupil for facilities, curriculums, and teachers. Others, prominent educators among them, are forecasting that education in the future will be more closely coordinated or integrated with other services and functions, such as public health, housing, social welfare, land use, recreation, employment and assistance for youth, and libraries. A 1972 article by Pennsylvania's commissioner of higher education, Jerome M. Ziegler, states that the traditional separation of city hall from the board of education is breaking down, that big-city mayors are either already involved in school problems or are on the threshold of involvement. He attributes this to at least four factors:

1. Citizen concern over the quality of public education;

2. Growing interaction between the school system and other departments and agencies of city government;

3. The interrelationship of the educational system with other city problems and conditions facing the mayor; and

4. Intervention by the federal government in local school affairs through the courts or federal social and educational programs.

Citizen concern over how well the schools perform has grown so insistent, so demanding, and so charged with emotion, Ziegler says, that mayors are no longer able to disregard it.

"Never mind that the mayor has no official responsibility for the management of the schools. He is the chief elected official in the city and he is being held accountable by his constituents!"[6]

Chicago's Mayor Richard J. Daley, for one, has been taking a new look at the role of public education in his city and its effect on policies affecting the city's future. At a June 1971 meeting of the National League of Cities' board of directors, for example, he took issue with a member of the staff who suggested that the debate on the merits of the Nixon administration's Education Special Revenue Sharing Act of that year should be left to the educators. Mayor Daley, acknowledging that historically mayors have not taken part in decisions relating to education, asked whether there was "anything so sacred about it that mayors should not become involved." He felt that "all mayors should begin to be concerned about education." The staff man, Sam Merrick, responded that since education is not a general government function of cities, most mayors have no expertise in the field. "They keep chasing us away," Mayor Daley replied. He added that the League of Cities should be asking: "Where are we going on education, even locally? How well are we doing? Where is the evaluation? Where is the study? If we are not getting the type of education that some people say we are not getting, why not?" And he questioned why city governments should not take a position on educational matters.

Daley's interest inspired the NLC's committee on human resources to recommend amendments to the "national municipal policy" on the subject, which were adopted by the organization at its annual Congress of Cities the following fall. The policy now includes the statement that "detachment of municipal government from educational problems is no longer possible," and recommends that "where possible, city governments should assume an active role in local education (i.e. planning, administration and budgeting)."[7]

In the years ahead we can expect to see shifts from the traditional control and management by independent boards of education to administrative structures more directly accountable to mayors. As Commissioner Ziegler said: "Perhaps it is time to try another form or structure of governance, one in which the school system is a department of city government, with the superintendent responsible to the mayor and through him to the people."

With mayors now becoming responsible for the coordination of the criminal justice system and for the coordination of manpower programs, the next challenge is to make them responsible for housing and for education. These are all functions basic to the quality of urban life. They are completely interrelated with all other governmental activities of the city that affect the urban environment. Since citizens have come to expect effectiveness as well as efficiency in local governments, it is essential that these structural changes take place.

As this book has attempted to indicate, change is a basic fact of urban life in America. And the shift in citizens' expectations has resulted in a demand that local government policy be oriented to accommodate change. This is the result of an awareness of the importance of cities in our national life and of the impact of their governmental decisionmaking on the daily lives of individuals and on the community. The shift is from a concern with the mechanics of efficient management of housekeeping functions to an equal concern with city government policy planning and the substance of actions by its decisionmakers.

Allen E. Pritchard, Jr., who became executive vice-president of the National League of Cities on July 1, 1972, has stated that the most significant change that has taken place in city government in the last hundred years is taking place right now.

"We are now finally developing in city government a concept of the city as a planner and resource allocater rather than just a housekeeper," he said. "I think that is the most significant change because the emphasis is shifting now from efficiency to effectiveness in shaping the quality of performance.

"As a policy planner, a resource allocater, and an advocate to shape it, the city is playing a role in influencing the whole social and economic system in the metropolitan area, even though it is not the government of that whole urban system which you might call the 'real city.' "

With the exception of the few years he served as administrative assistant to a United States senator, Pritchard has spent his entire career as a close participant in city government affairs. Following graduate study of public administration at the University of Colorado, he served a short time as executive director of the Colorado Municipal League, then on the staff of the League of Wisconsin Municipalities, and became executive director, successively, of the league of municipalities in Ohio and Kansas. This author then persuaded him to accept an offer by James E.

Webb to become staff director of the Municipal Manpower Commission, a citizen group established in 1959 by the National League of Cities, with the aid of a half-million-dollar grant from the Ford Foundation, to make a study of how best to train, recruit, and retain in city government qualified professional, technical, and administrative personnel. Webb served as its chairman until he left to accept appointment by President Kennedy in 1961 as administrator of the new space program that ultimately put the first man on the moon.

From studying municipal manpower problems Pritchard went to Capitol Hill, then in 1965 organized the new joint service for the League of Cities and the Conference of Mayors that provided a "Man in Washington" for individual cities under contract. A year later he became the League of Cities' director of congressional relations, then deputy executive vice-president until he accepted a top staff position in 1972.

Since assuming his new role, Pritchard's emphasis has been on policy planning, not only for cities but also for their state leagues and their national organizations. The National League of Cities and the United States Conference of Mayors established a joint Office of Policy Analysis. Under the direction of Philip J. Rutledge, an experienced city government administrator in Detroit and in Washington, D.C., and former deputy assistant secretary of the United States Department of Health, Education and Welfare, the mission of this office is to assist in undertaking a systematic organizational effort to exert a leadership role in the formulation of national urban policies before they become hardened into programs. It explores and suggests policies which lay the groundwork for constructive change and improvement in the quality of life in urban areas.

Policy analysis is an important tool for local decisionmakers—mayors, councilmen, managers, department heads—in their urban policy planning. It is a systems approach to decisionmaking. The International City Management Association published in 1973 an introduction to the techniques of analyzing information systematically to develop alternatives for making better policy choices. Written by Kenneth L. Kraemer, *Policy Analysis in Local Government* includes suggestions for administrative arrangements and financing of the process.

Whether a city can actually influence "the whole social and economic system in the metropolitan area, even though it is not the government of that whole urban system," depends upon how effectively it engages in policy planning and the choices it makes. From policy it then becomes a question of management. And the techniques of city management are becoming more sophisticated and improving even more rapidly than in the "efficiency" era of fifty years ago. The upgrading of professionalism in city administration is attracting top-quality, professionally prepared personnel. New technologies and new systems have found their way into city operations as standard tools. Training programs have become standard for administrative personnel, from entry-level firemen and policemen to city managers. Consultants, foundations, and universities devote resources and talent to improving capacities of city departments, ranging from the office of the mayor to the crew that mans the trash truck.

Even so, effective decisionmaking is still no easy task. The next challenge is to upgrade the capabilities of the part-time elected local legislators—city council members—to cope with their responsibilities for planning and overseeing today's complex urban activity. As Allen Pritchard said in a 1974 *Nation's Cities* editorial: "The future role of cities in the federal system, the success of 'decentralization' efforts, the productivity of general revenue sharing and block grants, and the level of public satisfaction with local government will rest increasingly on the capacity of local legislative bodies."[8] That will be the new emphasis on improving still further the quality of local government in the United States.

Despite these long strides in management techniques, the academic community is still concerned that the fragmentation of local government in metropolitan areas precludes the delivery of urban services that meet sufficient standards of equity, responsiveness, efficiency, and effectiveness. They view it as a chaotic condition that requires reorganization. However, as noted in Chapter 9, voters in most cases have rejected consolidation and other plans for metropolitan structural reform. Various forms of voluntary regional cooperation are now being tried.

At some point in the future, the new structure of local government inaugurated throughout England April 1, 1974, may begin to appeal to Americans. Simply stated, it makes the county responsible for certain area-wide functions, such as air pollution control, sewage disposal, solid waste disposal, public health, welfare assistance, transportation, and land-use planning. The cities and boroughs within the county continue to elect their own councils and to operate the strictly local functions. It is a "two-tier" system, the county being one tier, the municipalities being the other. In a counterpart system in Canada, thirteen municipalities were federated under a metropolitan council in the Toronto area in 1954. Dade County, Florida, might be considered an example in the United States. In most states of this country we already have in place the structure for two-tier government. All that is now necessary is to reassign functions. It would be a system similar to that advocated by the Committee for Economic Development in its 1970 report, *Reshaping Government in Metropolitan Areas.*

In that report, CED's Research and Policy Committee recognized the conflicting forces of centralization and decentralization in metropolitan areas. "The interdependence of activities within metropolitan areas requires area-wide institutions for some functions or parts of functions of government," the panel said. At the same time, the committee acknowledged the need for governmental units small enough "to enable the recipients of government services to have some voice and control over their quality and quantity."

The committee recommended a governmental system of two levels that is similar to the British model. It suggested that a "reconstituted county government could provide the framework for a new area-wide government in metropolitan areas contained within a single county." For metropolitan areas that cover more than one county, the committee recommended a federation of counties or an even more cohesive unit to embrace all the territory. The second level of the committee's model would consist of "community districts," local governments where they exist, and new districts in areas with no governmental units.[9]

Despite amply demonstrated progress in city governance, the prophets of doom and gloom continue to decry the "urban crisis." They seem to be unaware of the ingenious job that most city governments—not all—are doing in a complex, dynamic urban system. These governments are responsive, adaptive institutions. They take on new responsibilities and new ways of operating in order to meet the emerging and changing needs of the citizens and the community. They are growing, vital institutions, their roles constantly expanding and changing.

The range of new departments and special assistance which are part of a typical city hall demonstrates the increased breadth of city hall's involvement in the life of its citizens. These include:

Manpower coordinators or agencies whose task it is to relate to the entire employment and job creation situation of the metropolitan area.

Human resources agencies to blend the disjointed municipal, county, and private efforts into a coordinated and responsive network of human assistance.

Administration of large day care and child development networks.

Consumer agencies, environmental units, veterans' affairs task forces, drug abuse agencies, youth coordinators, and offices that attend to the problems of the elderly.

All these areas of concern—and there are many more—are new spheres cities have moved into within the past decade.

In meeting the problems of environmental control, city governments are in the forefront of applying new technology and entrepreneurial aptitude. Note these diverse examples:

Saint Louis is generating power by burning solid waste.
Portland cooperated with Boeing Aircraft in recycling its

solid and liquid wastes on land so that it could be used for agricultural purposes.

Atlanta converted many of its vehicles to propane gas to combat air pollution. It is also recycling steel cans at a profit.

Many cities are exploring ways of converting solid and liquid wastes into products to help offset the costs of collection.

Milwaukee has for many years produced and marketed a commercial fertilizer made from the sludge collected through its sewage system.

In the area of law enforcement, several cities, including San Francisco, Los Angeles, Seattle, Kansas City, and Washington, have introduced widespread use of computers to improve all phases of the criminal justice system. This has included the computerization of outstanding warrants, stolen vehicle and property information, and similar information for police; notification of appearance dates for prosecutors; and information on the status of cases, location of inmates, and the status of probationers and parolees for corrections officials. Examples of more specific innovations in the field of law enforcement include:

Detoxification centers intended to provide an alternative to incarceration for chronic alcoholics are found in cities like Saint Louis, Boston, and Houston.

Employment placement in lieu of trial is being tried in Manhattan.

Drug treatment referral which, if successful, will result in dismissal of charges is an approach being tried in Washington, D.C.

Many cities are testing halfway houses for drug addicts, convicts, juvenile offenders, the mentally ill.

In transportation, Atlanta is deeply involved in a rapid transit system which will include fifty miles of rail rapid transit, fourteen miles of busway, and 1,500 miles of local feeder buses. Other major cities are establishing balanced transportation systems—employing a variety of means of transit within one overall system. Chicago reviewed its zoning system to use zoning as a tool for influencing the relative desirability of various modes of transportation.

These are just a few examples of locally initiated experiments in meeting specific challenges. Of far greater significance is the fact that some cities are now on the threshold of being able to "put it all together." The pioneering efforts of the city of New Haven in the 1960s demonstrated that a city government could, in fact, develop a revitalization strategy, incorporating physical development, economic development, community services, health, education, and job development in one overall strategy for turning around a declining or stagnant local community.

Utilizing federal assistance, hopefully through the new community development block grant, other cities are getting the tools and the resources to take this long-range, broad-based strategic approach to governance.

The city of Hoboken, New Jersey, for example, has developed a plan for rehabilitating fully one-third of its existing housing stock. This effort, coupled with economic development plans for its long dormant waterfront (across the river from midtown Manhattan) and its large, underutilized warehousing district, will provide Hoboken the economic and employment base for community revitalization.

Another city, which is adopting a quite different strategic approach to revitalization, is Dayton, Ohio. Dayton in its Model City area has made a full-scale commitment to the concept of satellite corporations, which are community based, quasi-public agencies meeting a whole array of community needs—housing, health, economic development, employment, family counseling, legal and consumer services. Other neighborhoods of the city are developing their own tailor-made strategies for community improvement with the overall guidance of city hall.

There is no question that city governments are responding to the conditions imposed upon our cities by a variety of forces. Why, then, are these important contributions so consistently downgraded and minimized?

The answers lie in a kind of double standard that people unconsciously apply to city government. They tend to compare the performance of city government with that of private industry. In fact, the conditions under which private corporations and city government operate are so dissimilar that comparisons are very misleading. General Motors or Litton Industries can pick and choose what fields they want to get into, what people they want to reach, and what product they want to make. City governments have no such luxury. Private corporations may spend six or seven years designing, market researching, model building, field testing, and redesigning a product before the public even knows it exists. Even then they frequently produce an Edsel. City governments have no such privacy in which to work out the bugs of their programs.

Even the federal and state governments have more opportunity to design and test programs without the full glare of publicity. Local governments, however, operate in a perennial goldfish bowl. That the operators of local programs are so accessible accounts for some of this. How does a citizen complain about the way Medicare or Social Security is administered? There's no one to complain to. A locally run employment training program or a community health center is something else. People know whom to complain to, and they do.

Many of the programs administered by cities must be designed on a crash basis—witness the implementation of the 1971 Emergency Employment Act. The National League of Cities and the United States Conference of Mayors lobbied for passage of this critically important legislation for two years before it finally became law. The unemployment rate in our cities had been getting steadily worse for the preceding three or four years. Unemployment rates in some central cities reached 10, 12, and 15 percent. Finally, when the law was passed, cities were given two weeks to design their programs.

When the mechanical difficulty of putting together a local emergency employment program quickly is coupled with attitudinal and institutional problems, it is a wonder the program has operated as well as it has. First, city department heads had to be convinced that their participation was worthwhile, that the process of hiring for newly identified job slots would not be bound in by excessive red tape. The program then had to be adapted to the merit system if the city chose not to bypass its merit system. This frequently meant delay in actual hiring. Separate job slots had to be established in order to ensure that EEA applicants were competing only against each other, since under most civil service procedures several applicants would have to be interviewed and ranked for each job. The procedures for testing, interviewing, and other processing normally took a month or longer for each position. In this relatively simple "crash" program, requirements that most citizens consider essential to maintain quality accountability and fairness in city government operations all have the effect of slowing down and complicating an urgently needed program.

Cities are expected to design programs to meet problems created by failures in other parts of the system. Urban renewal is expected to proceed without delay, even though two decades of neglect in building an adequate stock of low- and moderate-income housing makes relocation an almost insoluble bottleneck.

Cities are called upon to stem the growth of crime when narcotics continue to flow into the country, and the penal system—which is largely outside the municipality's jurisdiction—continues to create hard-core criminals out of first offenders.

A related problem is that city governments often have to step in when other institutions in our society can no longer serve a function they once did. When private mass-transit systems can no longer function effectively, the municipal government must move in and make do. When the federal government fails to live up to its national commitment to full employment, local governments are expected to become the employer of last resort. When state governments fail to provide decent standards of welfare assistance, the poor flock to cities in search of supplemental services—like public housing, day care, medical care—which help sustain them. When basic industries in a region decline or mechanize, the people who lose their jobs come to cities seeking a means of support and survival.

Cities become the magnet of much of the uprootedness, the conflict and striving of our society.

The fact that cities are in "crisis" is not new. The fact that cities are the centers of conflict and demands for improvements is not new. Cities have always served this purpose. Only in America do we ask the question: Can the cities survive? Can Rome, or Paris, or London survive? Can Peking or Istanbul? These cities have survived not only thousands of years—and constant shifts in land use, commerce, population, and role within the nation— they have also survived the overthrow of nations and social systems and the decline of civilizations.

So the question should not be: Can the cities survive? The question should be: Shall city governments be expected to cope *all by themselves* with the demands and aspirations of the peoples who inhabit the cities? Can the cities cope *all by themselves* with the economic impact of national investment decisions made by huge corporations to shift from one area of the country to another, or to move out of city locations? Can cities restore or replace *all by themselves* the antiquated housing and industrial facilities they have inherited from outmoded technology, misdirected national policies, and private neglect?

The answer, of course, is no. They can't do any of these things all by themselves. But city governments and city leadership are capable of surmounting the tasks that confront them. They are adapting their organizational forms, their programmatic approaches, and their scope of concerns to meet the demands placed on them.

Of course, they can't do the job by themselves. They need:

Adequate resources from the states and the federal government.

Adequate authority to design and to carry out new and necessary measures.

Support—from the citizens, from the private sector, and from the state and federal governments—to help them adapt and respond to the demands placed on them.

Understanding of the vital role of the city in our economy, our social life, our culture. Understanding that the juxtaposition of the desire to serve and the demand to be served, of opportunity and waste, of inspiration and conflict, of the best and the worst, is a basic element of urban existence.

Commitment to build the best in our cities so that the great majority of our people can affirm their hopes that city living is indeed the "good life" in America.

Children playing in a city playground in New York epitomize the continuing emphasis by city officials on enhancing the quality of life of the nation's cities.

Notes

Chapter 1: City Governments in Transition

1. The historian Daniel J. Boorstin, in *The Americans: The Democratic Experience* (New York, 1973), p. 648, is critical of writers using the word "black" instead of "Negro." "Future historians," he says, "will doubtless begin to be wary of the books on the history of the Negro in the United States when they find the word 'Negro' being displaced by the word 'Black' in the 1960s and 1970s—just as they were wary of books in German history in the era when the word 'Aryan' became fashionable. 'Negro' is a neutral historical term. . . . The history of the Negro American began to be chronicled, and was being well chronicled in quite another spirit, before the word 'Black' became fashionable."

Nevertheless, this book will use the word now fashionable.

2. Earl and Miriam Selby, eds., *Odyssey: Journey Through Black America* (New York, 1971), p. 44.

3. *The State* (Columbia, S.C., January 7, 1924).

4. H. H. Proctor, D.D., "The Atlanta Plan of Inter-Racial Co-Operation," *Southern Workman,* January 1920, cited in H. R. Lynch, *The Black Urban Condition* (New York, 1973), pp. 139–40.

5. *Atlanta Journal,* January 8, 1924.

6. Daniel W. Hoan, *City Government: The Record of the Milwaukee Experiment* (New York, 1936), p. x.

7. Edward S. Kerstein, *Milwaukee's All-American Mayor: Portrait of Daniel Webster Hoan* (Englewood Cliffs, N.J., 1966), p. 25.

8. Ibid., p. 185.

9. Henry J. Schmandt et al., *Milwaukee: A Contemporary Urban Profile* (New York, 1971), p. 70.

10. Ibid., p. 68.

11. Ibid., p. 28.

12. Margaret T. Parker, *Lowell, A Study of Industrial Development* (Chicago, 1970).

13. Louis Edward Alfeld, John S. Miller, Walter W. Schroeder III, *A Guide to Using Urban Dynamics,* Report D–1953–2 to U. S. Department of Housing and Urban Development (November 1973).

Chapter 2: The Evolution of Cities in the United States

1. Constance McLaughlin Green, *The Rise of Urban America* (New York, 1965), on which much of the history of these early settlements is based (hereafter cited as C. M. Green, *The Rise of Urban America*).

2. Richard C. Wade, *The Urban Frontier* (Cambridge, Mass., 1967).

3. Arthur M. Schlesinger, "The City in American History," in J. John Palen and Karl H. Flaming, eds., *Urban America, Conflict and Change* (New York, 1972), pp. 32–33 (hereafter cited as Palen and Flaming, *Urban America*).

4. C. M. Green, *The Rise of Urban America,* p. 75.

5. Andrew D. White, "The Government of American Cities," *Forum* (New York), vol. X (December 1890), p. 25.

6. Ernest S. Griffith, *A History of American City Government: The Conspicuous Failure, 1870–1900* (New York, 1974), p. 82 (hereafter cited as E. S. Griffith, *History*).

7. Ibid., pp. 89–90.

8. Francis N. Thorpe, comp. and ed., *Federal and State Constitutions,* 7 vols. (Washington, 1909).

9. C. M. Green, *The Rise of Urban America,* p. 111.

10. E. S. Griffith, *History,* pp. 52–62.

11. Frank Stewart, *Half a Century of Municipal Reform* (Berkeley, Cal., 1950).

12. E. S. Griffith, *History,* p. 271.

13. Frank A. Neff, *Municipal Finance* (Wichita, 1939), p. 35, citing Charles Zueblin, *American Municipal Progress* (New York, 1916), pp. xi–xii.

14. Palen and Flaming, *Urban America,* p. 43.

Chapter 3: Cities Unite to Improve Efficiency

1. James A. Bryce, *The American Commonwealth* (New York, 1899 ed.), vol. I, p. 642.

2. Harold D. Smith, *Associations of Cities and of Municipal Officials,* Report of the Urbanism Committee of the U.S. Natural Resources Committee (Washington, 1939), p. 1.

3. John G. Stutz, "The Municipal League Compendium," *Proceedings*

First and Second Conferences, American Municipal Association (Lawrence, Kansas, 1926), pp. 129–30 (hereafter cited as *Proceedings).*

4. Louis Brownlow, *A Passion for Anonymity* (Chicago, 1958), p. 279.

5. For an excellent description of state leagues see Eddie M. Young, "The Roles and Functions of State Leagues of Municipalities: A Study in Intergovernmental Relations" (Ph.D. diss., American University, 1974).

6. *Proceedings,* p. 127.

7. Kenneth E. Kerle, "The League of Kansas Municipalities" (Ph.D. diss., American University, 1967), p. 733.

8. J. G. Stutz letter to the author, December 20, 1971.

9. Charles E. Merriam, "The Future Work of the American Municipal Association," *Proceedings,* pp. 109–12.

Chapter 4: The Golden Twenties—Boom!

1. Daniel J. Boorstin, *The Americans: The Democratic Experience* (New York, 1973), pp. 263–65. See also Sam Bass Warner, Jr., *Streetcar Suburbs: The Process of Growth in Boston, 1870–1900* (Cambridge, Mass., 1962).

2. Carl W. Condit, *The Rise of the Skyscraper* (Chicago, 1952), p. 112.

3. Automobile Manufacturers Association, *Automobiles of America* (Detroit, 1970), p. 259.

4. "A Model Traffic Ordinance," *City Manager Magazine,* January 1924, pp. 17–19.

5. Edgar M. Hoover, "Internal Mobility and the Location of Industry," in Harold F. Williamson, ed., *The Growth of the American Economy,* 2nd ed. (New York, 1951), p. 749.

6. Frederick Lewis Allen, *Only Yesterday: An Informal History of the Nineteen-Twenties* (New York, 1931; Perennial Library ed., 1964), pp. 132–40.

7. *National Municipal Review,* March 1917, pp. 202–6.

8. *Tenth Yearbook, The City Managers' Association* (Lawrence, Kansas, 1924), pp. 92–8.

9. Leonard D. White, "The Future of Public Administration," *Public Management,* January 1933, p. 11.

10. *Model City Charter* (6th ed., 1964), National Municipal League, 47 E. 68th St., New York, N.Y. 10021. 70 pp. $2.50.

11. J. P. Jervey, "City Managership—A Profession," *Tenth Yearbook, The City Managers' Association* (Lawrence, Kansas, 1924), p. 146.

12. Clifford W. Ham, "The Assistant City Manager," *City Manager Magazine,* August 1924, pp. 7–8.

13. *American Municipal Association News,* vols. I–V, *passim.*

Chapter 6: The Depression Thirties—Bust!

1. *American City,* January 1931, p. 5.

2. *City Managers Yearbook,* 1932, *passim.*

3. Daniel W. Hoan, *City Government: The Record of the Milwaukee Experiment* (New York, 1936), pp. 313–15.

4. *Proceedings of the American Municipal Association, 1931,* p. 102.

5. This account of the Maxwell School's founding is from Peter J. Johnson, "Stable Conservatism and Sane Progressivism: The Origins of the Maxwell School," *Maxwell Review,* Winter, 1973–74, pp. 1–10.

6. Paul V. Betters, *European Unions of Cities and the Fifth International Congress of Local Authorities,* American Municipal Association (Chicago, 1932).

7. *Conference of Mayors of the United States Held at Detroit, Michigan, June 1, 1932,* p. 8. Transcript of proceedings in the library of the National League of Cities and U.S. Conference of Mayors.

8. *Proceedings of the American Municipal Association,* 1932, pp. 135–41.

9. *Conference of Mayors Held at the Mayflower Hotel, Washington, D.C., on February 17, 1933,* pp. 97–114.

10. Paul V. Betters, "Memorandum to the Executive Committee, February 25, 1933," *Transcript of Proceedings of Executive Committee, November 2, 1935,* Exhibit H. Transcript in the files of the National League of Cities.

11. *Minute Book of the American Municipal Association,* vol. 1, p. 83.

Chapter 7: City-Federal Linkages Start Working—Recovery!

1. Louis Brownlow, *A Passion for Anonymity,* pp. 272–74.

2. F. H. La Guardia, "The Federal Work Program and Cities," *City Problems of 1935,* U.S. Conference of Mayors (Washington, D.C., 1935), p. 6.

3. *United States Municipal News,* vol. 4, no. 18 (September 15, 1937).

4. Jay W. Forrester, *Urban Dynamics* (Cambridge, Mass., 1969). For a description and criticism of Forrester's model, see Jerome Rothenberg, "Problems in the Modeling of Urban Development: A Review Article on *Urban Dynamics* by Jay W. Forrester," *Journal of Urban Economics,* vol. 1, no. 1 (January 1974), pp. 1–20.

5. See Norman Beckman, "Federal Long-Range Planning: The Heritage of the National Resources Planning Board," *Journal of the American Institute of Planners,* vol. 26, no. 2 (May 1960), pp. 89–97.

Chapter 8: World War II and Its Aftermath

1. Kelly Miller, "The City Negro," *Southern Workman,* April 1902, cited in Hollis R. Lynch, *The Black Urban Condition* (New York, 1973), p. 48.

2. Frances Fox Piven and Richard A. Gloward, *Regulating the Poor, The Functions of Public Welfare* (New York, 1971), pp. 130–32.

3. James MacGregor Burns, *Uncommon Sense* (New York, 1972), p. 24.

4. C.M. Green, *The Rise of Urban America,* p. 174.

5. *United States Municipal News,* vol. 8, no. 12 (June 1, 1941).

6. Norman Beckman, "Federal Long-Range Planning: The Heritage of the National Resources Planning Board," *Journal of the American Institute of Planners,* vol. 26, no. 2 (May 1960).

7. *United States Municipal News,* vol. 8, no. 19 (October 15, 1941).

Chapter 9: The Intergovernmental Mix and Mess

1. Jack Rosenthal, "The Outer City: U.S. In Suburban Turmoil," *New York Times,* May 30, 1971.

2. Roy W. Bahl and Robert E. Firestine, *Urban-Suburban Patterns and Migration Fiscal Structures,* Occasional Paper No. 8, Metropolitan and Regional Research Center, Maxwell School of Citizenship and Public Affairs (Syracuse, 1972).

3. Vance Packard, "The Loss of Roots," *Washington Post,* September 17, 1972.

4. John C. Bollens, *The States and the Metropolitan Problem* (Chicago, 1956), pp. 35–49.

5. U.S. Bureau of the Census, *Governmental Units in the United States, 1942* (Washington, D. C.: U.S. Government Printing Office, 1944).

6. Paul Studenski, and the Committee on Metropolitan Government of the National Municipal League, *The Government of Metropolitan Areas in the United States* (New York, 1930).

7. Among the far-reaching revisions adopted in 1947 was one that created a new category of AMA for "organizational members." These were to include nonprofit organizations with purposes compatible with those of the American Municipal Association. Such affiliates would be entitled to three votes at annual conventions and in other AMA business and could name a representative on the executive committee. Apparently it was intended that the various national societies and associations of functional, administrative officials headquartered at the Public Administration Clearing House in Chicago and elsewhere might be persuaded to become organization members of AMA. None ever did, and that membership category was dropped in 1953.

8. Carl H. Chatters, "The Place of the American Municipal Association in Municipal Government in the United States: A Statement for Consideration on April 10–11, 1948" (manuscript in the files of the National League of Cities).

9. Although he was back on the job, in apparent good health, a few months after his 1951 heart attack, Chatters notified the executive committee in late November 1953 that he wished to leave the position of executive director of the American Municipal Association on June 30, 1954. In his notice Chatters said: "I find that the combined efforts of travel, administration, research, speaking and politics are more of a load than I wish to carry. My two predecessors died as a result of their AMA tasks. I would like to avoid that."

10. Dr. Hamilton in 1972 became dean of the Graduate School of Public Administration, Golden Gate University, San Francisco. Kerstetter in 1965 became executive director of the International Institute of Municipal Clerks and then research director of the American Public Works Association.

11. Proceedings National Conference on Metropolitan Problems (New York: Government Affairs Foundation, Inc., 1956).

12. Robert G. Dixon and John R. Kerstetter, Adjusting Municipal Boundaries: The Law and Practice in 48 States (interim mimeo, American Municipal Association, Washington, D.C., 1966).

13. Department of Urban Studies, Adjusting Municipal Boundaries: Law and Practice (Washington, D. C.: National League of Cities, 1966).

14. Government Affairs Foundation, Metropolitan Surveys: A Digest (Chicago: Public Administration Service, 1958).

15. Woodrow W. Dumas, "The Politics of City-County Consolidation in Baton Rouge," in Lowell W. Culver, ed., Adopting Local Government to Urban Growth Problems (Tacoma, Wash.: Pacific Lutheran University, 1969), p. 52.

16. Council of State Governments, The States and the Metropolitan Problem: A Report to the Governors' Conference (Chicago, 1956).

17. Richard C. Hartman, "The State's Role in Regionalism," in Kent Mathewson, ed., The Regionalist Papers (Detroit: Metropolitan Fund, Inc., 1974).

18. Vincent L. Marando, "The Politics of Metropolitan Reform" (paper delivered at the Conference on Government Reform in the 1970s: Metropolitan Studies Program, Maxwell School, Syracuse University, March 1974), processed, pp. 45–50.

19. Ibid., p. 52.

20. William R. MacDougall, "Consolidation: How Is It Working?" Consolidation Partial or Total (Washington, D.C.: National Association of Counties, 1973), p. 2.

Chapter 11: City Hall's Worsening Fiscal Dilemma

1. Advisory Commission on Intergovernmental Relations, *City Financial Emergencies: The Intergovernmental Dimension* (Washington, D.C., 1973), p. 3.

2. Henry W. Maier, "President's Address," *Proceedings of the American Municipal Association 1965* (Washington, D.C., 1965), p. 4.

3. *Proceedings of the American Municipal Association 1931–1935* (Chicago, 1936), pp. 549–56.

Chapter 12: Mayors on the National Stage

1. Frederic N. Cleaveland and associates, *Congress and Urban Problems* (Washington, D.C., 1969), p. 17.

2. Suzanne Farkas, *Urban Lobbying: Mayors in the Federal Arena* (New York, 1971), p. 47.

3. U.S. Congress, Senate, Committee on Public Works, *Water and Air Pollution Control: Hearings on S. 890 and S. 928*, 84th Cong., 1st sess. (April 22–25, 1955), pp. 156–57.

4. Randall B. Ripley, "Congress Champions Aid to Airports," in Frederic N. Cleaveland and associates, *Congress and Urban Problems* (Washington, D.C., 1969), pp. 20–71.

5. Royce Hanson, "Congress Copes with Mass Transit, 1960–64," ibid., pp. 311–49.

6. Judith Heimlich Parris, "Congress Rejects the President's Urban Department, 1961–62," ibid., pp. 173–223.

7. Ibid., p. 15.

Chapter 13: The Long, Hot Sixties—Innovation and Turmoil

1. James L. Sundquist, *Politics and Policy, The Eisenhower, Kennedy, and Johnson Years* (Washington, D.C.: The Brookings Institution, 1968), p. 34. The author, a senior fellow at the Brookings Institution, was administrative assistant to Senator Joseph Clark and an official in the executive branch during much of the period he describes.

2. Ibid., p. 85.

3. Ibid., p. 92.

4. Michael Harrington, *The Other America* (Baltimore: Penguin Books, 1963, by arrangement with Macmillan, New York, 1962), p. 12.

5. James L. Sundquist, *Making Federalism Work* (Washington, D.C.: The Brookings Institution, 1969), p. 149.

6. *Creative Federalism*, hearings before the Subcommittee on Intergov-

ernmental Relations of the Senate Committee on Government Operations, 90th Cong., 1st sess. (1967), p. 734.

7. *Federal Role in Urban Affairs,* hearings before the Subcommittee on Executive Reorganization of the Senate Committee on Government Operations, 89th Cong., 2nd sess. (1966), p. 636.

8. "Historical Highlights of the Poverty Program" (paper prepared for an Airlie House conference at Warrenton, Va., sponsored by the Urban Coalition, January 1969), p. 8. Cited by Sundquist, *Making Federalism Work.*

9. *Federal Role in Urban Affairs,* see note 7 above.

10. The report of the commission is the source of most of the data about the disturbances discussed in this chapter.

11. October 1967.

12. Report of the National Advisory Commission on Civil Disorders, p. 1.

13. Joseph A. Califano, Jr., quoted in the *Washington Post,* October 17, 1968, p. 17. Cited by Anthony Platt, *The Politics of Riot Commissions, 1917–1970* (New York, 1971).

14. *City,* vol. 2, no. 3 (May 1968).

15. National Broadcasting Company, February 2, 1969.

Chapter 14: A Look at the Future—Challenge!

1. John C. Bollens, *Special District Governments in the United States* (Berkeley, Cal., 1961), pp. 130–32.

2. In a perceptive analysis of U.S. housing problems, prepared for the Department of Housing and Urban Development in 1972 to get an outsider's perspective, a veteran of forty-six years of experience in housing management in Great Britain compared U.S. and British policies and program. See John P. Macey, *Publicly Provided and Assisted Housing in the U.S.A.* (Washington, D.C.: The Urban Institute, 1972).

3. For a description of these programs see Nancy B. Nyman, *Locally Funded Low- and Moderate-Income Housing Programs* (Washington, D.C.: International City Management Association, April 1974), Management Information Service, vol. 6, no. 4.

4. Nelson B. Henry and Jerome G. Kerwin, *Schools and City Government: A Study of Municipal Relationships in Cities of 50,000 or More Population* (Chicago, 1938), chap. 8.

5. Roscoe C. Martin, *Government and the Suburban School* (Syracuse, 1962), pp. 90–2.

6. Jerome M. Ziegler, "Should the Mayors Run the Schools?" *City,* vol. 6, no. 5 (Winter 1972).

7. National League of Cities, *National Municipal Policy 1974* (Washington, D.C.), p. 31.

8. Allen Pritchard, "A New Era for City Councils," *Nation's Cities,* vol. 12, no. 6 (June 1974), p. 4.

9. Committee for Economic Development, *Reshaping Government in Metropolitan Areas* (New York, 1970), pp. 18–20.

Index

74 75 10 9 8 7 6 5 4 3 2